STATES OF PERFECT FREEDOM

STATES OF PERFECT FREEDOM

AUTOBIOGRAPHY AND AMERICAN POLITICAL THOUGHT

PHILIP ABBOTT

THE UNIVERSITY OF MASSACHUSETTS PRESS   AMHERST, 1987

MIDDLEBURY COLLEGE LIBRARY

A B A_ 3 4 0 5

PS
366
.A88
A23
1987

Copyright © 1987 by The University of Massachusetts Press
All rights reserved
Printed in the United States of America
LC 86-16248
ISBN 0−87023−542−7
Set in Linotron Optima at G & S Typesetters, Inc.
Printed by Cushing-Malloy and
bound by John Dekker & Sons.

Library of Congress Cataloging-in-Publication Data

Abbott, Philip.
States of perfect freedom.

Includes index.
1. American prose literature—History and
criticism.   2. Autobiography.   3. Politics and
literature—United States.   4. United States—
Politics and government.   5. Authors, American—
Biography.   I. Title.
PS366.A88A23   1987   973'.09'92   86−16248
ISBN 0−87023−542−7

To Patricia Abbott

If I could write the beauty of your eyes
And in fresh numbers number all your graces

SHAKESPEARE

To understand political power aright, and derive it from the original, we must consider what state all men are naturally in, and that is a state of perfect freedom to order their actions and dispose of their possessions and persons as they think fit, within the bounds of the law of nature, without asking leave, or depending upon the will of any other man.

J O H N   L O C K E

CONTENTS

If America is different and each individual is different, then we can learn about ourselves by telling about ourself. Such a syllogism may not be perfect but it expresses some of the hopes we entertain when we read autobiography. The autobiography celebrates our dual conception of uniqueness by affirming our self-consciousness. The entrees offered over coffee or a cocktail—"Let me tell you about my marriage . . ."; "When I was a child . . ."; "In those days . . ."—are presented in the same spirit of Thoreau, who explained that he talked so much about himself because there was no one else he knew so well. We learn from the telling and we learn from what others tell us. Out of this discreteness comes generalization. "That happened in my marriage too" is one response and the story telling becomes an act of sharing. The autobiographer knows intimately the phenomenology of this discourse. He or she tells a life story so that others may see themselves as characters. If we do not match up (and here lies a central function of the autobiography), we can. The uniqueness of a single life, once examined, becomes a model for imitation.

Autobiographers then tell us a story about how we ought to live. Their lives are the evidence; we learn how to be happy, rich, healthy. All this story telling produces an instruction-manual kind of political thought. "How to" political thought may appear pathetically naive, but it does have a complex architecture all its own, one not generally examined by students of American political thought. For the beliefs that like America itself we can always start over and be "new" again, that "How shall I live?" is a practical question, suggest a depth and a range of discourse that has startling implications. That Benjamin Franklin became an international figure from beginnings so modest tells a story that still captures the imagination of Americans. Present-day Franklins are still telling us the same story. Could anyone change more than Whittaker Chambers, who left a life of atheistic communism to witness for religion and American values? Or Henry Thoreau, who went to live in the woods? Autobiographers tell us how they have changed. In the logic of American thought, they have also told us how we can change, how America can change, how the world can change.

I have tried to show through discussion of eleven American autobiographers how telling lives legitimates the American political consensus. If we can't change, then it is our lives that we have wasted through lack of effort or skill. For every man or woman who successfully copies Franklin or his many imitators, many others have been left behind. Franklin himself described some of them. Perhaps we do not wish to change; perhaps we are too corrupted to live as the autobiographer tells us we can. Thoreau, Henry Adams, Lincoln Steffens, Lillian Hellman, and others have said so. Here too then, we deserve the lives we live. But most interesting in the study of autobiography as political thought is the discovery of the yearnings largely unfulfilled and the fears that are never overcome by these tellers of their own lives. Franklin suffers not in spite of but because of his success. Thoreau, Hellman, Malcolm X, Abbie Hoffman, Charlotte Perkins Gilman nearly lose themselves in their efforts to find themselves. Many autobiographers search their childhood memories in an unsuccessful attempt to recover lost places of happiness. It is in these "failures" that one finds an American political theory that is rich and poignant and wise. In short, here is a political theory with all the characteristics (flawed and often twisted, of course) that conventional American thought so commonly lacks.

Support for this effort was provided by the Earhart Foundation. A version of chapter 3 appeared in the *Journal of Politics*. The following individuals read all or parts of the manuscript: Jean Bethke Elshtain, Robert Booth Fowler, Larry Spence, Robert and Gay Zieger, and Michael Levy. Their advice is greatly appreciated. Richard Martin has been an especially helpful and kindly editor. Patricia Abbott helped conceive the project and, as always, provided encouragement and counsel.

Philip Abbott
Grosse Pointe Woods, Michigan

STATES OF PERFECT FREEDOM

I N T R O D U C T I O N

In each generation, students of American political thought reexamine and confirm the relative poverty of their subject. Sometimes this is concluded as a celebration, sometimes with regret. But with regularity we are reminded of the shallowness of American political thought, its inability to transcend American life, its mystic rigidity, its tenacious conformity to liberalism, its repetitious assumptions of formality and atomism.

One group of analysts traced these features to the distinctive history of America, especially to its lack of feudal origins. Louis Hartz's *Liberal Tradition in America* is still the most powerful examination of American political thought to pursue this theme. Hartz concluded that the extraordinary consensus of beliefs in America produced tragic and dangerous consequences. The absence of competing theories created the periodic emergence of an "irrational Locke" which led groups to frenetically demand adherence to "the American way of life."[1] Daniel Boorstin reached a more sanguine conclusion. American political thought is characterized by a sense of "givenness" that makes attempts to create a formal grammar of politics superfluous. This sense of givenness was a "hallmark of a decent, free, and God-fearing society."[2] The concept of givenness was described by Robert McCloskey as "reflective."[3] He used an analogy of a mirror to portray American political thought as an activity that expressed and ultimately reaffirmed the basic structure of American society. American political thought was markedly unlike traditional political theorizing in that it was "nondialectical." Rarely is there a systematic critique of the basic structure of American society. For this reason one can read American political thought as a relatively accurate guide to current political activity in any given period, a project that must be done with great caution in say, an analysis of Plato and Greek politics. There was for McCloskey a peculiarly close connection between theory and practices in America. It was, if you will, the stable praxis of a totally bourgeois society.

These consensus analyses were of course themselves derived from current political experience and one could conclude that these efforts themselves were examples of the reflective character of American political thought. But similar arguments had been offered a generation earlier (although with a different vocabulary) by writers conversant with the socialist tradition. The origins of the "American exceptionalist" argument can be traced to the analyses of Marx himself.[4] The significance of the absence of a feudal tradition continued to be accepted (and also furiously rejected) by American Communist and socialist parties throughout the twentieth century. For the Left, a commitment to exceptionalism represented a crucial decision because it precluded not only the use of certain organizational and strategic alternatives but also the use of an entire vocabulary of politics.[5]

Perhaps the most thoughtful examination of American political thought from an exceptionalist perspective is Leon Samson's *Toward a United Front*. Samson argued that Americans could not understand the political language of European socialism because they held onto "substitutive counter-concepts" that he called collectively "Americanisms." Every major socialist concept had its equivalent in American ideology. For instance, argued Samson, America was undoubtedly a capitalist nation but its conception of capitalism was a "socialist" one.

> Opportunity is a key word in the dictionary of American idealism. But opportunity is not, strictly speaking, a capitalist concept. It is, strictly speaking, a socialist or rather a "socialistic" concept. Opportunity is the bourgeois concept of competition as it is refracted by Americanism, that is to say, as it is brought down from its bourgeois base to the broadest layers of the population—and so it is made to take on a social-democratic meaning. The idea that everybody can become a capitalist is an American conception of capitalism. It is a socialist conception of capitalism. Socialism is of all systems the only one in which everybody is in it. Capitalism is, in theory, and in Europe, for the capitalists—just as feudalism is for the feudal lords.[6]

When one looks at more recent analyses, there are similar assessments. Writers accepted the Hartz thesis in basic outline but emphasized the role of force and elite manipulation in the formation and persistence of the liberal character of American political thought. For example, Bruce Johnson, in reluctant agreement with Hartz, admits to a "remarkable cultural and political uniformity" in American political thought and accepts its source in "the weakness of class community in the United States." But Johnson contends that efforts to create communities were "ruthlessly repressed" by American business elites whose ideological weapons were supplied by the liberal tradition.[7] Thus the

liberal consensus as an explanation of the character of American political thought was reinterpreted as "liberal hegemony." The later concept
is regarded by many writers today as the basic theoretical interpretive
tool for the analysis of American thought and society.[8] Nevertheless,
liberal hegemony, despite its distinctiveness as a potential metatheory
of American political thought, still presupposes the basic characterization outlined above.

One might still presume, however, that the absence of a feudal tradition, an immigrant past, America's origins in liberal revolution, and
even the special tasks undertaken by corporate elites in a liberal society
might produce patterns and forms of political thought that are unique
or in unique combination, forms other than those outlined by liberal
consensus, exceptionalist and hegemony theorists. There have been
scattered attempts to search for a "hidden" American political thought.
Often these searches have proven fruitless and generally the searchers
have returned to one of the basic theses discussed above. But their
efforts are worth reviewing because they do, I think, suggest the existence of alternate patterns of political thinking in America.

One intimation of the existence of "hidden" patterns can be found in
Alexis de Tocqueville's description of America. Although Tocqueville's
approach in general fits the liberal consensus model, *Democracy in
America* contains a series of observations on what for Tocqueville were
unusual and puzzling aspects of American political thinking. For instance, although Tocqueville emphasized the American inclination to
withdraw from public life, he also noted a tendency for individuals to
move erratically from private to public concerns: "An American will attend to *his private* interests as if he were alone in the world; *the moment afterward*, he will be deep *in public business* as if he had forgotten his own. Sometimes he seems to be animated by the most selfish
greed and sometimes by the most lively patriotism." A dramatic change
in speech occurred during the sudden movement from private to public. Language heretofore "clear and dry and without the slightest orna-
ment" now was full of "inflated imaginations." "Writer and public,"
Tocqueville observed, "join in corrupting each other." He wondered if
these alternately displayed passions might originate from "urges . . .
united and mingled in some part of their being" which he had not been
able to understand.[9]

An important reexamination and extension of Tocqueville's observations appear in Irving Howe's discussion of the American novel. Howe's comments can be profitably applied to American political thought as well. He writes:

> One of the most striking facts about American life and literature is the frequency with which political issues seem to arise in nonpolitical forms. Instead of confronting us as formidable systems of thought, or as parties locked in bitter combat, politics in America has often appeared in the guise of religious, cultural, and sexual issues, apparently far removed from the conventions of Europe yet difficult to understand except in regard to those conventions.

Howe contends that the American political novels from the *Blithdale Romance* to *Democracy* to *All the King's Men* are unable even to sustain a political theme: "It is a characteristic rhythm of such novels that they begin promisingly, even brilliantly, in the portrayal of American political life and then, about mid-way, withdraw from or collapse under the burden of their subject." Americans are simply unable to see political life as an "autonomous field of action" because they "personalize" every aspect of a political existence. Howe concludes that "those massive political institutions, parties and movements which in the European novel occupy the space between the abstractions of ideology and the intimacies of personal life are barely present in America."[10]

If we continue for a moment with the question of the treatment of politics in the novel, we can, I think, benefit from Leslie Fiedler's discussion of the personal in American fiction. Fiedler notes the preoccupation with the theme of beginning in the American novel, a theme consistent with Hartz's conception of American political culture. American novelists say "for the first time (without real tradition there can never be a second time) what it is like to stand alone before nature, or in a city as appallingly lonely as any virgin forest." But Fiedler also discovered what he characterized as obsessive concerns within this theme: a fear of women, a recurrent examination of terror and violence, an unconscious flirtation with homosexuality. Our literature, Fiedler concludes, is a "literature of horror for schoolboys." The American novel is best summarized as "innocent, unfallen in a disturbing way, almost juvenile." The great works of American fiction are best suited for the childrens' section of the library because "their level of sentimentality is precisely that of a pre-adolescent." Fiedler reaches conclusions similar to those of Tocqueville and Howe: there is some cultural explanation for the "incapacity of the American novelist to develop" a mature vision. Instead of reaching maturation, the American novelist seems neurotically compelled "to return to a limited world of experience, usually associated with his childhood, writing the same book over and over again until he lapses into silence or self-parody."[11]

A number of writers have made assessments of American political thought similar to those offered by Howe and Fiedler on the American novel. Daniel DeLeon has recently pursued Samson's version of the exceptionalist thesis in this direction. He acknowledges the dominance of American liberalism but argues that the liberal consensus has itself produced an unusual radicalism that is antistatist, anti-institutionalist, and utopian. DeLeon identifies two indigenous radical traditions in America, a right- and left-wing libertarianism that extends from Thoreau to Josiah Warren and Benjamin Tucker to Murray Rothbard on the one hand and to Henry Demerest Lloyd, Bill Haywood, and Tom Hayden on the other. Although DeLeon is generally optimistic about the potential of these traditions, he admits that neither part of American radicalism has ever established itself as a real tradition, rather both have "always lived in the world of immediate sensation." His remarks on this point are especially relevant for our efforts:

> American radicalism has always lived in the eternal present of childlike innocence. Its speech has been the infantile or adolescent expression of a cluster of assumptions ingrained in our society, never formulated as a conscious philosophy. At times this has allowed powerful immediacy, but more often it prevents radicalism from perceiving its place within this culture, critically reapportioning from our heritage a clear and native identity. Instead we find uncertainty and occasional retreats to artificial constructs imported from elsewhere or mechanically developed without a concern for evolution.[12]

Thus DeLeon uncovers a paradox in American political thought: the existence of a radical tradition that is traditionless. The theme of individual self-assertion is given a much more negative interpretation in Christopher Lasch's *Culture of Narcissism.* Lasch outlines a progressive descent in the history of American individualism which begins with Cotton Mather's concept of personal calling and now rests with the openly manipulative hedonism of the author of the *Happy Hooker.* American thought is now so ahistorical and so self-absorbed that it can only be understood in terms of psychological pathology:

> The concept of narcissism provides us . . . with a way of understanding the psychological impact of recent social changes. . . . It provides us, in other words, with a tolerably accurate portrait of the "liberated" personality of our time, with his charm, his pseudo-awareness of his own condition, his promiscuous pansexuality, his fascination with oral sex, his fear of the castrating mother, his hypochondria, his protective shallowness, his avoidance of dependence, his inability to mourn, his dread of old age and death.[13]

For Lasch the categories of political thought are simply beyond the comprehension of the narcissistic mind. Political concepts, should they appear, represent direct projections of mental states.

Finally, a recent study by Wilson Carey McWilliams also accepts the existence of the patterns of political thought disclosed by the above writers but still insists that there is a submerged tradition of American political thought that is neither hedonistic, competitive, individualistic, nor privatistic. McWilliams's history emphasizes a recurrent and persistent yearning, not always openly expressed, for a sense of community that transcends the limits of liberal society. Writers such as John Winthrop, Nathaniel Hawthorne, Lloyd, and Richard Wright have explored the possibilities of fraternal life. But like Lasch, McWilliams's models of thought come early in America's history and are all but buried under the liberal. Today, writes McWilliams, the "worst errors" of judgment have been committed by those who yearn for fraternity.[14]

"How ought I live?"

All these assessments, despite major differences in scope and emphasis, suggest a common form of political thinking in America, which I call "sermonic." Rather than interpreting this form of discourse as a defective or truncated political thought, it may be worthwhile to view it as some kind of different political thought, one that originates from America's unique historical position.

What are the essential features of the sermonic tradition?

First, it repeatedly asks the same type question: "How can I be saved/successful/virtuous/rich/healthy/happy?" Emerson once remarked that each person was confronted with a very practical question: "How ought I live?" That a question such as this should be regarded as practical reveals a central aspect of American thought. The sermonic tradition suffers less from an inability to grasp political categories than from a belief that this "practical" question is a logically (and morally) prior one. Thus the question "How ought I live?" involves a conscious attempt to politicize personal life and indirectly (and often unwittingly) challenges the liberal distinction between state and society and public and private.

Second, it is atheoretical. This is not to suggest that sermonic literature represents Boorstin's conception of "givenness." On the contrary, this kind of political thought is anything but cautious and incremental. Sermonic thought is intuitive but radically and often carelessly so. Thus the sermonic tradition is best characterized as propositional. Lurking behind assertions such as "all men are created equal . . ."; "A vast conspiracy against mankind has been organized across two continents . . ."; "the history of mankind is a history of repeated injuries and usurpations on the part of man and toward woman . . ."; "If the inexpressible cruelties of slavery could not stop us, the opposition we now face will surely fail . . ." are theories that form what Hartz has called the "liberal settlement." But because that settlement is what is being challenged, sermonic discourse offers no more than a demand to recast consensus.[15] The act of return to first principles is generally the only theoretical advance that appears to be offered.

Third, it is ahistorical. Sermonic literature may employ historical precedents but it does so selectively. The core of sermonic thought is personal experience. As we shall discuss shortly, the real sense of history often extends no further than one's childhood.

Fourth, it takes the form of the tract, the speech, the pamphlet, the resolution, the manual. Jonathan Mayhew's "Resistance to the Higher Powers," Thoreau's "Civil Disobedience," William Lloyd Garrison's "Declaration of Sentiments," the Seneca Falls Resolution, the Peoples Party Platform, the manifesto of the I.W.W., the Port Huron Statement, the *Liberator, McClure's, Graham's Journal, The Whole Earth Catalogue, Our Bodies, Ourselves* are only a few examples.

Fifth, it expresses the entire range of American individualism. Sermonic literature can be alarmingly amoral as well as rigorously pietist. It can be totally self-absorbed and privatistic and it can be reformist and public spirited. It can be eagerly violent and amazingly gentle. It can be uncompromisingly reactionary or radical. But most of all, the sermonic tradition, whether it is a book recommending home-baked bread, better sex, or massive political resistence, assumes that each individual is responsible for the rightness and wrongness of an issue, that he or she must make a decision on the issue in question, that upon making that decision must act on it at once, that while such action has national, even worldwide import, above all it has personal significance. Those who do not accept such a change of heart are regarded with suspicion and often open hostility.[16]

What we have come to regard as American political thought functions against this background of sermonic activity. Its main purpose is to forge a national legitimization out of the sermonic tradition (a point pursued by both Hartz and the liberal hegemony theorists). Thus James Madison provides a theory to deal with "factions," Lincoln offers civil religion to contain ambitious men who prey upon the public's search for salvation, Herbert Croly begs us to abandon our archaic Jeffersonian prejudices, Robert Dahl offers polyarchy to restrain a "restless and immoderate people," John Rawls seeks to find a theory of justice in the context of so many different life plans, Ronald Dworkin presents a "covering principle" that will resolve liberal "inconsistencies." In its effort to provide consensus in the context of the sermonic character of American political thinking, the classics of American political thought do indeed portray individuals from an Olympian perspective that transforms them into troublesome, self-contained atoms.

From the vantage point of the legitimizing tradition, it does not matter whether individuals pursue a life dedicated to material con-

sumption or asceticism. What matters is the social and political consequences of these pursuits. As always, James Madison is the unmatched
figure in stating the conditions for the mission of the legitimizing tradition: "So strong is this propensity of mankind to fall into mutual
animosities that where no substantial occasion presents itself the most
frivolous and fanciful distinctions have been sufficient to kindle their
unfriendly passions and excite their most violent conflicts."[17]

If one thinks of American political thought in terms of two antagonistic
traditions locked in the vise of the shifting liberal consensus, one does
have a more complete picture than those offered by the liberal consensus, exceptionalist, liberal hegemony theorists. One is also able to
incorporate some of the observations made by Tocqueville, Howe,
Fiedler, Lasch, and McWilliams. The sermonic tradition does transform
political questions into social and sexual ones as Howe suggests American novelists do. It does suffer from an ahistorical and atheoretical bias,
although the sermonic tradition does so consciously in its effort to discover "practical" first principles and the legitimizing tradition does so
in an effort to generalize terms for a new settlement. It is persistently
individualist but not in the mechanistic terms posited by the legitimizers and those who focus their analyses on them.

But important questions remain unanswered: How does one explain
the repeated assertions that American political thought is somehow "in-
fantile"? Can one simply extrapolate a yearning for community from
sermonic propositions? Is the sense of self-examination as limited and
indeed as pathological as both Fiedler and Lasch suggest? Is the sermonic tradition so steeped in "the world of immediate sensation" (De-
Leon) that it is doomed to experience only a present?

There is a portion of the sermonic tradition that provides some answers to these questions. For this propositional literature does not rest
solely upon an antagonistic embrace with the liberal consensus. The
American autobiography is the submerged theoretical base of sermonic
tradition. If one treats autobiography as part of sermonic assertion one
discovers a form of political thought all its own, one with a common
structure and common concerns. It not only tells us about the process
of individual political commitment but it also reveals a great deal about
the formation of the self in liberal society.

"Frequent self-examination is the duty of all"

The autobiography is not a uniquely American prose form nor is it strictly speaking even a modern one. Saint Augustine, Cellini, Montaigne, and Casanova all wrote in a form that can be called autobiographical. But the term "autobiography" did not exist until the early nineteenth century. When he wrote the first portion of the account of his life in 1771, Benjamin Franklin used the term "memoir." Yet the autobiography has always been an immensely popular form of expression in America. Some writers have contended that it is the most fitting written structure for a democratic society.[18]

Alfred Kazin has complained that he does not know what autobiography is, that "the genre changes with each new example."[19] But there is a commonality to autobiographical forms. The "memoir" is foremost a rendering of one's public life. As such this form is generally available only to the "famous." Thus Franklin's "memoir" of a self-made man holds a special significance for the American. The memoir was pushed in a democratic direction. Anyone could, with a proper sense of purpose, become eligible to write one. The confession is the interior side of the memoir for it places self-reflection at its center. Self-doubts, inner triumphs, remorse and accommodation are the stuff of the confession narrative, aspects that Franklin carefully and artfully repressed. The diary, journal, and notebook are also autobiographical forms. Here the present moment, rather than the career or self, is the anchoring point of expression. The standard autobiographical purpose, the assessment of one's life across time through the exclusion and emphasis of historical events, is avoided in the diary. But even here the present moment is often used as a method for assessing a life. Thoreau's *Journal* used the examination of the passing moment to illustrate life opportunities that can be missed. The Christian diaries of Jonathan Edwards and John Woolman are meant in part to serve as an individual's historical record of waiting for a sign of grace.

In some ways the modern autobiography is a combination of the confession, the memoir, and the diary. The individual is at the center of history, not simply as reporter of historical events but he or she is nevertheless anchored in historical time. Thus the autobiography as a form attempts to explore both the public and private self, recounting the development of the private to the public and at the same time, exposing to the reader the private self beneath the public. There is then a double private-public connection in the autobiography: first, in the very act of deciding to commit one's own life to autobiography, and second, in reading an autobiography as a guide to one's own self-knowledge.

Of course, the autobiography will perform different functions in different cultures. In America the autobiography is a mode for the examination of the individual self that permits more historical and psychological complexity than sermonic propositions or the automatons posited by the tradition that extends from Madison to Rawls to Robert Nozick. The autobiography is an attempt to understand the relationship between personal and public life in a self-consciously systematic fashion.

Cotton Mather claimed that "frequent self-examination is the duty and the prudence of all that would *know themselves* and would not *lose themselves*." [20] The American Puritan's informal exchange of diaries was seen in terms of social reinforcement and self-criticism and in some periods was presented as evidence of election. The Christian narrative itself is a genre that predates the modern autobiographical form. Its structure survives in the most secular modern autobiography and still gives a sense of power and grace to the most poorly conceived account of a life. The recounting of the Christian's journey from outward piety or a life of sinfulness to conversion and pilgrimage is a story that is both self-centered and other-regarding. In the modern autobiography the path from private to public is less clear than that provided for by the Christian (or even Franklinesque) example. Connections are agonizingly incomplete as suggested, for instance, in Kate Millet's autobiography: "I can't be Kate Millet anymore. It's an object, a thing. It's no one. I'm only the fear in my gut. Just let me watch it from the sidelines." [21] But the attempt is still made, often with greater intensity than in the past.

Whatever changes have occurred in general structure and form, the American autobiographer engages in an openly didactic enterprise. Franklin, although clearly altering the Christian narrative, still begins his work with the stated hope that posterity will see his life "fit to be imitated." [22] Even Henry Adams, whose autobiography is written in a style of eloquent self-deprecation, passionately attempts to find out and tell the reader "what part of education has, in his personal experience, turned out to be useful, and what not." [23]

It is not uncommon for the American autobiography to contain, usually at its closing, a full-scale political tract. Autobiographies of reformers and revolutionaries nearly always conclude in this manner. Jane Addams's experiences at Hull House are expanded to include an analysis of poverty. Lincoln Steffens's career in reportage climaxes with a review of trends in corporate capitalism and a not too subtle plea for revolution. Malcolm X sums up his life with a plea for black nationalism. But less conventional autobiographers frequently employ the same structure. Thoreau's *Walden* contains an extended sermon on political economy. Henry Adams shows how one can come to terms with American civilization. Walt Whitman halts his musings long enough to provide us with a remarkably incisive commentary on the Civil War. Even Gertrude Stein's Proustian commitments succumb to generalization as she attempts to find a new stability in a "restless and disturbed world."

But the didactic aim is deeper and broader than the inclusion of the tract in the autobiography. For the autobiographical form suggests an alternate epistemology in American liberal political thought. Nearly all the great American autobiographers wrote conventional political works both before and after setting down their life. But the autobiography is written with the appreciation of the knowledge that the retelling of personal experience reveals public truths that might not be acceptable or even understandable if presented in another manner. Alexis de Tocqueville's complaint that the social structure of American society prevented the development of true philosophical traditions is an appropriate observation in this context. Because men and women cannot derive their beliefs or opinions from their class, they tend to "seek the courses of truth in themselves or like themselves." [24] The account of a single life is by implication an account of everyone else's life and a theoretical base is established. Thus the autobiography represents a structure for political reflection, one consistent with the Tocquevillian prophecy that the truth is to be sought in ourselves or in those like ourselves.

Perhaps a brief illustration will help. In the *Genius of American Politics,* Daniel Boorstin attempts to prove the validity of his givenness thesis by showing that even during the conflicts preceding the Civil War public debate between North and South centered around relatively narrow legal and sociological issues. Anyone who today reads the guarded addresses of Lincoln or the *real politik* constitutionalism of Calhoun sees support for Boorstin's thesis. The abolitionist political literature, although anything but restrained, does fit squarely in the tradition of American sermonic pamphleteering. Garrison and Wendell Phillips offer an outraged political pietism, which in terms of theory seems to do no more than appeal to a new standard in an American liberal consensus.

Yet alongside both pro- and antislavery writing stood the slave narrative as an equal to the American conscience. Several hundred autobiographies of fugitive slaves appeared after the prototype offered in *Narrative of the Uncommon Suffering and Deliverance of Briton Hamman, a Negro Man* was published in 1760. Abolitionists regularly "found" runaway slaves from whom narratives could be "told."[25] The best and one of the most effective of this subgenre is, of course, *Narrative of the Life of Frederick Douglass* which went through seven editions in publications by the Boston Anti-Slavery Society from 1845 to 1849. The success of the slave narrative can be traced to its artful combination of the Christian search for salvation and the liberal injunction to be free. Douglass's story of his banishment to a rural plantation and his encounter with a satanic foreman (nicknamed "the snake") reveals a merger of both Bunyan and Jefferson at an intensely personal level: "This battle . . . was the turning point in my career as a slave. . . . It was a glorious resurrection from the tomb of slavery, to the heaven of freedom. My long crushed spirit rose, cowardice departed, bold defiance took its place; and I now resolved that, however long I might remain a slave in form, the day had passed when I could be a slave in fact."[26] The self-evidence of the abolitionist tracts on natural rights emerges from the autobiography itself. The truth about slavery is revealed in the slave's own account of his condition which a more abstract appeal to natural right only confirms in shorthand form. The legal and sociological arguments over slavery paled before what in America is an epistemologically more reliable form. This point was always missed by southern retorters like Stephen Pearl Andrews and George Fitzhugh. For southern sociology could only reply with "scientific" generalization. How could Douglass be a malcontent or an eccentric when he lived the role that defined his very existence, a role that Douglass accepted and recounted, the role of slavery?

This process of autobiographical persuasion occurs with great frequency in American history. During periods in which waves of sermonic tracts exhort Americans to change, autobiographies explain the rightness of propositional assertion. If an actual autobiography is not forthcoming, a novel set in autobiographical form will serve almost as well.[27]

"No gains without pains"

If American autobiography performs an openly political function in attempting to recast the prevailing liberal consensus, it also reveals a set of desires and goals that rarely appears in America's two great political traditions. In its general structure the American autobiography does support and explain the propositional demands of the sermonic tradition. All American autobiographies recount some conversion experience. The movement from a life of sin to one of grace, from poverty to wealth, from egoism to altruism (or vice versa), from dependence to liberation forms the praxis for American political theory. One establishes a clear vision of the self as it currently exists, then as one would like it to be, with steps to achieve the latter. The life thus improved becomes a living model for others to imitate. Sometimes the actors become lost, lost in the relation of their steps to improvement, lost in the vision itself. However, as long as the plan is ultimately successful, these doubts only add drama to the effort itself. The tradition of self-improvement is thus a literature of self-sacrifice, self-denial, and especially exchange: sex for purity, purity for sex, money for comfort, comfort for money, privacy for fame, fame for privacy, and so on.

But a close reading of the American autobiography also shows that this conversion is never quite complete, that the converted self has not quite found the answers required by sermonic tradition, that a sense of exile threatens the autobiographer's own unification to self with his or her goals. In a sense the autobiography subverts the ideological function of the sermonic tradition.

Beginning with Benjamin Franklin, who first broke through the confines of Christian self-examination and thus created the first "modern" American autobiography, I have selected eleven American autobiographers as an illustration of this pattern in American political thought.

Other writers—Walt Whitman, Alfred Jay Nock, Emma Goldman, W. E. B. Du Bois, Jonathan Edwards, Margaret Sanger, Norman Mailer among many more—flourished as sermonic writers who wrote autobiographies. Innumerable others, whose activities led to instant celebrity, chose to try to explain their politics through an account of their lives. What their lives "stood for" generally exhausted their autobiographical (and theoretical) talent. But even these works (and Abbie Hoffman's is a possible representative of this category) still illustrate the mimetic structures of American political thought. For the most part, however, these are great writers in the sermonic tradition. Each writer spoke eloquently of the necessity for change in the American consensus. Each writer told how America had changed him or her and how he or she could change America.

Franklin's essays and aphorisms delineated a new conception of the virtuous life. Malcolm X's speeches inverted America's tradition of racism. Thoreau lived differently and urged his countrymen to "Simplify, Simplify, Simplify." Abbie Hoffman also "invented" a new way of life. Chambers and Hellman "witnessed" for their interpretation of American virtues. Addams and Gilman spoke for the plight of women. Henry Adams expressed his disgust for postbellum America. Steffens exposed our toleration for corruption and claimed to have seen a future that worked in the Soviet Union. Richard Wright examined the "ethics" of Jim Crow. The new lives demanded by these women and men challenged current received opinion on the great issues of their days: poverty, racism, sexism, war, communism, slavery, corruption, reform.

Each wrote in the idiom of the sermonic tradition:

So what signifies wishing and hoping for better times. We may make these times better, if we bestir ourselves. Industry need not wish . . . and he that lives upon hope will die fasting. There are no gains without pains. . . . (Franklin, "The Way to Wealth," 1774)

It is criminal to teach a man not to defend himself when he is the constant victim of brutal attacks. . . . In areas where our people are the constant victims of brutality, and the government seems unable or unwilling to protect them, we should form rifle clubs that can be used to defend ourselves and our property in times of emergency. . . . When our people are being bitten by dogs, they are within their rights to kill those dogs. (Malcolm X, "A Declaration of Independence," 1963)

The single great end to which all reformers, whatever their private theories may be, must look is distinct enough; it is to overcome the tendency of our political system to corruption. All political systems, no doubt, have some tendency, greater or less, towards corruption. The peculiarity of ours is that it moves, and for fifty years has moved, in that direction with accelerating pace, and it has now arrived at a point where even the blindest patriots see that, unless the evil is checked, our political system must break down and some new experiment must be substituted in its place. The ground, therefore, and the only ground on which all honest men can unite and insist with one voice upon reform, is that of resistence to the corruptions of our political system. (Henry Adams, "The 'Independents' in the Canvass," 1876)

Capitalism is license to steal; the government simply regulates who steals and how much. (Abbie Hoffman, *Steal This Book,* 1968)

The mass of men serve the State thus, not as men mainly, but as machines, with their bodies. They are the standing army, and the militia, jailers, constables, posse comitatus, and c. In most cases there is no free exercise whatever of the judgment or of the moral sense; but they put themselves on a level with wood and earth and stones; and wooden men can perhaps be manufactured that will serve the purpose as well. Such command no more respect than men of straw, or a lump of dirt. They have the same sort of worth only as horses and dogs. Yet such as these even are commonly esteemed good citizens. (Thoreau, "Civil Disobedience," 1848)

The last war simplified the balance of political forces in the world by reducing them to two. For the first time, it made the power of the Communist sector of mankind (embodied in the Soviet Union) roughly equal to the power of the free sector of mankind (embodied in the United States). It made the collision of these powers all but inevitable. For the world wars did not end the crisis. They raised the crisis to a new pitch. They raised the crisis to a new stage. . . . Few men are so dull that they do not know that the crisis exists and that it threatens lives at every point. It is popular to call it a social crisis. It is in fact a total crisis—religious, moral, intellectual, social, political, economic. It is popular to call it a crisis of the Western world. It is in fact a crisis of the whole world. (Whittaker Chambers, "A Letter to My Children," 1952)

I cannot cut my conscience to fit this year's fashions. (Lillian Hellman, Congressional Testimony, 1952)

Never again on earth will a man have a whole private cook to himself, to consider, before anything else, his special tastes and preferences. (Charlotte Perkins Gilman, The Home, 1903)

Society cares more for the products [youths] manufacture than for their immemorial ability to reaffirm the charm of existence. (Jane Addams, "The Spirit of Youth and the City Streets," 1909)

He saw millions of black soldiers marching in black armies; he saw a black battleship flying a black flag; he himself was standing on the deck of that black battleship surrounded by black generals; he heard a voice commanding: "Fire!" Booooooom! A black shell screamed through black smoke and he saw the white head of the Statue of Liberty topple, explode and tumble into the Atlantic Ocean. (Richard Wright, Lawd Today, 1963)

No one class is at fault, nor any breed, nor any particular interest or group or party. The misgovernment of the American people is misgovernment by the American people. (Lincoln Steffens, The Shame of the Cities, 1904)

These statements exhibit all the characteristics of sermonic thought. They are atheoretical and propositional challenges to the liberal consensus written in a hurry as speeches, pamphlets, compilations. All call for immediate action to meet a threat to popular government (Communists, politicians, capitalists). All call for the arousal of a complacent citizenry through a change of the heart. In a sense they reveal the democratic nature of American political thought in that each writer by rooting his or her assertions in immediate experience assumes a connection between public and private, the personal and the political, and asserts that new foundings are possible, that utopias begin with practical proposals. Thus both Howe's and Lasch's contention that American thought is forever mired in the personal misses the fundamental democratic assumption of the sermonic mode of analysis. From Franklin's advice, "no pain—no gain" to the same homey sermonizing of the Jane Fonda work-out tapes, there exists a belief that the future is within the grasp of each individual, blocked only by the amorphous but powerful forces of conventional political theory. The practicality contained in the utopian question "How ought I live?" gives sermonic thought its sense (and illusion) of irresistible power.

But what is also evident is the degree of frustration, anger, flirtation with violence, and apocalyptic visions in many of these selections. Wright's fiction and essays show an obsessive preoccupation with violence. Hyperbole abounds: Thoreau compares the citizenry to horses and dogs; Hellman writes disgustedly of the likely sexual activities of the "McCarthy boys"; Malcolm X speaks of all whites as "devils'; Hoffman writes obscenities on his forehead.

The autobiographies of these writers explore the basis of these sentiments. Franklin tells us that industry is the way to happiness; his autobiography details the relationship between gains and pains. Chambers's international crisis is illuminated in *Witness* through an examination of his own crisis. Gilman's own home causes her to seek the abolition of all homes. Addams shows how her work among immigrants clarified her own self as an "immigrant." I speak here not of psychological reduction as a key to the understanding of sermonic thought. The sermonic theorist invites the dissection of the personal. The personal is his or her mode of justification. What the analysis of the autobiography reveals is the full statement of the political claim, a claim that is already stated in political-personal terms, not simply in terms of exposing its origins but in terms of understanding what the autobiographer understands as its praxis. Of course, the liberation is liberal. Some readers may reach conclusions about the absurdity of praxis in a liberal society. Others may question the advisability of the quest itself. The efforts of many of these autobiographers may support such assessments. But another point deserves attention as well. The sermonic theorist-cum-autobiographer does explore the concept of emancipation in a way that most liberals do not. Lockean possessive individualism pervades the American autobiography but even its huckstering is part of a preoccupation with attaining an allusive state of grace.

CHAPTER TWO

HUSTLING

BENJAMIN FRANKLIN

MALCOLM X

ABBIE HOFFMAN

Benjamin Franklin's *Autobiography* is generally regarded as the first "modern" American autobiography. Franklin certainly has religious sentiments, but they come to rest upon a thinly self-constructed deism. There are also some traditional spiritual crises that are reported and he even flirts with conversion during the Great Awakening. Puritan religious earnestness, however, is absent from Franklin's life as he tells it. In its place is a different kind of quest. The *Autobiography* is generally read as a recasting of the Christian narrative in terms of material success, the beginning of a long descent that extends to P. T. Barnum and even to Xaviera Hollander's *Happy Hooker.*[1] There is some truth to this assessment. Franklin's autobiographical purpose is as open as the sermonic pronouncements of *Poor Richard's Almanac:* salvation is success, success is money, fame, and status.

Because the *Autobiography* presents such a clear picture of the real nature of the new modern success ethic, it rises to the level of political theory. The Puritan model of salvation is never completely rejected; in fact, it stands as an alternative to Franklin's own conception of life. But the new image of life in American society that Franklin creates always overtakes the old model, in part because it is the psychologically stronger one. Franklin is a hustler. Whether he sells, or writes pamphlets, or discourses in Parisian salons, he can never abandon the role of hustler. This chapter compares Franklin's life as he tells it to those of two other hustlers, Malcolm X and Abbie Hoffman. Taken together, these autobiographies present a single personality type; they also help explain the inventive character of American society and politics as well as the tragic consequences of its individualism.

There are two senses of hustling. They describe two aspects of the lives of Franklin, Malcolm X, and Hoffman. On the one hand hustling denotes a method of survival and advancement. Hard work, willingness to assume risks, and dedication are the features of hustling that Franklin emphasizes. Franklin sleeps very little; he seeks "improvement by constant study." Those who don't follow Franklin's regimen are "poor devils" who "keep themselves always under."[2] The life of the hustler is a never-ending swirl of activity, and rest can translate to failure.

Malcolm X presents the underside of hustling:

I was a true hustler—uneducated, unskilled at anything honorable, and I considered myself nervy and cunning enough to live by

my wits, exploiting any prey that presented itself. I would risk just
about anything. . . . Full-time hustlers never can relax to appraise
what they are doing and where they are bound. As is the case in
any jungle, the hustler's every waking hour is lived with both the
practical and the subconscious knowledge that if he ever relaxes,
if he ever slows down, the other hungry, restless foxes, ferrets,
wolves, and vultures out there with him won't hesitate to make
him their prey.[3]

Franklin sold newspapers; Malcolm X sold dope. Malcolm X emphasizes the exploitive role of hustling. The hustler cheats, lies, and
steals—all for his own benefit.

There are some similarities between the two. The hustler as self-
aggrandizer is, nevertheless, a hard worker, a "practical" man, a risk
taker. The hustler as self-improver is rarely without his exploitive aspects.
Franklin has his troubles distinguishing between these two types. He is
cheated by Governor Keith, stranded in England without money and
references after he had assumed that a mutual agreement had been
struck. The governor has out-hustled him in the second sense of the term.
As we shall see, Franklin himself manipulates others for his own ends.

In his autobiography Abbie Hoffman is extremely defensive about
this distinction. "I could have become a millionaire," he asserts. He did
not. But he bristles all the more from reportage that describes him as
"shrewd," "cunning," and "dangerous." It is the system, exploitive by
nature, that encourages and tempts the honest hustlers: "The opportunities that existed were among the most inventive contradictions any
capitalist society ever contrived. It is indeed possible in the good old
U. S. of A. to be wanted equally by the FBI and Universal Pictures."
Hoffman received offers for permission to market an "Abbie Doll," to
allow a writer to compile a counterculture "Dear Abbie" column, to
head up a division of Random House, to be marketed as a new "multi-
talented property" by the William Morris agency. He turned all these
offers down and was even "guilt-tripped" (hustled?) by Jean Genet to
donating the $65,000 screen rights to *Revolution for the Hell of It* to
the Black Panthers. But, as we shall see, it was Hoffman's public persona as a hustler that precipitated this critical response. "I read *Variety*,

Show Business, Billboard, and other trade papers far more probably than any other radical organizer in history" was one of Hoffman's boasts.[4]

Franklin, Malcolm X, and Hoffman were American revolutionaries, and revolutionaries with varying degrees of success. How did their self-constructed roles as hustlers (in either or both senses) affect their political theory? To answer this we need to examine in more detail the phenomenology of the hustler. It appears axiomatic that the hustler as self-improver (let us call him hustler$_1$) represents the approved model of the good man for a bourgeois society, while the hustler as exploiter (hustler$_2$) is its antithesis. But the relationship between the two is not a neat dialectical one. For both kinds of hustlers social and political arrangements are obstacles or objects to be used. Thus the hustler assumes a peculiar archetypal role in bourgeois society. He is outside society in an important sense even when he behaves as hustler$_1$ and still, in a sense, socially approved when he assumes the role of hustler$_2$ (Hoffman's inventive contradiction of capitalist society).

"I never became totally anything"

I think these aspects of hustling as a cultural type can be sketched by looking at the central activity of the American hustler: selling. All three men under consideration rejected the more settled occupations of their fathers. All of Franklin's elder brothers were apprenticed to trades. At ten Franklin was removed from grammar school to help in his father's tallow chandler and soap boiler business. Franklin in old age realized that a large family kept his bright father "close to trade," but as a youth he hated this business and begged to go to sea. Quarrels followed, the young Franklin turned to the freedom of the streets (a universal training ground and object of fond remembrance for all hustlers). There he was "a leader among boys," who "sometimes led them into scrapes." This rebellion provides Franklin with the first of many incidents in his picaresque autobiography. He had led his gang to steal stones to be sold to build a wharf. Franklin carefully reminds his readers of the distinction between hustler$_1$ and hustler$_2$: although this was an example of "an early projecting spirit" and "tho' I demonstrated the utility of our work, mine convinced me that that which was not honest could not be truly useful." A despairing father sends Benjamin off to apprentice as a printer with his brother. There are bitter fights. Franklin offers a personal lesson: "I fancy his harsh and arbitrary treatment of me might be a means of impressing me with that aversion to arbitrary power that has stuck to me through my whole life."[5] Benjamin refuses to sign an indenture renewal and begins his new life.

Malcolm X's origins are expectedly somewhat different, but they follow the same general pattern. Earl Little was a Baptist minister who was killed when Malcolm was six. The family struggled to hold one another together. The emotional and economic loss of the father was too great, however: "about in late 1934, I would guess, something began to happen. Some kind of psychological deterioration hit our family circle. . . ." Louise Little had a nervous breakdown and state authorities sent Malcolm to live with another family. Malcolm remained a well-behaved and bright student. His first obstacle to success was not paternal plans but the pronouncements of a high school counselor. Malcolm announced his intention to become a lawyer. The counselor responded: "Malcolm, one of life's first needs is for us to be realistic. Don't misunderstand me, now. We all here like you, you know that. But you've got to be realistic about being a nigger. . . . You need to think about something you *can* be." Carpentry was suggested. Thirty years later Malcolm X's anger is still vividly expressed. He assails "so-called 'middle-class'" Negroes—"the typical status-symbol-oriented, integration-seeking type Negroes." In the thirties "successful" Negroes were waiters, bootjacks, and janitors. Today, black lawyers and professors were their exact counterparts—"sipping cocktails" and grabbing "a few more crumbs from the groaning board of the two-faced whites with whom they're begging to 'integrate.'"[6] Had he stayed in Michigan he too would have been "successful," "even become a carpenter." Instead Malcolm Little set out from Mason to become "Detroit Red," hustler$_2$.

Abbot Hoffman was born in 1936 (eleven years after Malcolm X) to a different marginal group in American society. The autobiography begins with a description of personal destiny reminiscent of Henry Adams's. Abbott was "the first born son of a first born son of a Jewish family." In the twentieth century upward mobility has become institutionalized for the white middle class. Thus Hoffman is able to avoid the exercise of paternal power that Franklin faced and, of course, the obstacles placed before Malcolm Little. But a college also offers an Enlightenment education turned antibourgeois and the young Hoffman is enthralled by the teaching of Herbert Marcuse, Abraham Maslow, and Frank Manuel. "Most other students . . . seemed used to this exchange of ideas, and familiar with names like Descartes and Rousseau. I was a comparative hick. Every new idea hit me like a thunderclap."[7] Manuel tells Hoffman that the Bible "is all made up. Nothing but *Grimm's Fairy Tales.*" He learns about "your basic 'proletariat class.'" From Maslow, Hoffman discovered self-actualization: "Existential, altruistic, and upbeat, his teachings became my personal code." But Hoffman insists, in the true spirit of the hustler he was to become, "I never became totally anything." At this point Hoffman is still on a conventional, although upwardly mobile life track. He enters Berkeley as a graduate student in psychology. An unplanned pregnancy leads to marriage and Hoffman begins his career as hustler through a series of jobs as mental hospital orderly, movie theater manager, pharmaceutical salesperson, and, simultaneously, political activist. But his father always "mumbled in pained litany, 'If it hadn't been for Brandeis. . . .'"[8]

The movement of these men out of the confines of the lower-middle class gives their lives a sense of personal destiny very different from that of the Puritan autobiographies. Jonathan Edwards knew that his life was subject to a plan; his search involved a means of discovering it. The sociological origins of the lives (and decisions and accidents) of Franklin, Malcolm X, and Hoffman create a perception of a large arena of freedom. Their destinies are seen as unformed and subject only to personal effort and luck. Of course, as we shall see, the hustler's life is not nearly so free as he pretends, but in an important sense the hustler's role outside of society gives him a unique conception of equality of opportunity.

Robert F. Sayre describes Franklin's perception of his life as so free that "whatever actions he took were in a dramatic sense 'acts,' roles to some degree thrust upon him but also consciously selected and therefore open to whatever interpretations he wished to make of them."[9] This is a good description of the hustler's self-image. As a salesperson he must present himself in such a light that other's will identify his product. The hustler is a schemer; to sell his product he must sell himself.

But he can never offer his "real" self because then his range of freedom so necessary for the sale is limited. Thus one finds in these men an inordinate, even obsessive concern with appearances.

Franklin reports having made a major discovery early in his life by studying books on rhetoric. He found a "method the safest for myself and very embarrassing to those against whom it was used." By feigning a stance of "modest diffidence," avoiding "anything that may be disputed with words," Franklin found that he "grew very artful and expert in drawing people, even of superior knowledge, into concessions the consequences of which they could not foresee, entangling them in difficulties out of which they could not extricate themselves, and so obtaining victories that neither myself nor my cause always deserved." As a good hustler, he would abandon the method later, only to return to it "when I have had occasion to inculcate my opinions and persuade men into measures that I have been from time to time engaged in promoting." [10]

Appearance is really the only persona that Franklin ever reveals. As a young businessman he "dressed plain and was seen at no places of idle diversion." He went to great effort "not only to be in reality industrious and frugal, but to avoid all *appearances* of the contrary." [11] He would carry the paper he purchased through the streets in a wheelbarrow to convey the image of "an industrious, thriving, young man." Franklin is very careful to instruct his readers that all this hustling is honest. He really is industrious and frugal but one must also show the world that this is so. Still, the *Autobiography* contains activities that border on hustler$_2$. Franklin writes an anonymous pamphlet on the need for paper money. The House approves a currency bill and Franklin is rewarded by his grateful friends by the gift of a monopoly in the printing of the money. The only lesson that Franklin draws from this incident is simply that it pays to be able to write. Franklin bribes couriers to distribute his paper. He writes anonymously in another paper in order to drive a new competitor out of business and open up the field for himself. Of course this may be described as good business, and Franklin does have good reasons for his actions, but Part 1 of the *Autobiography*, the first step in Franklin's journey away from poverty and obscurity, reveals a willingness to use appearances for reasons other than establishing his industriousness. Franklin is not above scheming and creating "false" appearances for his own benefit. In fact, the emphasis on the utility of appearances is so great and so repeated that a reader can become suspicious. Is the scene in which Franklin tells of his "unlikely" beginnings in Philadelphia, shipwrecked, confused, and penniless, a concoction designed to heighten his present role? Is the project to attain moral perfection a ruse? Are both and other appearances carefully constructed, as Franklin's use of his wheelbarrow was designed to produce a certain reaction? Whenever the hustler celebrates his success, or even attempts to instruct (that posterity "may know the use of that virtue"), he risks suspicion. How much, the reader can legitimately ask, am I being hustled?

Both Malcolm X and Hoffman tell of this trade in appearances. The hustler, by the nature of his role, always works for an instant reaction. He does so for two reasons. First, because he is a salesman; he must establish as quickly as possible a basis for a productive relationship with his customer. He must be seen as competent, ready to deliver, able to provide a service or product. Without an immediately constructed basis for social interaction, the hustler remains a stranger. Second, of course, because the hustler must be able to assume the role of stranger as soon as the transaction is complete. The sale buttoned-down, the hustler has no more immediate interest in the client, at least not until the next sale. The hustler knows that this must be so because what he has presented is after all only appearance. It cannot be kept up for long because it is not real. General reputation is of course very important as appearance but it has none of the intensity of the sale itself. We can see this role enacted whenever we buy a product or service that requires any kind of selling. Insurance, auto, or refrigerator salespeople exhibit an instant friendliness. They chat about family, any mutual acquaintances, and the product, all casually, but on a hidden schedule. When the sale is made, or if it falls through, their eyes move toward another potential customer; a more remote politeness takes over.

Perhaps the most important feature of this instant relationship is dress. Most business journals contain a column on proper attire. Dress varies depending on the hustle, but it must show success above all. Sometimes this requires a certain understatement, sometimes bravado. Just after Franklin had established himself in a print shop, he went back to his old employer "in a genteel new suit from head to foot, a watch, and my pockets lined with near five pounds sterling in silver."[12] But Franklin was still a young and inexperienced man. He came to treat dressing "like a gentleman" as a badge of indebtedness. He carefully dressed in Quaker style, plain but neater than that of a journeyman. The young Malcolm Little repeated Franklin's "errata." The costume of the street hustler, style in extremis, was out of place when he revisited rural Michigan. "My conk and whole costume were so wild that I might have been taken as a man from Mars."[13] "Harlem Red" did not play in Mason, Michigan. Little, broke and dispirited, returns to Harlem. His account of his transformation to a waiter, his zoot suit and four-inch-brimmed pearl gray hat discarded for a waiter's jacket, "pleased and surprised" the customers who "couldn't have been more happy" with the new role. Malcolm Little's description of his new job rivals Sartre's famous account of alienation of the waiter: "I learned very quickly dozens of little things that could really ingratiate a new waiter with the cooks and bartenders. Both of these, depending on how they liked the waiter, could make his job miserable or pleasant—and I meant to become indispensable. Inside of a week, I had succeeded with both. . . . I couldn't have been more solicitous."[13] At night Malcolm would change his attire and "sell reefers like a wild man."

Hoffman's career as salesman began in college. He sold subs at night to hungry dorm students. He set up a charter air-flight service. For three years he was a pharmaceutical salesman. "Blessed with souped-up adrenal glands, the gift of gab, and chutzpah, I had all the makings of a first-class Willy Loman." Hoffman describes selling at Westwood Pharmaceutical as his "last job." But he really continues selling almost anything: Mississippi handicrafts, used clothes, and especially his own talents. After quitting as traveling salesman, Hoffman ("jobless but free") studies another kind of sales pitch. He listens to Stokely Carmichael and quickly works on a new style: "I studied him hard that night. . . . I, too, wanted to develop my own style of speech. . . . I built my style of verbal riffing on Stokely's spoken R&B."[14] In his new role as movement jester, Hoffman imaginatively invents a sales persona based upon fashion. He is painted, hairy, beaded, and flower laden. But directness is usually the salesman's best strategy and Hoffman's favorite costume was the word "fuck" imprinted on his forehead.

The hustler's ability to manipulate appearances represents the basis for his freedom. Because he is not locked into any single identity he is able to move in and out of various classes, at least temporarily. But this freedom does have its price. Malcolm X expressed (although I do not think he understood) this paradox with great clarity. During his days as "Detroit Red" he conveys his sense of elation with hustling: "Every day, I cleared at least fifty or sixty dollars. In those days (or for that matter these days), this was a fortune to a seventeen-year-old Negro. I felt, for the first time in my life, that great feeling of *free!*" But in the same chapter we are told of a different aspect of hustling: "What I was learning was the hustling society's first rule; that you never trusted anyone outside of your own close-mouthed circle, and that you selected with time and care before you made any intimates even among these." [15]

The hustler views society at large as a huge, powerful but lumbering giant that can be tricked and fooled. Society (or at least basic aspects of it) is exploitive and hypocritical. This belief provides the hustler with his rationalization for his own activities. But if fellow hustlers are comrades in this kind of guerrilla war against convention, they are also potential adversaries. Betrayal or deceit is one of the hustler's basic fears. I think this concern produces a peculiar conception of community for the hustler, and a particular style of political activity as well.

The view of society offered by Franklin is one of two basic classes. On the one hand are the rich and well born. Franklin is careful to give polite credit to those "leading men" who helped him. But in general members of Philadelphia's business aristocracy are at best unreliable and at worst slothfully venal. They show an interest in his efforts but fail to deliver (Sir Sloane); they use their political influence to place obstacles before his business enterprise (Andrew Bradford); they even trick him (Governor William Keith). On the other hand there are the artisans like Keimer and Franklin's own father and brother who tyrannically exploit Franklin's talents. Between these two classes is a group of journeymen, men anxious to better themselves. But like James Ralph and John Collins, they frequently succumb to alcoholism or, like George Webb, betray Franklin's confidences for their own betterment.

Franklin does manage, however, to find men he can trust. They are hustler, types like him. Franklin's sweetest memories are reserved for Joseph Brieinthal (copier of deeds), a "good-natured, friendly, middle-aged man, a great lover of poetry"; Thomas Godfrey ("a self-taught mathematician"); Nicholas Scull (surveyor) "who loved books, and sometimes made a few verses"; William Coleman (merchant's clerk) "who had the coolest, clearest head, the best heart, and the exactest morals of almost any man I ever met with." [16] These were the intimates Franklin carefully chose. These were the hustlers with whom he built his political career.

Malcolm Little's world is more threatening. Some of his clients "had the instinct of animals." They would follow him, dart out of a doorway and rip at his drugs "like a chicken on corn." The outlines of his own sociology are stark. Ghetto blacks for the most part hustled one another. Whites hovered over the ghetto like vultures. For Malcolm the essence of this relationship between black and white is revealed in the prostitution business in Harlem. As a chauffeur for white clients of call girls, Little lived in a "black-white nether world" where the cash nexus and sexual longing provided opportunities for racial fantasies. "Anything they could name, anything they could imagine, anything they could describe, they could do . . . as long as they paid." Little thought he saw the white world with its mask lifted. "The hypocritical white man will talk about the Negro's 'low morals.' But who has the world's lowest morals if not whites?" Here in Little's car were "rich men," "Ivy League fathers. . . . Society leaders. Big politicians. Tycoons. . . . City government big shots." [17]

Twentieth-century Detroit or Harlem is not a replica of eighteenth-century Philadelphia, but, like Franklin, Malcolm Little recalls his small cadre of comrades affectionately: "Cadillac, Drake and Sammy" (pimps), "Fewclothes" (pickpocket), "Jump-steady" (burglar). After his conversion to the Nation of Islam he manages to visit his old friends as a kind of subsidiary pilgrimage to his life as hustler.

Hoffman's sociology in broad outline is the same as Franklin's and Malcolm X's. He lives, as all hustlers do, in a society that is sufficiently slack to allow him to ply his trade but also so corrupt as to cheat him and even threaten his freedom as a hustler. Hoffman makes his living off the "Establishment." Franklin had to rely upon the help of Philadelphia gentlemen. Despite Malcolm's disgust, it was the lascivious clients whom he chauffeured who provided him with a living. Hoffman insisted that he was part of an emerging new social order, but the confession that "personally, I always held my flower in my fist" reveals more than he intends. His status and livelihood are dependent upon a public confrontation with the establishment. Thus when Hoffman scatters money over the gallery of the New York Stock Exchange, or sends pot to 300 people selected at random on Valentine's Day, or publishes *Steal This Book*, he is as dependent upon the needs of the media as Malcolm X was on the needs of his clients. "Pimping" is a harsh description, certainly too harsh to describe Hoffman's actions, but he certainly stands in the traditional hustler's role in relation to society. He exploits and in turn is exploited. Unfortunately, he insists on conceiving his role in terms of a countercultural hustler$_1$, providing services and direction for the movement. The Chicago trial is seen as "part vaudeville, part insurrection, part communal recreation" and the cocaine bust as simply the provision of entertainment for a friend. But the establishment on occasion will behave in ways that Hoffman says it would. It lashes out as it does at any hustler$_2$ and treats Hoffman as an insurrectionist and a drug dealer. Hoffman is reduced to insisting that everything was really all only for fun and profit.

Hoffman too must carefully pick his comrades. A co-writer sues him; agents pretend to be buddies; comrades compete for the attention of the media; the hippie culture of the Lower East Side has its "Mansonesque moments." But Hoffman has his pals and he devotes a chapter to them: Jerry Rubin (just as "Che needed Fidel and Costello needed Abbott, Jerry Rubin and I were destined to join forces"), Paul Krassner, Bob Fass, Ed Sanders, Emmet Grogan.

Before we leave the subject of the hustler's conception of society and his attempts at inventing his own community, it is important to note the role of women in the hustler's life. These fragile communities are male societies. The hustler does have problems with women. As usual, Franklin's narrative sets the pattern. Franklin's reputation as a womanizer is confirmed by his *Autobiography*. This aspect of his life is confessional. Franklin, anxious to portray a life "fit to be imitated," admits that the "hard-to-be-governed passion of youth" had led to "intrigues with low women that fell in my way." These affairs "were attended with some expense and great inconvenience, besides a continual risk to my health by a distemper, which of all things I dreaded, tho' by great good luck I escaped it."[18] At twenty-four, Franklin marries Deborah Reed, the young woman he alleges originally to have seen during the first day of his arrival in Philadelphia and whom he had broken an engagement with as a result of his "giddiness and inconstancy" in London. Deborah Reed proved a "good and helpful helpmate, assisted me much by attending the shop." Franklin is able to say that he had "corrected that great erratum as well as I could."

In the long moral lesson that is Franklin's *Autobiography,* there are two kinds of women, "low women" and "helpmates." In one of the narrative's incidents Franklin reports meeting two young women on a coach to Newport. A "grave, sensible matron-like Quaker lady" (someone's helpmate, no doubt) warns him: "Young man, I am concerned for thee, as thou hast no friend with thee and seems not to know much of the world or of the snares youth is exposed to; depend upon it, these are very bad women; I can see it by all their actions; and if thee are not upon thy guard, they will draw thee into some danger; they are strangers to thee, and I advise thee, in a friendly concern for thy welfare, to have no acquaintance with them." The two women invited the young Franklin to visit them in New York, but he "avoided it." Later Franklin learns that these were indeed a "couple of strumpets" when stolen goods were found in their lodgings. The incident leads Franklin to conclusions commonly reached in his autobiography. Beware of appearances and make your own luck. "So though we escaped a sunken rock which we scraped upon in the passage, I thought this escape of rather more importance to me."[19]

If the hustler must choose his comrades carefully, he must be especially cautious with women. The "hard-to-be governed" passions make the hustler subject to a hustle. Moreover, sexual activity can lead the hustler away from his own very dangerous trade. Women, "low women," have an enervating effect on the hustler that he must escape. It is probably no accident that both of Franklin's accounts are described in terms of flight, but like all the accounts of hustlers this stance in relation to women entails the shedding of appearances, the exposure of two selves. None of the hustlers we are examining can make that sort of commitment. Instead they select a "helpmate," a woman at least partially removed from the hustler's public persona and one whose sexuality is safely contained. The hustler's "helpmate" is no madonna. After all, the hustler is too cynical to adopt that role and, more important, too psychically wary. And the helpmate is not a friend in the sense that the hustler sees his close circle of comrades. She is sort of a minor friend, standing somewhere between a close acquaintance and an employee. Franklin ostensibly marries Deborah Reed to correct a moral errata but is it too judgmental to suggest that a woman twice jilted, "generally dejected," and "pitied" is the ideally safe marriage partner for a hustler?

There are two potential helpmates in *The Autobiography of Malcolm X*. One, Laura, is presented to show how Malcolm Little treated women; the other, Betty, arrives after his conversion to the Nation of Islam. She is to be the helpmate of Malcolm X. Laura is a bright young woman with aspirations to go to college. She meets Malcolm Little at a drug store where he is a soda jerk. Laura soon discovers that Little has a nighttime persona as hustler and, we are told, is enthralled by the zoot suit and Detroit Red's circle of pals. But Little leaves her for a white woman. "Up to then I had been just another among all of the conked and zooted youngsters. But now, with the best-looking white woman who ever walked in those bars and clubs . . . even the big, important black hustlers and 'smart boys'—the club managers, name gamblers, numbers bankers, and others—were clapping me on the back, setting us up to drinks at special tables and calling me 'Red.'"[20] Laura never recovered from the rejection. She became an alcoholic, a prostitute, and a lesbian. Malcolm X confesses to his own "moral errata." Of course, he never corrected his mistake with Laura as Franklin did with Deborah Reed.

But Malcolm is able to describe the attitude of Malcolm Little toward women:

> in those days I had my own personal reasons. I wouldn't have considered it possible for me to love any woman. I'd had too much experience that women were only tricky, deceitful, untrustworthy flesh. I had seen too many men ruined, or at least tied down, or in some other way messed up by women. Women talked too much.

For ten years Malcolm X had no lover. He assiduously avoids the sisters in the Nation of Islam and "yes, I did tell the brothers to be careful." In 1956 he meets a new sister, Betty X, at Temple Seven. The moral errata is corrected at least in terms of gender. Or is it? Malcolm X will not propose in a conventional way: "I wasn't about to say any of that romance stuff that Hollywood and television had filled women's heads with." The hustler's sense of fear of and disgust with women still animates Malcolm X. Here is his account of the announcement of the marriage:

> The news really shook everybody in Temple Seven. Some younger brothers looked at me as though I had betrayed them. But everybody else was grinning like Chesire cats. The sisters just about ate up Betty. I never will forget hearing one exclaim, "You got him!" That's like I was telling you, the *nature* of women. She'd *got* me.[21]

Certainly Malcolm X had a "good" marriage; Betty X was a "good" helpmate. "Betty understands" that Malcolm X's work "is a full-time job."

There are three women in Abbie Hoffman's life: Sheila, Anita, and his underground lover (unmentioned in the autobiography). At the close of *Soon to Be a Major Motion Picture* Hoffman attempts to come to terms with feminism. As it turns out, the reflections reveal only Hoffman's "woman problem." He begins his discussion with an account of his own vasectomy as a kind of illustration of his commitment to sexual equality: "Somehow this whole contraception business just didn't seem fair. Why should it be the woman's responsibility?" But he quickly reminds the reader that he, after all, had other reasons for the operation: "Sometimes women balled me less for kicks than to get pregnant." He reasserts his belief in "equality between the sexes" and proclaims his love for Anita. Of course he was never monogamous. The marriage was an "open-ended relationship," "with my end considerably more open than hers (Much more!)." But he "in your double-standard way was faithful to Anita" even though he stated that "I balled my way through the movement." What Hoffman wants to talk about most in his discussion of the "women's movement" as "a healthy step up the human ladder" to "a higher level of honesty" between the sexes is his own sexual performance. Anita "marveled at my sexual appetite." "Whenever I look at one of those charts surveying how often men do it I end up falling off the right end of the bell-shaped curve. In other words, a lot."[22] Hoffman does not know if he is bragging or confessing a weakness. He decides to consider himself a "macho-feminist." He will have none of Midge Dexter or George Gilder or Norman Mailer, although he regards the latter's *Prisoner of Sex* as a "brave, honest description of the sexual tensions and conflicts experienced by the American male." Hoffman does tend to see women as sex objects but he is trying to "escape" from this prison and he insists that his life so far "implies more determinism than warranted." Perhaps Hoffman, like Franklin and Malcolm X, is really trying to escape from the consequences of "hard-to-be governed" passions and "unworthy flesh."

"It was wonderful to see the change"

We have examined the lives of these three men in terms of hustling, but Franklin, Malcolm X, and Hoffman are foremost political actors. How does their role as hustler, with its moral ambiguities, its constantly shifting social personalities, its view of society as alternately prey and predator, its network of compatriots, effect the construction of political theory and action? In order to answer this question we must first note that for each of these men accession to the world of politics involves an act of conversion similar in structure to that described in the religious autobiographical narrative.

In the traditional religious narrative a central question always is "How genuine is the conversion?" Has a new self really been born? Without underestimating the significance of the changes in each of these men's lives that led them to politics, I think it is reasonable to say that the old self of the hustler never really disappears. In fact, the most that can be said is that hustling is transformed into a political act.

It appears that Franklin's autobiography does not contain a conversion at its center, but his account of his life is a portrayal of two tremendous conversions, one from a life of poverty to wealth, another from a private life to a public one. Certainly no sense of religious awe accompanies these conversions; Franklin's quests are worldly. But like the theologians of the Great Awakening, Franklin practices his own kind of "experimental" religion. Change, radical change, in his life is the result of personal effort. The moral of his life, those aspects of it "fit to be imitated," is Arminian. Moreover, he leaves no doubt that his old self, the self of his birth as the "youngest son of the youngest son" for five consecutive generations of artisans, has been shed: "I have raised myself to a state of affluence and some degree of celebrity in the world." [23]

Hustling then is interpreted by Franklin as a substitute for grace. The four-part structure of the *Autobiography* is submitted as proof of the utility of hustling₁. We have reviewed the account in Part 1 in which Franklin uses the picaresque to describe the life of the hustler: his battles with his father, brothers, and employers; his efforts at self-education; his sacrifices, including his efforts to avoid meat (too expensive), beer, women, theater, and cafés. But read as conversion narrative, the core of Part 1 is the voyage from Boston to Philadelphia. Franklin found that the opportunities for hustling in Boston had diminished. "I had already made myself a little obnoxious to the governing party. . . . it was likely I might if I stayed soon bring myself into scrapes, and further that my indiscreet disputations about religion began to make me pointed at with horror by good people as an infidel or atheist." He certainly needs a "new life." At seventeen he was "too saucy and provoking." The boat trip to Philadelphia represented a crisis for Franklin, one that was severe enough to bring forth the hustler who avoided disputes with words and cultivated the appearance of industry and frugality. The boat crashed in a storm. Franklin spent the night along a beach. He was feverish and "without victuals or any drink but a bottle of filthy rum." He walked fifty miles to Burlington and found a boat to take him to Philadelphia. Thus Franklin arrives to undertake his new life:

> I was in my working dress, my best clothes being to come round by sea. I was dirty from my journey; my pockets were stuffed out with shirts and stockings; I knew no soul, nor where to look for lodging. Fatigued with walking, rowing, and want of sleep, I was hungry, and my whole stock of cash consisted of a Dutch dollar and about a shilling in copper coin, which I gave to the boatman for my passage.

Franklin is acutely conscious of his role as outsider. He walks among the many "clean dressed people." "Unemployed," "penniless," "lost," "awkward," "ridiculous," he tells us that he "wished he never left home" and details the embarrassment he suffers in the simple act of buying bread: "Not knowing the different prices nor the names of the different sorts of any bread, I told him to give me three pennyworth of any sort."²⁴ Franklin receives several loaves, stuffs some in his pocket and manages to give the extra offending rolls to a woman and child he passes near the wharf. He walks into a Quaker meetinghouse and sleeps through the evening. He is befriended by a young Quaker who steers him away from a disreputable lodging and finds him a place to stay. He submits to "several sly questions." Franklin is suspected of being a runaway.

Part 2 is a summary of the lessons Franklin drew from his "first entry" into the city. It contains his famous "bold and arduous plan at arriving at moral perfection." Many critics have found this effort laughable or disgusting or even an exercise in self-parody.[25] Each of these reactions carries weight. The retelling of the plan openly invites these descriptions and therefore makes it a puzzling exercise. Morality is reduced to the behavior of the good shopkeeper. It is to be inculcated like an accountant keeps track of the profits of a firm. Franklin makes a little book in which he allots a page for each virtue:

> I ruled each page with red ink so as to have seven columns, one for each day of the week, marking each column with a letter for the day. I crossed these columns with thirteen red lines, marking the beginning of each line with the first letter of one of the virtues, on which line and its proper column I might mark by a little black spot every fault I found upon examination to have been committed respecting that upon that day.

Although Franklin plays the game straight for the reader ("It may be well my posterity should be informed that to this little artifice, with the blessing of God, their ancestor owed the constant felicity of his life down to his seventy-ninth year, in which this is written"),[26] there is a certain comic touch to the description of the exercise. Franklin had anticipated the "encouraging pleasure" of viewing a clean book. This was not to be. In fact, order, the central aspect as a self-improvement procedure that requires the daily recording of faults, is a virtue that Franklin cannot ever master. But look at the plan from the perspective of Franklin as a hustler. Franklin never lived the life of the stolid bourgeois shopkeeper. He did, however, see the need to *appear* as one. But if the plan is the artifice of a hustler, it also reveals the inner life of that profession. This daily regimen in which time is mechanistically parcelled into hourly units for self-reflection and projects is an account, veiled, as are all the pronouncements of hustlers, of Franklin's enormous psychic efforts to avoid the fate of his father and his journeymen friends. It is the codification of a conversion, a kind of hustler's personal religion.

Part 3 is an account of Franklin's second conversion, again self-willed: "I began to turn my thoughts a little to public affairs. . . ." As a hustler, he conceives of political activity in terms of "projects," projects to get streets paved and lit, to build hospitals, colleges, and orphanages. One critic writes that Franklin sees street drainage and lighting as equivalent to law making and political theory.[27] He had defended this charge in his *Autobiography;* even a street lighting project is not a "trifling matter, human felicity is produced . . . by little advantages that occur every day." But Franklin's petit bourgeois utilitarianism suggests only part of his approach. The plan had treated cleanliness and justice as virtues of equal importance. Beneath the utilitarianism is a fascination with the project itself. Political life is a series of projects, "scams" in the vocabulary of the hustler$_2$, which taken together lead to fame and political power. Franklin is not insincere when he celebrates his projects as "useful to the city I love" but the utilitarianism that propels the projects is the utilitarianism of the hustler, not of the shopkeeper.

How does the hustler approach his political projects? He does so with the same manipulation of appearances, the same connivance to learn the motivations of others, the same self-constructed sets of pals that he uses in his private hustles. Franklin wrote *Poor Richard's Almanac* under the pseudonym of Richard Saunders and in the style of "the harangue of an old man." He knew that "common people bought scarce any other books" and "considered it as a proper vehicle for conveying instruction." The maxims on industry and frugality were interspersed throughout the calendar. The clergy and gentry distributed the sayings to their poor parishioners and tenants gratis. In Pennsylvania "some thought it had its share of influence in producing that growing plenty of money." Franklin himself "reaped considerable profit from it, vending annually near ten thousand." As in any project of a hustler$_1$, everyone ends up "happy"—and a little bit tricked.

The plan was Franklin's self-improvement guide for success in business. When he turned to public affairs he developed "a great and extensive project" for a new kind of hustle. He first conceived the project in 1731 and its description forms the introduction for Part 3 of the *Au-*

tobiography. Proposed as a series of axioms, the new plan outlines the sources of political conflict in the world:

That the great affairs of the world, the wars, revolutions, etc., are carried on and effected by parties.

That the view of these parties is their present general interest, or what they take to be as such.

That while a party is carrying on a general design, each man has his particular private interest in view.

That as soon as a party has gained its general point, each member becomes intent upon his particular interest, which thwarting others, breaks that party into divisions and occasions more confusion.

That few in public affairs act from a mere view of the good of their country, whatever they may pretend. . . .

That fewer still in public affairs act with a view to the good of mankind.

Franklin's conception of pluralism required the creation of a "united party of virtue"—"whoever attempts this aright and is well qualified, cannot fail of pleasing God and of meeting with success." This new party would be organized as a secret sect. Admission would at first be limited to young, single men who would receive indoctrination for thirteen weeks in the plan. Members would "engage to afford their advice, assistance and support to each other in promoting one another's interest, business, and advancement in life. . . ."[28]

The Society of the Free and Easy (Franklin's name for the new party of virtue) is not an Enlightenment flirtation with benevolent despotism. It is an idealization of Franklin's hustler pals. Franklin has been "saved" by the plan and when he goes political he fantasizes that it will not only save others but save society as well. But the Society of the Free and Easy has all the earmarks of the hustler's worldview. It stands outside society, its true goals are secret, it is a vehicle for individual advancement.

The party of virtue never reformed the world, but Franklin did create his own quite successful model. The junto, composed of Franklin's friends described earlier, did act as a kind of hustler's version of a front group. The junto replicated itself. New groups were formed by the original members under different names (the Vine, the Union, the Band, etc.). New members were not informed of the relationship of their group to the mother junto. The junto and its affiliates formed the basis for the implementation of Franklin's projects. He would write an anonymous article "to prepare the minds of the people." Affiliated organizations would discuss the proposal and a campaign would be planned for the legislature to undertake the project. Often at this point Franklin would propose some matching grant to initiate the project on an experimental basis. In the case of the project for Philadelphia's first hospital, he proposed that if £ 2,000 were donated privately, another 2,000 in public funds be appropriated. The junto then provided the organizational structure for fund raising. In the same manner, Franklin describes "influencing public opinion" to reform the constable system and to create an orphanage, co-op library, and academy, as well as those "trifling" projects of street paving and lighting.

The junto is the archetypal political form of the hustler. In Franklin's narrative it is firmly drawn on the model of hustling$_1$. The junto does good work, but the image of society at large as an obstacle to the hustler's goals and as an object to prey upon is the basis for its organizational structure. Franklin could not "remember any of my political manoeuvres, the success of which gave me at the time more pleasure" than the construction of that hospital. "I more easily excused myself for having made use of cunning," Franklin concedes, as he also tacitly admits that the leader of the party of virtue, like the industrious and frugal shopkeeper, is still trading in appearances.

Malcolm Little's transformation to Malcolm X is more dramatic, more explosive than the conversions of Franklin. This is so in part because *The Autobiography of Malcolm X* is an account of the transition, vividly expressed, from hustler$_2$ to hustler$_1$. Of course Malcolm X does not see his life this way. For him his story involves a momentous conversion from hustling to religious salvation. There is, however, hustling, and a lot of it, after the conversion. Moreover, there is more than one conversion in Malcolm's life, perhaps as many as four.

Compare Franklin's description of his arrival in Philadelphia to Little's account of his journey to Boston:

> I looked like Li'l Abner. Mason, Michigan, was written all over
> me. My kinky, reddish hair was cut hick style, and I didn't even

use grease on it. My green suit's coat sleeves stopped above my wrists, the pants legs showed three inches of socks. Just a shade lighter green than the suit was my narrow-collared, three-quarter length Lansing department store topcoat.

Years later, Malcolm X's half-sister tried to sooth the embarrassment: "she told me later she had seen countrified members of the Little family come up from Georgia in even worse shape than I was." [29]

The first conversion begins. Malcolm Little is quickly transformed into an urban hustler$_2$, but in the tradition of the conversion narrative Malcolm X underplays certain aspects of his life. For a time he lives as hustler$_1$. Under the sponsorship of his half-sister Ella, Malcolm Little hustles through a series of jobs—waiter, soda jerk, shoe-shine boy— that are the urban black equivalent of Franklin's indentures. But Little begins to hustle$_2$ at night and finally takes to the street full time as a dope peddler. Franklin's entire autobiography is a didactic tract extolling the virtues of hustling$_1$. Malcolm X emphasizes his transformation to a hustler$_2$ in order to underscore the enormity of the conversion to the Nation of Islam. Of course, Malcolm Little is caught in his role as hustler$_2$ and sentenced to Charlestown State Prison for burglary. He had "sunk to the very bottom of the American white man's society." [30]

Franklin obtained his rhetorical skills by reconstructing articles in the *Spectator* by memory; Malcolm Little copied and memorized a dictionary. At the same time Little begins writing to Elijah Muhammad. The two transformations are reported simultaneously. A "new world" opens up. He reads compulsively. Histories appear to account for most of his studies. Durant, Toynbee, Olmstead, H. G. Wells, Woodson are remembered. The entry into the new world of books emphasizes his personal limitations as a hustler. His daily letters to Muhammad are especially painful to write. Little's career as a hustler required specialized verbal skills:

I became increasingly frustrated at not being able to express what I wanted to convey in letters that I wrote, especially those to Mr. Elijah Muhammad. In the street, I had been the most articulate hustler out there—I had commanded attention when I said something. But now, trying to write simple English, I not only wasn't articulate, I wasn't even functional. How would I sound writing in slang, the way I would *say* it, something such as, "Look, daddy, let me pull your coat about a cat, Elijah Muhammad—." [31]

Little was a very young man when he went to prison. ("I wasn't quite twenty-one. I had not even started shaving.") Prison had shattered his newly acquired persona as hustler. His "homemade education" further tore away at his "old" self. I want to argue that, despite the religious conversion, "Detroit Red" still forms the core of Malcolm X's personality. Still, it must be mentioned that Little's conversion is felt as genuine. The account has all the poignancy of the Puritan narrative: Little's old personality "slid away . . . like snow off a roof. . . . I would be startled to catch myself thinking in a remote way of my earlier self as another person." Of course a reader's fascination with such a transformation should not neglect an evaluation of substance. Malcolm Little was a hustler$_2$, preying on the weaknesses of an oppressed people. But Malcolm X is a racist, a preacher of hatred against "white devils." There is as well the problem of the autonomy of the new Malcolm X's self. The "new world" that opened up as a result of Malcolm's self-education stands in opposition to his role as disciple. Malcolm Little who is saved as Malcolm X is an open and slavish follower of Muhammad. "Every Muslim said that never would you do as much for Mr. Muhammad as he could do for you." [32] He receives his new name from him, follows his orders on political questions, accepts the mythology of the Nation of Islam. It is true that the new self born of conversion is a fragile one that requires nurture from external sources, but one need not have a phobia of organized religion to see that Malcolm X's new self looks at the world with eyes hypnotized.

This hero worship would end, of course. "In years to come," Malcolm X reminds us, "I was going to have to face a psychological and spiritual crisis." Ironically it is the old Malcolm Little, the hustler, who sets up the standards for the eventual reevaluation of Elijah Muhammad. For this final conversion Malcolm X would pay with his life, but when he leaves prison in 1952, he returns to Detroit with all the newness about him that characterized him in his trip from Mason. "It was in August when they gave me a lecture, a cheap L'il Abner suit, and a small amount of money, and I walked out of the gate." [33] He begins a new kind of hustling.

Again, let me say that selling religion is morally distinct from selling dope. There are, however, unavoidable similarities. Malcolm starts, as he did at his first conversion, as a hustler, in the daytime. At night he hustles for Temple One. He rises quickly, as assistant minister, as minister, as builder of new temples in other cities. The *Autobiography* is filled with accounts of his sermons. They are delivered in a feverish, staccato style: "Every time I spoke . . . my voice would still be hoarse from the last time." The pitch is always the same. White men are "blue-eyed devils," Christianity is another crime of the white man, slavery is only one aspect of the white man's "orgy of greed and lust and murder." After I "had them fired up with slavery, I would shift the scene to themselves." The speech would close with a request, evangelist style, for those who wished to follow Muhammad to stand up.

Malcolm X built his own kind of junto. His assistants varied their pitches to meet different audiences. The selling was referred to as "fishing." The rule was: "You have to be careful, very careful, introducing the truth to the black man who has never previously heard the truth about himself, his own kind, and the white man." The market was, after all, very competitive: "we were only one among the many voices of black discontent on every busy Harlem corner." Malcolm X and his pals "fished" at the meetings of other groups. The method has "many refinements . . . it consisted of working the always shifting edges of audiences that others had managed to draw." Black Nationalist audiences were interested in revolution; "visible results" were obtained when five or six Muslim brothers would pass out leaflets that announced the cure for the black man's "moral, economic, and political sickness." The "best 'fishing'" audience of all were the Christian churches. Malcolm X and his band of brothers would race "fast and furiously" to arrive before each evangelical storefront let out. "Come to hear us, brother, sister—You haven't heard anything until you have heard the teachings of The Honorable Elijah Muhammad—" was the pitch here. Malcolm X knew his customers: "These congregations were usually Southern migrant people, usually older, who would go anywhere to hear what they called 'good preaching.'" When these Christians came to an Islam meeting, they were "conditioned, I found, by the very shock I could give them about what had been happening to them while they worshiped a blond, blue-eyed God. . . . I tailored the teachings for them."[34]

The junto that Malcolm X built within the Nation of Islam explains part of the reasons for his separation from Elijah Muhammad. A totalitarian organization will permit no independent hustlers. Malcolm X tended to see the "divorce" with the eyes of a hustler. Other ministers (those comrades whom every hustler ought to choose carefully) were jealous of him. He was enraged when he learned that Muhammad had affairs with Muslim women. Brothers had been summarily suspended from the church for adultery (including Malcolm X's own brother). He flew to Arizona to confront Muhammad and was given what he recognized as a hustler's line. Malcolm X's reaction is revealing. The old self reemerged as a judge of the new one:

> Both in New York and Chicago, non-Muslims whom I knew began to tell me indirectly they had heard—or they would ask me if I had heard. I would act as if I had no idea whatever of what they were talking about—and I was grateful when they chose not to spell out what they knew. I went around knowing that I looked to them like a total fool. I felt like a total fool, out there every day preaching, and apparently not knowing what was going on right under my nose, in my own organization, involving the very man I was praising so. *To look like a fool unearthed emotions I hadn't felt since my Harlem hustler days. The worst thing in the hustler's world was to be a dupe.*[35]

After a period of confusion Malcolm X underwent another conversion. He accused Muhammad of "religious fakery" and "immorality"; set up his own rival organization (the Organization of Afro-American Unity); and changed his name again (El-Hajj Malik El-Shabazz).

Abbie Hoffman's transformations are more like Franklin's. The conversions are self-willed. Hoffman cultivates his persona as countercultural model as carefully as Franklin did in constructing his role as the industrious and frugal shopkeeper. He remembers his marriage to Anita in these terms: "We were *the* hippie wedding that June, the one featured in *Time.*"[36] Hoffman's life changes are so Arminian in structure that religious experience is largely metaphorical. Still, new selves are born. When at the Chicago trial Hoffman is asked when he was born, he replies, "Psychologically, 1960. . . ." Hoffman experiences all the Franklinesque problems associated with the self-construction of the new persona. He insists that he is a hustler for the movement. Or is he selling the movement for himself? The moral ambiguity of the hustler, his inability to distinguish between hustling$_1$ and hustling$_2$, creates serious consequences for Hoffman's own self-identity. His appearance as Yippie entails the manipulation of the establishment. Thus his identity is in part a media construction, if only as a result of his own deception. To the extent that the actions and tastes of the establishment change in ways that Hoffman cannot control, his new identity is threatened. His autonomy is, in important ways, as incomplete as the more Old Light conversion of Malcolm X. Franklin had to rely upon well-placed friends as well as his pals; so does Hoffman.

All of this is not meant to suggest that Hoffman's rejection of the bourgeoisie and his new beginning as a "child of the sixties" is not psychically felt. But again it is hustling that links up to the new self. The constructing of a political organization from one's hip pals is also part of Hoffman's modus operandi. During his stint as salesman for Westwood he decides to take over the Worcester chapter of the NAACP. With the help of an Irish priest and a "hungry black law student," Hoffman declares that within months he had created the "most militant chapter in the country." [37] He does for a time do political work in a conventional mode. He is a campaign worker for several peace candidates and he labors bravely for SNCC in Mississippi and Georgia.

It is Hoffman's encounter with the "hippie" immigration to the Lower East Side that awakens his instincts as a hustler. These youth were like the Jews who had arrived two generations earlier, but with a difference. Hoffman's forebears came to New York and survived by building family networks. These new immigrants were more "concerned with keeping the family away." Instead they formed a "fugitive colony, on the run from parents and bounty hunters sent to track them down." Hoffman was initially hostile to his new neighbors. He was fifteen years older than the average runaway. To him, the hippies were "just so many glassy-eyed zombies"; to them, he was too much of a "politico," "just another power freak." But the hustler is, above all, adaptable. Hoffman insists that he had "left my old hustler's sales rap back in Worcester, with my suit and my sample case." Yet this was an "organizer's paradise." Hoffman studied "karmic salesmanship." "I thought more about how I should say what I wanted." In short, he hustled those kids. The thirty-one-year-old "power freak" became the official national hippie. Hoffman tells us his secret of hustling: "The times required a new organizing style. Organizers are almost always outside agitators. Like anthropologists, they study the locals, learn their dialect, begin mimicking the style of speaking. This is what I had done in the civil rights and antiwar movements."[38]

There was a conversion at work here of sorts. Hippie youth did represent for Hoffman a culture that was the inverse of that of his grandparents and parents. The hippies were provocatively antibourgeois and Hoffman enjoyed the "dirtiness" of it all: "As a kid I was taught that everything bad happened on the street. Disease lurked in the gutter. When you got fired you were 'out on the street.' Night and day we were warned about the dangers of the street. Just being there was liberation. I walked the soles off my boots three times that first year of the hippies."[39] But hustling was what Hoffman did "in the streets." He did it the same way that Franklin did, by adapting appearances to meet the expectations of his prey and by keeping his true motives hidden from the inhabitants and half-hidden from his own junto.

As I said in chapter one, critics often bemoan the absence of an architectonic structure in American political thought. The autobiographies of Franklin, Malcolm X, and Hoffman provide a partial explanation of this phenomena. The worldview of the hustler forbids the order not just of the organization chart but also of a society composed of legitimately justified relationships. Hustling$_1$ requires a rejection of a natural order of society. Hustling$_2$ views social relationships as hypocritical and supported only by appearances. Thus the hustler builds his own political organizations outside society. Yet, although these new institutions may be elaborately constructed and more or less effective (especially in a society itself given over to a hustler ethic), they always exhibit a gimcrack quality. There appears to be a whole world that separates Franklin's creation of the society of "new leaders of virtue" and Hoffman's Yippie International, but there is an unmistakable similarity between Franklin's imagination and Hoffman's:

> A word was born on New Year's Day. *Yippie!* Five conspirators lay scattered on the pillows adorning the postage-stamp living room of our Lower East Side flat. Paul Krassner, suffering from an acid hangover, staggered around asking, "Why? Why? Why?" . . .

"I, EYE! EYE! EYE! I love you very much," chimed in Anita. "PEE-PEEE," piped Jerry Rubin, his Rolodex brain already connecting the concept to structure. "You need a little pee-pee in every movement."

"I again. I am a walrus, I am the Eggman," said Abbie. "E is for everybody's energy," exclaimed Jerry's girlfriend, Nancy Kurshan. "Yippie!" shouted the chorus. The exclamation point would carry us to victory. Its good vibes would conquer all question marks and get us to Chicago. If the press had created the "hippie," could not we five hatch the "yippie"? A political hippie.[40]

When the hustler approaches politics he treats the existing order as a joke. Even when he is earnest (as in the case of Malcolm X) he is most concerned that the joke not be played on him. A psychoanalyst would no doubt see special connection in the reference to urine in the above recollection. There is indeed a revealing aspect to the passage. The concept is immediately connected to structure. But the structure is itself cynically conceived even when it is presented as a joke: "You need a little pee-pee in every movement." Franklin had preyed upon the anxieties and ambitions of the struggling artisan class, Malcolm X on the anger of blacks, and Hoffman on the yearnings of middle-class youth.

The hustler's entire world is ad hoc. His political theory is a direct reflection of this "freedom."

"Like a man travelling in foggy weather"

Do the many conversions of these hustlers have any impact upon their activities? Is the hustler condemned in some Calvinist sense to always remain a hustler? I have argued that he is. But these autobiographies do suggest that there are moments when the identity of the hustler is at least temporarily shed. These moments of revelation are brief (and, significantly, briefly reported) and of course any real conversion is incomplete. The experiences, however, do show us something about the "true" self of the hustler and, by implication, about the nature of American individualism.

Franklin's autobiography is the least helpful on this point. In fact, a sympathetic reader can ask why Franklin chose to reveal the hustler beneath the famous international personage. There must be a self that is not scheming, that does not measure every encounter in terms of a hustler's felicific calculus. Alas, with the exception of the implications of the strain of hustling, the *Autobiography* offers us little evidence that Franklin has any personality other than that of the hustler.

Franklin does not even offer the reader glimpses at a self that is not a self-conscious social role. A few hints are all we get. For example, look at this passage:

> In 1736, I lost one of my sons, a fine boy of four years old, by the small pox taken in the common way. I long regretted bitterly, and still regret that I had not given it to him by inoculation. This I mention for the sake of parents who omit that operation on the supposition that they should never forgive themselves if a child died under it—my example showing that the regret may be the same either way, and therefore the safer should be chosen.[41]

This account (which precedes one that tells of a visit to and reconciliation with his dying brother) concerns an errata that cannot be corrected. Franklin's heartfelt guilt is not explored nor is remembrance employed to assay grief. We certainly cannot judge Franklin for not dwelling on this tragedy; the regret may have been still too bitter to discuss. But what is important here is Franklin's attempt to justify the inclusion of the event in didactic terms. There are risks at every turn; select a course that minimizes pain. Franklin's account quickly hurries on. The death of a brother and a son are sandwiched between displays of his skills at learning languages and organizing the Junto. There may be a person beneath the hustler's persona, but Franklin may have calculated that the effort of finding him was not worth the risk.

Franklin, whose secular Arminianism led him to worldly conversions, displayed a curious sympathy for religious sects. He was positively disposed toward the Great Awakening; he regularly paid his annual subscription to the Presbyterian church (although forgoing Sunday attendance for independent study); he never refused to contribute to new sects. This special regard was in part the result of Franklin's belief in the social utility of religion in general, in part good politics for a businessman and public official and in part the result of one hustler's natural sympathy for another (some ministers were "projectors" just like him). But there was another reason as well. Franklin wanted to be good. True, his was a hustler's conception of goodness, but still, he was willing to take any advice on how to be good. We saw how both Malcolm X and Abbie Hoffman carried hustling over to their new lives. Franklin always kept a hustler's epistemology. Truth was provisional; its value lay in how it helped you. But because the world offered almost no guidelines for goodness (fortune and success), truth was tentative. Pascal's wager is too timid for a hustler's ethic, but Franklin does admire the believer's desire to find truth. He tells us that he would have given up his Sundays of study if his church had a "good" preacher. The sermons only told how to be a good believer. "These might be all good things, but they were not the kind of good things that I expected. . . ." Franklin wanted to know how to act, how to survive. As we saw, he drew up his own plan, but he was especially impressed with the doctrinal position of the Dunkers who refused to publish their beliefs because they were not sure that they had arrived at the "perfection of spiritual or theological knowledge." His defense of the Dunkers, expressed in allegorical form, provides us with the only hint of a posthustler ethic: "This modesty in a sect is perhaps a singular instance in the history of mankind, every other sect supposing itself in possession of all truth, and that those who differ are so far in the wrong—like a man travelling in foggy weather: Those at some distance before him on the road he sees wrapped up in the fog, as well as those behind him, and also the people in the fields on each side: but near him all appears clear, tho' in truth he is as much in the fog as them." [42] Here is a conception of tolerance that is different from the hustler's. Franklin does not advocate a cynical laissez-faire for all beliefs on the premise that all forms of authority are hypocritical bases for advancement. For Franklin to say that he is not sure of what he is doing violates the hustler's code of self-confidence. Is the plan a proposal of a man "travelling in foggy weather"? Is hustling the "good" life for such a man? Franklin does not consider these questions. There is no conversion away from hustling. There is not even any sustained self-doubt. There is only the germ of an idea of another way of life.

Much has been made about Malcolm X's postconversion experience. Had he abandoned the politics of racial hatred? Was the break with Elijah Muhammad evidence of the beginnings of personal autonomy? To say yes to these questions with any certainty is to participate in the romance of the conversion narrative itself. Malcolm X was shot before he could live out these alternatives and recall them. Speculation is all that can be offered, and speculation requires us to ask if Malcolm X, now El-Hajj Malik El-Shabazz, would continue hustling as leader of his new junto, the Organization of Afro-American Unity.

Abbie Hoffman's postconversion experience is provisional as well, but it does reveal a good deal about the hustler's dilemma. The hustler's greatest fear is the loss of his ability to manipulate appearances. The episodes of the hustler trapped are the most chilling aspects of these autobiographies. Franklin was momentarily without resources in London, but Malcolm X and Hoffman were placed in jail. The experience brought on a conversion (or two) for Malcolm X; Hoffman's six weeks in the Tombs leads him to risk his carefully constructed public persona ("I became something of a brand name") in order to go underground. But initially he had no idea how psychologically difficult this transformation would be. He begins his new journey in the manner of a salesman's briefing. He seeks advice from the underground. The response asks no more of Hoffman than Hoffman the hustler has undertaken himself in the past: "Concentrate on your walk and your voice. You must become very conscious of how you project yourself in the world."[43] Hoffman "worked diligently to develop a new identity."

"On a yellow pad I wrote the autobiography of my new life."[44] Abbie is now Frank. He goes to Georgia and has his hair straightened, then to Los Angeles for plastic surgery. In some respects, Frank has a life similar to Hoffman's. There are a series of temporary jobs and moves. The hustler as prankster is still evident: "I called the New York City Police Department and reported myself missing." Frank occasionally emerges as Abbie for interviews.

Then there is a crack-up. Has Hoffman the hustler assumed one appearance too many?

Alone, in a strange city, the whirly-wheels in my brain took off. I pictured myself growing old. I became old. I experienced false heart attacks. I talked to machines, people on the other side of the world, and finally to the dead. I became obsessed with visions of my father, the grief over his death finally came pouring out. Often I would get lost in the streets. A fugitive's brain is filled with a mass of data—social security numbers, job histories, birthdates, coded contracts, even different birth signs. There are at least two dozen names I use. If I examine the problem of who I am, something everyone does in introspective moods, the problem only gets magnified. A simple "What's your name?" can produce insane giggles.[45]

The man with a dozen names is able to contact a psychiatrist and the "mental wounds began to heal." Did Hoffman's spiritual crisis lead him to shed his life as a hustler? This is the interpretation that his account suggests. The act of autobiography is recalled as a transformation process: "Talk about being reborn! I never was quite sure I was writing an autobiography or a biography." Hoffman settles down. He lives in a "heartland paradise" of a thousand people; "the locals started to accept me." He leads a group of townspeople in opposition to the installation of nuclear reactor plants in the valley. "This struggle was different, though; it was *our* home, *our* land under attack." Hoffman wins. "It is probably the best organizing I have ever done. . . ."[46]

Is this community activity part of a discovery of Hoffman's true calling? Hoffman thinks so. ("I have never seen myself as anything more than a good community organizer. It was just the Vietnam War that made the community bigger, that's all.") Here ends a classical conversion narrative. Hoffman finds himself in upstate New York. The pranks, the interview shows, the cosmopolitan world of the Lower East Side are left behind him as he takes on his "real" role as a kind of Jeffersonian activist.

But is the hustler really dead? Is local antinuke activity the base for a new junto? Is the hustler's conception of politics still operative? Hoffman's life lesson, expressed in a hip version of *Poor Richard,* indicates the tenacity of the hustler's personality: "There is absolutely no greater high than challenging the power structure as a nobody, giving it your all, and winning." Politics still is a trick; Hoffman ends his autobiography with the mock wistfulness of a hustler, "I've had some good times, had some bad. Took some lumps. Scored some points. Half-way through life, at 43, I still say, 'go for broke.' . . . Now as then, let the game continue."[47]

CHAPTER THREE

REDEEMING

HENRY DAVID THOREAU

The political thought of Henry David Thoreau has all the characteristics of a sermon. "Civil Disobedience," Thoreau's masterpiece, is apocalyptic, exhortatory, and above all, stridently moralistic. The inherent brutality of slavery is declared, as are the commercial motives behind the war with Mexico. Thoreau, American Jeremiah, complains that the "children of Washington and Franklin sit down with their hands in their pockets, and say that they know not what to do, and do nothing." Americans today practice a "counterfeit" virtue. They "hesitate" and regret and "sometimes they petition; but they do nothing in earnest and with effect."[1] The essay bristles with statements literally made to become revolutionary slogans: Action from principle changes things and relations! Break the law! Stop the machine! The State is half-witted! Declare war with the State! Refuse allegiance!

Thoreau does not recommend revolution, however, or even concerted direct action. Both reform and revolution "take too much time." He has "other affairs to attend to." Thoreau declares that it is not his duty to eradicate even "the most enormous wrong."[2] Other concerns engage him; his duty is to "wash his hands" of those evils. Even after Thoreau so unreservedly defended John Brown, he reminded an abolitionist that "I do not so much regret the present condition of things in this country (provided I regret it at all) as I do that I ever heard of it."[3]

Thus ends this peculiarly American radicalism. Thoreau recommends withdrawal while hoping for a conversion in the American heart. Emerson's criticism of the Transcendentalist personality seems to accurately reflect upon Thoreau and American political thought in general:

> they are not good citizens, not good members of society; unwillingly they bear their part of the public and private burdens; they do not willingly share in the public charities, in the public rites, in the enterprises of education, of missions foreign and domestic, in the abolition of the slave trade, or in the temperance society. They do not even like to vote.[4]

There appears then to be an ironic conclusion to an essay that is one of the few recognized classics of American political thought. Thoreau as political theorist is a remarkably antipolitical writer; as a reformer he is openly disdainful of reformers; as a revolutionary he refuses to accept the personal burdens of a revolutionary.[5] In short, it seems that one is forced to conclude that although Thoreau is driven on occasion to attack and even critique American society, his major preoccupations are solipsistic. In his own words: "I should not talk so much about myself if there were anybody else whom I knew so well." In this vein (of which there is overwhelming evidence) Thoreau's political works are distractions from his own lifelong spiritual pilgrimage. In *Walden,* society is left behind so that he might have "a little world all to myself."[6] It should be noted, however, that the combination of political radicalism and self-absorption is a common trait in American culture. There may be linkages between both forms of thought and behavior that an examination of Thoreau would disclose. *Walden* was not Thoreau's only experiment in pursuit of individual and spiritual salvation. *A Week on the Concord and Merrimack Rivers* and *Cape Cod* were other efforts to find or retrieve a sense of self outside of society.[7] Taken together, all these works can be seen as pilgrimages in which America's social and political problems are treated as secondary, even epiphenomenal concerns, compared to Thoreau's egoistic obsession with self-discovery.

But each of these pilgrimages also reveals attempts to reach beyond Thoreau's personal search in order to portray the outlines of alternative social orders. How were lives lived before the rise of the village and, later, the state? How do people "outside" of society, in both a physical and psychological sense, live today? What new social order can be imagined? What principle binds people to society? These questions, along with Thoreau's own painful search for a sense of individual peace, are prominent and repeated in *Walden* as well as in *A Week* and *Cape Cod.* Woven into the stylized autobiography is a systematic search for and evaluation of utopias. In the American context it is fitting that Thoreau pursued utopian thought, not only in the context of romantic autobiography but also broadly within the structure of a state of nature, for each of Thoreau's pilgrimages are cast in prepolitical environments (outside a village, along a river, and on a beach), in Locke's words, in "states of perfect freedom" to order our actions.

"Our fates at least are social"

A Week on the Concord and Merrimack Rivers has been praised by some as a travel book. Others have seen it as a kind of preliminary to *Walden*. Walter Harding expresses conventional wisdom when he describes *A Week* as a "typically Transcendentalist" work, often wandering into "the abstract and occasionally into the vapid."[8] Indeed, Thoreau does allow himself long self-indulgent discursions in Hindu texts and minor classical poets, but if one studies the autobiographical structure of *A Week* its political purpose becomes visible.

It has been suggested that the writing of *A Week* was itself an exercise in "grief work."[9] Thoreau's brother, John, who accompanied him on the trip, died shortly after their return. Thoreau wrote the manuscript at Walden Pond, his best-known retreat. The vacation with John had become a model for the comradeship that had been thus far denied him by the townspeople of Concord. Thoreau had already become a local pariah. In fact, his retreat to Walden was a public and self-imposed recognition of this role. *A Week* was a description both of a withdrawal from society (albeit a temporary one) and of a search for answers as to why withdrawal was necessary. Was there comradeship in a state of nature? What was its material basis? Did it differ substantially from what passed for friendship in nineteenth-century America? Locke has argued that the world "never was, nor ever will be, without numbers of men" in a state of nature. Thoreau, quite self-consciously, attempted to discover if the Lockean conditions of "perfect equality" could be recovered.

The river itself becomes for Thoreau a metaphor for his own liberation from false human relationships in society. The book begins with a reminder that the Concord river is a natural archetype: the "Musketaquid or grass-ground river" was "probably as old as the Nile." Thoreau watches the current and tells of his resolve to launch himself "on its bosom," and "float whither it would bear" him. The two young men weighed anchor and immediately their reflections acquired "an historical remoteness from the scenes we had left. . . ." We are told that this trip is an "unusual enterprise":

You shall see men you never heard of before, whose names you don't know. . . . You shall see rude and sturdy, experienced and wise men, keeping their castles or teaming up their summer's wood, or chopping alone in the woods, men fuller of talk and rare adventures in the sun and wind and rain, than a chestnut is of meat; who were out not only in '75 and 1812, but have been out every day of their lives; greater men than Homer, or Chaucer, or Shakespeare. . . .[10]

Thus begins *A Week,* a seven-day pilgrimage in which Thoreau attempts to find evidence for a new model of friendship derived from an eyewitness account of how men lived before the Lockean social compact makes one "body politik." This "unusual enterprise" is composed of three layers of analysis, each interspersed within the daily structure in which Thoreau divides the trip itself. First and most prominent is the presentation of the autobiographical relation of Thoreau to his travels. Second is the description of the social order observed through the journey. Third is an analysis of the historical past in the region visited.

On the first day, childhood memories flash before him. The child, after all, is not quite part of society and Thoreau notes that the childhood fondness for fishing can be recaptured by the adult fisherman. Thoreau links his childhood to the comradeship of all fishermen: "The characteristics and pursuits of various ages and races of men are always existing in epitome in every neighborhood. The pleasures of my earliest youth have become the inheritance of other men."[11] In a tentative way, Thoreau tries to argue that his own solitude is less a state of personal estrangement than a part of some sort of submerged fellowship. He remembers an old fisherman from his youth and concludes that his fishing was not a sport or even a means of subsistence but a "solemn sacrament." At this point, despite the bravado of the embarkment from Concord, Thoreau's attempt at universalizing personal experience is cautious and even poignant.

The Sunday chapter which follows is an ebullient pastoral, an alternative to the Christian sabbath and, not surprisingly, a stylized obituary for Thoreau's dead brother. Thoreau, writing up his account at Walden, is overwhelmed by the peace and beauty of a Sunday morning:

The stillness was intense and almost conscious, as if it were a natural Sabbath and we fancied that the morning was the evening of a celestial day. The air was so elastic and crystalline that it had the same effect on the landscape that a glass has on a picture, to give it an ideal remoteness and perfection. The landscape was clothed in a mild and quiet light, in which the woods and fences checkered and partitioned it with new regularity, and rough and uneven fields stretched away with lawn-like smoothness to the horizon, and the clouds, finely distinct and picturesque, seemed a fit drapery to hang over fairyland. The world seemed decked for some holiday or prouder pageantry, with silken streamers flying, and the course of our lives to wind on before us like a green lane into a country maze, at the season when first trees are in blossom.

He asks, "Why should not our whole life and its scenery be actually this fine and distinct?" But Thoreau and his brother are the object of stares by churchgoers. The comradely pastoral seems to have been shattered and Thoreau is driven to a furious attack on Christianity. The Gospels are simply not pastoral enough. "A healthy man, with steady employment, as wood chopping at fifty a cord, and a camp in the woods, will not be a good subject for Christianity." Religious morality is "too subtle," finer even than that of the politicians. Preaching is "disheartening and disgusting"; "the church is the ugliest looking building" in the village.[12]

At noon on Monday, Thoreau and his brother break from their travels for lunch. Time appears to stop and a sense of place expands. The brothers lunch on melons, "the fruit of the east." Anxiety is becalmed in the "infinite leisure and repose of nature." The brothers find the moment so perfect their thoughts turn to drugs as an enhancer of the special moment. Thoreau notes that a French traveler reported that the leaves of the Oriental kat tree "produce an agreeable soothing excitement, restoring from fatigue, banishing sleep, and disposing to the enjoyment of conversation." Thoreau and his brother ask if they might lead a dignified Oriental life along this stream as well, and the "maple and alders would be our kat trees."[13]

Again this pastoral comradeship is broken as Thoreau's thoughts turn to reformers. In light of the reality of the noontime pastoral moment, "escape" is the "great pleasure" and the political state is "incredible and insignificant." "Revolutions in society have no power to interest"; conventions are not necessary for reform. In bold defiance, Thoreau asks: "What if these grievances do exist?" State and society, animated by the "restless" class of reformers, are more dangerous than "any Cossack or Chippeway" one might come across in the wood.[14]

On Tuesday, the brothers leave the river and Thoreau climbs the Saddleback mountain. He insists that he is not "lost": "I am not alone if I stand by myself." The day is spent observing the "uncivil" men and women in this pastoral state of nature. Thoreau is transfixed by the "noble and poetic" boatmen, stone masons, and lumberers he observes along the river. Here work was transformed: "Their commerce did not look like toil" but more like "a game of chess." By the following day the outbursts against reformers and preachers are less prominent. The river has carried Thoreau both physically and psychologically deep into an Edenic state of nature: "There are no more quiet Tempes, or more poetic or Arcadian lives than may be lived in these New England dwellings. We thought that the employment of their inhabitants by day would be to tend the flowers and herds, and at night, like shepherds of old, to cluster and give names to the stars from the river banks." Now the two brothers float on the river, not so much as escapees from a hostile society, but alongside banks where "friends and kindred dwell." Thoreau's thoughts turn to kindness. The movement of the stars reveals laws, "not of kindred merely, but of kindness, whose pulse still beats at any distance and forever." He remembers past kindness unacknowledged as "winds of heaven unnoticed."[15]

The long discourse that follows begins with a description of friendship firmly encased in the pastoral setting:

> Friendship is evanescent in every man's experience, and remembered like heat lightning in past summers. Faint and flitting like a summer cloud; there is always some vapor in the air, no matter how long the drought; there are even April showers. Surely from time to time, for its vestiges never depart, it floats through our atmosphere. It takes place, like vegetation in so many materials, because there is such a law, but always without permanent form, though ancient and familiar as the sun and moon, and as sure to come again. The heart is forever inexperienced.[16]

Friendship lies outside organized society. There is "no institution which friendship has established; it is not taught by my religion, no scripture contains its maxims." Christianity has so codified love that for Thoreau friendship must be "essentially heathenish." When a friend treats a friend as a Christian, the special bond has been broken. Charity is now the controlling relation. The "principle which established the almshouse takes its place." The State thinks it succeeds when it is able to establish conduct "hardly more than rogues practice." If only the dreaded reformers and philanthropists could see that all the abuses of society would be "unconsciously amended in the intercourse of friends."[17]

Even the town fails to base social relationships on friendship. Instead it accepts a "cheap civility." One who loans a neighbor his wagon or discounts a cord of wood is judged a friend. These are only "accidental and trifling" aspects of friendship. No one is "transfigured and translated by love" in another's presence. In fact, to say that a man is your friend means commonly that he is not your enemy. Nevertheless, friendship is the "secret of the universe." "Men naturally though feebly, seek this alliance, and their actions faintly foretell it." Thoreau, the individualist, concludes that "our fates at least are social."[18]

The journey down the Merrimack begins as a rejection of society and as a spiritual pilgrimage. The pastoral life that Thoreau thought he saw in the woods offered a utopian alternative that renewed a sense of the social in Thoreau. Although the country seemed so new, Thoreau remarked that he did not have to travel far to find "where men inhabited, like wild bees, and had sunk wells in the loose sand and loam of the Merrimack." "There dwelt the subject of the Hebrew scriptures, and the *Esprit des Lois,* where a thin vaporous smoke curled up through the noon." History becomes universal here: "All that is told of mankind, of the inhabitants of the Upper Nile and the Sunderburds and Timbuctoo, and the Orinoko, was experience here." The state of nature was real. Thoreau had, of course, in a sense experienced a state of nature. In Concord, he had been estranged from local society. He had been alone, without the pleasures of a social life, alienated from both the social order and the political system. The journey now cast him literally in a state of nature and, as a consequence, Thoreau found that there was no "Arcadian life which surpassed the luxury and serenity" of these river people. This state of nature was real enough; it offered an environment without alienation. Now it was possible for Thoreau to deal with those complaints of his friends in society. His friends castigated him for his silence. But here in Arcadia "true hospitality" and "ancient civility" did not demand the amenities of conversation. His friends criticized him for his political opinions. But here there were no slaves, no taxes, no commerce. Lovers demand so much, "cheap and passionate emotions," commitments that are "extravagant and insane." Yet when lovers meet "not on carpets and cushions, but on the ground and rocks," they can part "without any outcry, and part without loud sorrow." And perhaps most important of all, the memory of his dead brother would no longer occasion an unbearable sense of loss and guilt. Friendship cemented along these Arcadian rivers would leave memories "incrusted over with sublime and pleasing thought, as monuments of other men are overgrown with moss." Friends "have no place in the graveyard." [19]

On Thursday, the penultimate day of Thoreau's journey, there are signs of a resolution of the personal crisis, but they are ambiguous ones, sometimes hinting as much of resignation as of triumph. The Edenic character of brotherly friendship continues. The young men buy a melon. Thoreau is pleased by the naturalness of the economic transaction in the midst of a wood. The river had been a tangible source of renewal. Now he remarks how difficult it is to remain on this path. There is a note of wistfulness as he remarks that "the world reposes in beauty to him who preserves equipose in his life, and moves serenely on his path without secret violence." The men must leave their boat. They had glided down the river but now "trod the unyielding land like pilgrims." Thoreau is travel weary and now not quite certain of the whole enterprise. He inserts a local historian's account of the first plowing of the land at Haverhill. Maybe his pastoral state of nature was not real. Maybe his generation had come into the world fatally late for some enterprises. The mythic basis of his travels seems to be evaporating. He wishes he had written more in his journal. Could the pastoral be recaptured if it had been more meticulously recorded? Too many "indifferent things" were set down. "It is not easy to write in a journal what interests us at any time, because to write it is not what interests us." Maybe, after all, the frontier is not to be found in this state of nature at all. "We do not avoid evil by fleeing before it, but by rising above or diving below its plane. . . ." "The frontiers are not east or west, north or south, but wherever a man fronts a fact, though that fact be his neighbor, there is an unsettled wilderness between him and Canada, between him and the setting sun, or further still, between him and it." [20]

Thoreau, the self-described sojourner, begins to doubt the utility of traveling. Can he continue the vaguely defined pilgrimage he had set out upon? Can he stop? Traveling develops a sense of self-sufficiency and independence, but there may be no purpose to the effort. Thoreau, the obsessive punster, offers a deadly serious joke. Traveling, and by implication self-searching, wears away the soles of the shoes. Before long it "will wear a man clean up, after making his heart sore into the bargain." [21] Can Thoreau stop his search? Will he continue to be a traveler, a stranger in both society and the woods?

During his trip Thoreau sporadically interspersed his pastoral with historical summaries of the villages that he passed. In general, he was impressed with the stolid bravery of the pioneers. For him some of the villages were now in their "dotage," yet we "have need to be as sturdy pioneers as Miles Standish, or Church, or Lovewell." But at the same time Thoreau was horrified by the Indian wars. No histories were written nor monument raised to these "crippled" and "exterminated" people. Locke had carefully distinguished a "state of nature" from a "state of war," but there still was an unquestionably gothic element in the former. "Unjust violence and slaughter" did occur in the state of nature. At points, Thoreau had noted historical scenes of violence, the murder of a fur trader and a battle with Indians, but the pastoral effect is so strong that he remains incredulous: "It did not look as if men had ever had to run for their lives on this now open and peaceful interval." [22]

Thursday's account, however, reintroduces anarchic terror into the pastoral. This time it is not so easily pushed aside. Thoreau tells the story of an attempted Indian massacre of a frontier family and of the capture and flight of two young women. The story is retold by Thoreau in a kind of breathless detail that rivals Poe. The mother sees her infant's brains dashed against an apple tree. The following morning she and her comrade kill and scalp their captors and after placing the scalps of the dead in a bag as proof of what they had done, begin their escape by canoe for Haverhill sixty miles away by the river. Thoreau now narrates as if the event is occurring before him:

> Early this morning this deed was performed, and now these tired women and this boy, their clothes stained with blood, and their minds racked with alternate resolution and fear, are making a hasty meal of parched corn and moosemeat, while their canoe glides under these pine roots whose stumps are still standing in the bank. They are thinking of the dead whom they have left behind on that solitary isle far up the stream, and of the relentless living warriors who are in pursuit. Every withered leaf which the winter has left seems to know their story, and in its rustling to repeat it and betray them.[23]

The story ends happily enough, all things considered. Miraculously, the women escape the roving bands of Indians, are reunited with their family, and are paid fifty pounds by the General Court for their trophies. Thoreau concludes that there have been many who in later times have lived to say that they had eaten the fruit of the same apple tree that marks the place of the infant's murder.

Thoreau still insists upon the remoteness of the murder but now he uses the event to remark that the event did, after all, occur since Milton wrote his *Paradise Lost*. Had the pastoral that Thoreau just discovered already been shattered, not by some emptying of mythic structure, but by another myth? Was the murder of the infant against the Edenic apple tree (which later inhabitants also tasted), and the murders that followed, the rebirth of another myth? Were the crimes of the settlers and the Indians a kind of biblical repetition that now afflicted America? Thoreau continues with the thinly disguised analogy:

> The age of the world is great enough for our imaginations, even according to the Mosaic account, without borrowing any years from the geologist. From Adam and Eve at one leap sheer down to deluge, and then through the ancient monarchies, through Babylon and Thebes, Brahma and Abraham, to Greece and the Argonauts; whence we might start again with Orpheus and the Tro-

jan war, the Pyramids and the Olympic games, and Homer and Athens, for our stages; and after a breathing space at the building of Rome, continue our journey down through Odin and Christ—to America.

Perhaps the history of the world can best be understood as the personal history of "but sixty old women, such as live under the hill, say of a century each, strung together." The old woman fourth removed from Thoreau would have suckled Columbus; the ninth, Norman the conqueror; the nineteenth was the Virgin Mary; the sixtieth was "Eve, the mother of mankind." The infanticide took place 142 years before Thoreau's journey, so that the mother of the dead baby was in a direct mythic line to Thoreau himself. In any case, Thoreau explains that if these "sixty old women would hold hands they would span the eternal from Eve to my own mother."²⁴ Thoreau, the anti-Christian of Sunday, now includes himself in the biblical myth of original sin. The timelessness of the pastoral described in Sunday's pagan fraternal celebration is now replaced by the timelessness of the horror of American origins. To celebrate the fraternal myth of pastoral America is to unavoidably accept the fratricidal myth of what is also a "howling wilderness."

Two myths in hand, Thoreau returns to reconsider his own pilgrimage of self-identity. Friday is a poignant closing of A Week. Walden would close with the spring, but here the fall provides the background for Thoreau's mood. The men went to sleep in summer and "awoke in autumn." Thoreau does not return to the pastoral in a presentation of harvest festivals in Concord and other New England towns. He speaks in praise of fairs—the sober farmer folk, with "an unusual springiness to their gait, jabbering earnestly to one another," are unconsciously acting out the ancient festivals of the Greeks and Etruscans. But Thoreau watches them as a detached outsider. He confesses that he can never really be a farmer. He tries to tell himself that great poets and geniuses who were unknown to their generation have "their high estimate beyond the stars." There is the same defiance here that one finds in his political writings. The poet is "no tender slip of fairy stock." He needs no "peculiar institutions and edicts for his defence." His "fainting companions" will eventually "recognize the god in him." After all, it is "the worshippers of beauty. . . . who have done the real pioneer work of the world."[25]

Yet the attempt to construct a myth that will strengthen his own identity is for Thoreau at this point a failure. He is plagued with self-doubt. His library contains books in which "immortal works stand side by side with anthologies which did not survive their month, and cobweb and mildew have already spread from these to the binding of those. . . ."[26] Moreover, the mythic role of the heroic poet, detached from society and contemptuous of fame and popularity, is a repudiation and retreat from Thoreau's own fraternal myth outlined earlier in A Week.

But even the rejection of the pastoral, which he had so earnestly sought, produced for Thoreau a sense of discovery: "I have seen a bunch of violets in a glass vase, tied loosely with a straw, which reminded me of myself." Thoreau is still determined to hold to Tuesday's maxim ("I am not alone if I stand by myself"). The image here is not one of a Carlylean poet, or even of a serene shepherd or rustic farmer. The violets are unmasculine, fragile, without roots. There are "some tender buds . . . left upon my stem / In mimicry of life / But ah! the children will not know them / Till time has withered them / The woe / With which they're rife."[27]

"The sun is but a morning star"

Walden is universally regarded as Thoreau's literary masterpiece. It is acclaimed as an autobiography stylized and condensed into a year and forged into a structural and stylistic work of art.[28] The experiment at Walden was, of course, only one of Thoreau's autobiographical travels and one can ask why, literary achievement aside, generation after generation it has been this account that has so captured the American imagination. One reason, I suspect, is that at the moment Thoreau recalled his Walden experiment he was able to summon up enough will to convince himself and his readers that he had undergone a genuine and lasting conversion. Thus Walden succeeds where A Week failed. Thoreau had found "what to live for" and gave a "true account of it." Walden links up with Pilgrim's Progress and Jonathan Edwards's Narrative and countless tracts of American culture. It is, in the words of Sherman Paul, "an experience of the microcosmic and cosmic travels of the self."[29] In a more limited sense Thoreau showed that a Transcendentalist could find true conversion. But even more important, when Thoreau tells us in the last lines of *Walden* that the "sun is but a morning star" he has told generations of Americans that individual salvation is possible and they, one by one, can be happy.

Two themes provide the framework for Thoreau's account of his conversion. Both merge to prove the validity of the experiment. One, like *A Week* and *Cape Cod*, is the autobiographical account of the flight from society. Thoreau writes from the perspective of the village. He is now a "sojourner in civilized life again" and so he would have us believe he is now a happy and rested man. He is so contented that he would not even bother to tell his story, save that people are curious about his experiment. Thoreau consents to tell a "simple and sincere account" of his life at Walden.

Thoreau's reticence is, of course, feigned. Very shortly he assumes the classic jeremiadic style of his political essays: Why if men are free are they so enslaved? "Who made them serfs of the soil? Why should they eat their sixty acres, when man is condemned to eat only his peck of dirt? Why should they begin digging their graves as soon as they are born?" These Rousseauean questions are followed by a Marxist observation: "There is no play in them, for this comes after work."[30] But the answers that Thoreau offers are in anticipation neither of Rousseau nor Marx but of traditional American evangelism. We are not free or happy because we do not have the will to be so. The constant motion of the American is Augean labor never completed. Thoreau recommends one single act of motion, a flight out of society to a state of nature. In the woods, motion can be kept to an essential minimum, "cut" and "shaved close," "reduced to its lowest terms," and thus be made meaningful.

The Thoreauvian critique in *Walden* is then a purification of bourgeois value. Time *is* important and not to be wasted. But work in society, even careful, simple, honest work, is itself a waste of time. Faith, not work alone, brings liberation. Thoreau confesses he has little to say to the poor; he addresses those who are said to be in "*moderate* circumstances." Because the flight to the woods is temporary, the bourgeois life can be cleansed, doubly cleansed at that. The fear, the "quiet desperation," that time spent in work and thrift is still wasted can be

dispelled by returning to a state of nature. Moreover, peace and happiness can come only to the converted. A new life can offer solace to
the tormented ego. Thus despite Thoreau's critique of trade, despite his
attack on materialism, despite his disdain for organized religion, in
Walden he offers advice to the middle class that is not only full of hope
but relatively painless. Ignore reformers; ignore demands for charity;
ignore the poor. Free yourselves and you will be happy. Thoreau, the
social critic, knows bourgeois fears intimately and above all he knows
the solutions the bourgeois seek.

But the success of *Walden* is explained by more than the injunction
to flee to "live a primitive and frontier life." Thoreau is painfully explicit
in explaining precisely how happiness can be recovered. *Walden* is a
work that literally reeks with practicality. In fact, it is the juxtaposition
of the romance of flight with blueprints for practical living that make
Walden the cultural success that it is. Between the poignant reflections
on the pond in winter and the delicate balance among birds, fish, in-
sects, and animals are instructions and advice on how to build a house,
how to entertain, how to eat, how to plant a garden, how to build furniture, how to budget. The chapter on "Higher Laws" turns out to be a
discussion of the virtues of vegetarianism.

In each of these manuallike exercises Thoreau is as conscious of time
fruitfully spent as any bourgeois. He wants simple furniture and no ornaments to save time in dusting. Weeding a bean field becomes a long
war against time, and he wonders if he has not undertaken some
new Augean labor. More to the point, however, we find Thoreau,
sometimes openly, sometimes surreptitiously, sometimes even unconsciously, reaffirming the sins (or virtues) of middle America. The journey to a state of nature at Walden is a personal act of redemption. Thoreau hopes to redeem himself in the eyes of Concord by retrieving the
principles of bourgeois life itself.

Walden undoubtedly begins in the spirit of *épater les bourgeois*. Thoreau adds to the polemic his own rejection by the middle class:
"it became more and more evident that my townsmen would not after
all admit me into the list of town officers, nor make my place a sinecure
with a moderate allowance." Bourgeois Concord did not need a "self-
appointed inspector of snow storms" nor a tender of huckleberry
bushes and red pine. So Thoreau found that he must shift for himself: "I

turned my face more exclusively than ever to the woods, where I was better known. I determined to go into business at once, and not wait to organize the usual capital using such slender means as I had already got."[31] The tone is ironic, but it is evident from subsequent business-derived metaphors on how to dress, eat, and live cheaply that Thoreau often saw his flight as analogous to an entrepreneurial venture, although of course, one on his own terms.[32]

In his Franklinesque sermon on economy, Thoreau goes as far as to suggest that coffinlike railroad boxes can provide a fine serviceable means of shelter. Yet when he sets out to build his own house, the six-foot box is abandoned. Likewise, he does not take up residence in the shanty of James Collins despite the fact that the shack "was considered an uncommonly fine one." A good business deal is struck, even the exact time of possession is detailed. The shanty is torn down and the boards used for Thoreau's own house. There are several disclaimers that he is not house proud ("my excuse is that I brag for humanity rather than for myself") but can we deny that Thoreau's description of his cabin nevertheless has the ring of the realtor's pitch?—"the walls being of rough weather-stained boards, with wide chinks, which made it cool at night. The upright white hewn studs and freshly planed door and window casing gave it a clean and airy look. . . ."[33] And then, of course, what a view!

Thoreau admits this is his first house and he is conscious of its impact upon him. He "had made some progress toward settling in the world." A pleasant sense of order arose from this possession. "This frame, so slightly clad, was a sort of crystallization around me, and reacted on the builder." The house, transformed from the poor Irishman's shanty, is both bourgeois and antibourgeois. Thoreau chides his villagers for their architectural ornaments and *their* reliance on Irish labor. He reminds us that he is only a "squatter." But possession at Walden has its psychological impact and Thoreau's chanticleering about the low cost of his cabin is itself a bourgeois habit not even turned inside out.

Many years later E. M. Forster would buy a woods with his royalties from *A Passage to India*. Here is his reaction to ownership: "The other day I heard a twig snap in it. I was annoyed at first, for I thought that someone was blackberrying, and depreciating the value of the under-growth. On coming nearer, I saw it was not a man who had trodden the twig and snapped it, but a bird, and I felt pleased. My bird." Forster wondered if "his" forest would make him become "enormously stout, endlessly avaricious, pseudo-creative, intensely selfish."[34] Of course, Thoreau's two years at Walden Pond never produced the kind of character described in Forster's nightmare. Yet there is a noticeable absence of whimsy in Thoreau's own experiment with private ownership. Not only does the cabin become his to admire, but Walden woods is inhabited by *his* birds, *his* ants, *his* flowers, as well as by *his* bean field and *his* woodpile. Only the "best" visit *his* woods; the railroad is an intrusion upon *his* solitude; the Irish ice cutters deface *his* pond.

Thoreau was a bachelor, but *Walden* is laced with domestic preoccupations. Thoreau tells us of the joy of baking bread. He makes some of his own furniture, listing items he did buy: "a bed, table, desk, three chairs, looking glass, tongs and andirons, kettle, skillet, frying pan, dipper, wash bowl, two knives and forks, three plates, one cup, one spoon, a jug for oil, a jug for molasses, and a japanned lamp." Of course, Thoreau extols the virtues of freedom from domestic possession, but we are told a great deal more about Thoreau's kitchen and cooking habits than one would expect or even wish to learn. Thoreau's real point, one that American readers undoubtedly appreciate, is not based upon an argument for the destruction of consumer-oriented domesticity. Like all of Thoreau's statements in *Walden,* his position is one of purification. The creation of an "ideal" kitchen is Thoreau's goal. In this respect, Thoreau illustrates the link between *Better Homes & Gardens* and the *Whole Earth Catalogue.* Look at Thoreau's advice on the curtain question:

> I would observe, by the way, that it costs me nothing for curtains, for I have no gazers to shut out the sun and the moon, and I am willing that they should look in. The moon will not sour milk nor taint meat of mine, nor will the sun injure my furniture or fade my carpet, and if he is sometimes too warm a friend, I find it still better economy to retreat behind some curtain which nature has provided, than to add a single item to the details of housekeeping.[35]

This is certainly sound, reasonable advice, but it is advice offered in the context of domestic aesthetics, one that attempts to answer the question: "How can I make my home both pleasing and efficient?" Thoreau can marvel over the beauty of a water dipper in the same manner that his twentieth-century counterparts enjoy their Cuisinarts. In fact, in more general terms, Thoreau's conception of domesticity anticipates the contemporary model. It is a domesticity highly purified, stripped of spouse, children, and neighborhood. It is the domesticity of single-hood—well-managed, isolated, and visually pleasing.

Locke had argued that private property did exist in a state of nature. The "partage of things, in an inequality of private possessions, men have made practicable out of the bounds of Societie. . . ."[36] Thoreau establishes this point effectively in both an experimental and a psychological sense at Walden. The power of *Walden* in the American imagination is not simply pride of ownership. Private property as a certain avenue for the inculcation of virtue is regarded as self-evident in American culture. The power of *Walden* is its success in combining the pride of ownership *with* the romance of a primitive life. Thoreau had not only established domicile in the state of nature but also domesticated the entire wood. The fact that he had done so without obviously becoming enormously stout and endlessly avaricious makes the American romance all the more sweet.

Thoreau's affirmation at Walden is anything but a defense of capitalism. Of course, he did use wage labor to plough his field. But he described it sheepishly: "I was obliged to hire a team and a man for the ploughing, though I held the plough myself."[37] He did sell his vegetables in the market and carefully recorded his profits along with a quote from Cato's *De Agri Cultura* on selling. He did use his mother's labor to clean his laundry, a point on which the author of *Walden* is silent. It is not these incidents per se that so rivet Thoreau's experiment to American political economy. Although fuel for Thoreau's iconoclasts, they are trivial matters at Walden. It is, rather, Thoreau's complex approach toward economic institutions that are so instructive. Thoreau captures these attitudes as sharply and beautifully as he does the glints and shimmers on Walden Pond.

In the chapter on the Baker farm, Thoreau, the "free man," strolls through the pine groves. The scene is redolently pastoral. The morning light especially fascinates Thoreau: "I stood in the very abatement of a rainbow's arch, which filled the lower stratum of the atmosphere, tinging the grass and leaves around, and dazzling me as if I looked through colored crystal." For a moment he wonders if the halo of light around him is a sign of election. He shakes off the thought as superstition but soon returns to ask: "But are they not indeed distinguished who are conscious that they are regarded at all?"[38]

The walk had taken him near the dreaded railroad, and Thoreau remembers a friend's comment that no halo surrounds the shadows of Irishmen: "it was only natives that were so distinguished." What follows is a revealing dialogue between Thoreau and John Field, an Irishman who clearly cannot attain the halo that Thoreau so admires. The encounter is a kind of inverse pastoral. A summer shower forces Thoreau to seek shelter. He half-expected a Vergilian character to emerge from the hut a half mile from the road—"And here a poet builded / In the completed years, / For behold a trivial cabin / That to destruction steers." Instead of an image of a "noble infant sitting on his father's knee," Thoreau sees John Field and "his poor starveling brat." Field is "honest, hard-working, but shiftless," his wife "brave" but "greasy" and dirty. John Field complains to Thoreau about how hard he works "bogging" a field for a neighbor farmer at the rate of ten dollars an acre. Thoreau attempts to speak to him "as if he were a philosopher": "Give up bogging and wear light clothes like me; give up meat and catch fish; live simply and go a-huckleberrying in the summer." But John "heaved sigh at this" and "his wife stared with arms a-kimbo." Thoreau concludes that "alas! the culture of an Irishman is a enterprise to be undertaken with a sort of moral bog hoe." The shower ends, Thoreau leaves the leaking hut to return to his own idyll singing advice like verse: "Go fish and hunt far and wide day by day"; "Rise free from care before the dawn, and seek adventures"; "Let not to get a living by thy trade, but thy sport."[39] Well, he had tried to transfer that halo to the Field family.

Thoreau's attitudes toward wage laborers involved both a condemnation of wage labor and a justification of the status of the wage laborer. The working man and woman ought to be free; they ought to free themselves; everyone ought to work only for himself. In Thoreau's words, "Through want of enterprise and faith men are where they are. . . ." As for "poor John Field": "With his horizon all his own, yet he is a poor man, born to be poor, with his inherited Irish poverty or poor life, his Adam's grandmother and boggy ways, not to rise in this world, he nor his posterity, till their wading webbed bog-trotting feet get talaria to their heel."[40] No American halo here.

If *Walden* has any single clear message as to how to achieve happiness, it is in the doctrine of self-improvement. The concept enjoys a fascinating plasticity in American society. It can provide the justification for the most brutal economic opportunism, for upward social mobility, for religious salvation, for political reform. It can also be used as a defense against psychological disintegration, as a model for political change, as a critique of bourgeois smugness. Thus Benjamin Franklin, Andrew Carnegie, Malcolm X, Jonathan Edwards, and Lincoln Steffens have all used the concept in describing their lives. Thoreau's *Walden* rests firmly in the self-improvement tradition. Thoreau, as all the writers mentioned above, sees life in terms of a series of actions which properly focused and planned can individually lead to happiness/virtue/salvation. That *Walden* is an exercise in conversion explains the American fascination with Thoreau as much as the continuing interest in his political pronouncements. Stanley Hyman commends *Walden* on these terms: it is a "vast rebirth ritual, the purest and most complete in our literature."[41] There are crises to be sure. The long winter at Walden Pond provides the context for self-doubt and melancholy. But Thoreau does burst forth in spring: "What is man but a mass of thawing day?" He concludes that "the coming in of spring is like the creation of Cosmos out of Chaos." The concluding image of *Walden,* that of the insect long buried in the leaf of an old table is so perfect, so American homey that Thoreau cannot resist its repetition as a symbol of "faith in a resurrection and immortality." He also had woven himself a silken web and, nymphlike, explodes as a "more perfect creature," thus passing from "the lumpish grub in the earth to the airy and fluttery butterfly."[42]

In addition to self-doubt, there is temptation. In a chapter called "Higher Laws" Thoreau feels the urge to transmogrify not to a butterfly but to a predator. At twilight Thoreau glimpses a woodchuck (the nemesis of his bean garden) and feels a "strange thrill of savage delight." He was not hungry but how he was "tempted to seize and devour him raw!" On other occasions, he reports that he found himself "ranging the woods, like a half-starved hound, with a strange abandonment, seeking some kind of venison which I might devour, and no morsel could have been too savage for me." These urges might be passed off as the natural lapses any vegetarian might endure (or even as the consequences of the displaced desires of a celibate). But this temptation to succumb to a "primitive rank" is connected to the same general depression that accompanies viewing the pond in the winter. One emotion is active, even adventurous; the other passive and melancholy. Spiritual life led to dissipation of energy. The primitive life was simply too animallike. In an inversion of his own concerns, the foxes in winter remind Thoreau of rudimental, burrowing men. Each way of life, higher and lower, can lead away from self-improvement. Thoreau insists that "chastity is the flowering of man," but he is forced to admit that, even when we are conscious of the animal in us, we must realize that the "reptile and sensual cannot be totally expelled." They are, he writes, "like the worms which, even in life and health, occupy our bodies."[43]

The Thoreauvian fear is loss of control and the subsequent dissipation of the self. In the individualist ethos of the conversion narrative, the dissolution of the self destroys the hope of redemption. In this we find an explanation for the recurrent preoccupation with diet and sexuality in the sermonic tradition. Franklin's vegetarianism, Malcolm X's strict regimen, and now Thoreau's fear of the sensual, all reflect an attempt to retain at least a rudimentary control of a threatened self. No wonder then that American political thought so frequently lapses into bodily concerns.

Nowhere is this more evident than in Thoreau's reaction to the American primitive Alex Therien. This woodchopper puzzles, fascinates, and repels Thoreau. He is described as quiet and humble, simple and natural, good-humored and content. "Vice and disease, which cast such a somber moral hue over the world seemed to have hardly any existence for him." But Thoreau's physical description is more revealing:

He was about twenty-eight years old, and had left Canada and his father's house a dozen years before to work in the States, and earn money to buy a farm with at last, perhaps in his native country. He was cast in the coarsest mould; a stout but sluggish body, yet gracefully carried, with a thick sunburnt neck, dark bushy hair, and dull sleepy blue eyes, which were occasionally lit up with expression. He wore a flat gray cloth cap, a dingy wool-colored greatcoat and cowhide boots. He was a great consumer of meat, usually carrying his dinner to his work a couple of miles past my house,—for he chopped all summer,—in a tin pail; cold meats often cold woodchucks, and coffee in a stone bottle which dangled by a string from his belt; and sometimes he offered me a drink. He came along early, crossing my bean-field, though without anxiety or haste to get to his work, such as Yankees exhibit. He wasn't a-going to hurt himself. He didn't care if he only earned his board.[44]

In A Week on the Concord and Merrimack, men of Therien's type— woodchoppers, stonecutters, boatmen—were praised as men greater than "Homer, or Chaucer or Shakespeare." Here, close up, Thoreau finds that Therien reads Homer all right but he understands none of it. Only the rhythms and sounds enchant him. Thoreau questions him incessantly for his opinions on money, reform, work, religion, and charity and concludes that "I did not know whether he was as wise as Shakespeare or as simply ignorant as a child, whether to suspect him of a fine poetic consciousness or of stupidity."[45] When Thoreau had that urge to leap up and devour that woodchuck, was it the image of a transformation to Therien, tin pail of cold meat swinging in hand, that so repulsed him? Hidden behind the self-improvement narrative written as a redemptive moral for American society is the fear of loss of the only possession Thoreau really cannot surrender: his own sense of self. Its very prominence in Walden is, in some respects, evidence of its potential collapse.

"It was a wild, rank place . . . a vast morgue. . . ."

Cape Cod, the last of Thoreau's autobiographical travels, is a presentation of a truly horrific state of nature. Thoreau had hoped to discover America's origins by visiting the villages along the Cape. The historical accounts of early settlements are often excised from editions of Cape Cod, but Thoreau's purpose in writing history is clear: "Let no one think that I do not love the old ministers. They were, probably, the best men of their generation, and they deserve that their biographies should fill the pages of the town histories." He even regrets that his identification could not be stronger: "If I could but hear the 'glad tidings' of which they tell, and which, prechance, they heard, I might write in a worthier strain than this."[46]

The personal history of village foundings, however, is overwhelmed by Thoreau's reactions to nature on the Cape. He was well acquainted with the ecology of Walden Pond. The beaches on the Cape, however, exhibit none of the gentleness of a river shore. The immensity of the ocean terrifies Thoreau. "Chaos reigns" on the beaches. The sounds of the breakers continually startle him. The beach violates his senses. Without an object to measure against, the landscape is a "constant mirage." Men look like boys, beached whales, like men. Standing at the Highland Light, he feels as if the whole Cape is shifting beneath his feet. Nature had been Thoreau's refuge from a hostile society and from his inability to form personal relationships. Here it seemed to attack him as well.

On one of his trips to the Cape, Thoreau witnessed a shipwreck. The *St. John,* filled with Irish immigrants, had crashed against the rocky shore at Cohasset. One hundred and forty-five people died. This event forms the theme of the entire account of his travels on the Cape. Thoreau does not explicitly mention his experience with another disaster. In 1850 Margaret Fuller Ossoli, one of the very few women who could be said to have had any semblance of a romance with Thoreau, had perished in the wreckage of the *Elizabeth* off Fire Island. Thoreau had attempted to retrieve her personal effects, including her manuscript on the Italian revolution, but his efforts were unsuccessful because the wreck had been pilfered by locals. A body had been reported several miles downshore. When Thoreau had reached the scene, all that remained were a few bones.[47]

Given this earlier experience, Thoreau's reportage at Cohasset would understandably then be a difficult assignment. He offers a cinematic description. The villagers who owned wagons were made temporary undertakers. They retrieved and identified bodies. Above the rubble and carnage were neatly spaced rows of coffins. Thoreau asks questions: Where did the ship strike the rocks? Did all the passengers drown or were some killed by the wreckage? He tries to interview a survivor who "seemed unwilling to talk." His descriptions verge on the clinical:

I saw many marble feet and matted heads as the cloths were raised, and one livid, swollen, and mangled body of a drowned girl, who probably had intended to go out to service in some American family,—to which some rags still adhered, with a string, half concealed by the flesh, about its swollen neck; the coiled up wreck of a human hulk, gashed by the rocks or fishes, so that the bone and muscle were exposed, but quite bloodless,—merely red and white,—with wide-open and staring eyes, yet lustreless, dead-lights; or like cabin windows of a stranded vessel, filled with sand. Sometimes there were two or more children, or a parent and a child, in the same box, and on the lid would perhaps be written with red chalk, "Bridget such-a-one, and sister's child." [48]

Despite his own restraint, Thoreau is critical of the apparent lack of grief among the residents. In the crowd men are collecting sea weed, "though they were often obliged to separate fragments of clothing from it, and they might at any moment have found a human body under it." "Drown who might," concludes Thoreau, "they did not forget that this weed was a valuable manure. This shipwreck had not produced a visible vibration in the fabric of society." [49]

But what of Thoreau's own response? He had seen a grief-stricken mother. He reports making no attempt to console her. He carefully observes survivors; he offers no personal aid. The next day he swims at the Cohasset Rocks. The sea-bathing was "perfect," the water "purer and more transparent than any I have ever seen." Where is the concern with discovering corpses? Was Thoreau collecting impressions as callously as the villagers gathered seaweed? Are these dead Irish to be regarded as moral bog hoes, as the ice cutters or as "poor John Fields" of *Walden?* It would seem so. Thoreau insists that the carnage was "not so impressive a scene as I might have expected." There were just too many bodies: "If I had found one body cast upon the beach in some lonely place, it would have affected me more." So many corpses suggest the stiffling majorities that he so dreads in his political essays. "A man can attend but one funeral in the course of his life. . . ." [50]

Still, the attempts to maintain indifference multiply. He "sympathized" more with the winds and the waves. If this disaster was "the law of Nature, why waste any time in awe and in pity?" Darwinist rationalization is then exchanged for ministerial consolation. The Irish had arrived at a better world than the Pilgrims. Thoreau had seen only "empty hulks," the spirits of the victims had really reached the "safest port in Heaven."[51]

None of these exorcisms works. The specter of the *St. John* haunts Thoreau as he travels along the Cape. The beach near Provincetown is "a vast morgue": "the carcasses of men and beasts together lie stately up upon its shelf, rotting and bleaching in the sun and the waves, and each tide turns them in their beds, and trucks fresh sand under them." Thoreau had discovered another state of nature. The beach is "a sort of neutral ground, a most advantageous point from which to contemplate the world," but it is a "trivial place," one which reason cannot order, a place where "only anomalous creatures can inhabit." It is a place of chaos and death. There are no fences, nothing to remind us that man is "proprietor." The gulls are of "a wilder, less human, nature" than the larks and robins of Walden. Packs of wild dogs roam the shore, sometimes emerging unexpectedly from carcasses with mouthfuls of offal. "Cold-hearted wreckers" (human scavengers) stalk the beaches in search of firewood and booty. But most important of all is the "vast and wild" ocean which reigns over this kingdom of "monsters and bears thus the waste and wrecks of human art to its remotest shore." "There is no telling what it may vomit up."[52]

Generally Thoreau bravely keeps to the beaches. When he does wander inland he finds that the villagers have been marked by the forces of the ocean. The houses are "bleak and cheerless," the trees are stunted and half-dead. The women are witchlike. One old woman, "singularly masculine" with "jaws of iron" looked like "one who had committed infanticide." These were no bourgeois villagers. They seemed half-mad. Camp revivals were held before a full moon. The hysterical shouting of the participants reproduced the sounds of the ocean. At Wellfleet Thoreau spends the night with an oysterman and his family. The oysterman is harmlessly eccentric but he is surrounded by suspicious women whom he complains run a "petticoat government" as well as a "brutish-looking man." The latter brags about shooting book peddlers from the porch. Thoreau subsequently learned that he had been mistaken for a peddler (and, later, for a bank robber).

There are few moments of peace for Thoreau on the Cape. At Truro he confesses that he "shuddered at the thought" of living there. The walker "must soon eat his heart." But Thoreau had made a discovery of sorts. He had found an inverse pastoral, a "naked Nature,—inhumanly sincere, wasting no thought on man."[53] There was no escape from this state of nature save death.

"This then is what charity hides"

A Week does demonstrate a serious attempt by Thoreau to develop a political theory that extends beyond the jeremiadic outbursts of "Civil Disobedience" and the John Brown essays. Thoreau had called upon his fellow citizens to "act from principle" in order to change "relations and things." A Week was an actual experiment, at least as Thoreau remembered and reconstructed it, to discover not simply an alternate individual life-style, but a different society. The pastoral and the state of nature, the two devices that Thoreau used to reconstruct his experience, did provide a basis for an examination of utopia. The state of nature is used ruthlessly as an analytic device in liberal political thought. It defines the obligations citizens have to one another and to the State. By combining it with the communal premises of the pastoral, Thoreau could present a radical utopianism. The chesslike movement of the boatmen, the noble grace of the farm wife, the folk wisdom of the settler—all these pastoral personalities who live and work near the river demonstrated the existence of community that was more casual and natural than the conformity of the small town. Moreover, Thoreau had made the one great concession that united his efforts with both radicalism and American liberalism. He was no armchair traveler; he had undertaken the trip himself. Thoreau, the superfluous man in bourgeois Concord, had been practical. He undertook this "unusual enterprise" as the Concord children and passers-by watched. He had proved that he could leave society and he had proved that other societies existed, just as he was to prove at Walden that he could reconstruct our own.

The problem with the effort in A Week lay with Thoreau's own disintegrating personality and his attempt to recover it. His pastoral moments are continually shattered by other memories which trigger sermons against the society he has left. Even his moments of fraternal serenity at the close of each day are marred by the sounds of Irish laborers or noises from a nearby village. Thoreau needs solitude for peace of mind, but that very solitude produced fraternal longings. No myth seems to give Thoreau permanent solace. The Merrimack could be the Euphrates or the Nile but Thoreau knows that the attempt at universalization will end in the "Concord mud." The boatmen could be ancient navigators and the farmers Etruscans but Thoreau knows that both are bourgeois New Englanders. In his desperate imagination, he observes that two travelers in the distance could be Vergil and Dante, wandering through a pastoral purgatory. A second look shows them to be ministers "with sermons in their valises all read and gutted." The pastoral never quite stays in place. The fraternal pagan sabbath is lost in Monday's doubts. Wednesday's sermon on friendship is retracted on Thursday. Friday's majestic poet is transformed into a few cut flowers. And perhaps most of all, lurking behind the trees on the river banks, lie dead Indians, murdered trappers, and a massacred infant. The American original sin is the only myth in the pastoral state of nature that does not seem to evaporate.

It may be that the limitations of Thoreau's conventional political thought can be explained through his own inability to permanently transcend his own sense of personal crisis. How many seven-day periods of alternate anxiety and exhilaration did Thoreau experience in his short life? There was to be a resolution of sorts at Walden Pond, but not only is the victory at Walden a mixed one, it also was followed by other journeys far less promising. In *Cape Cod*, Thoreau travels through a state of nature that is surrealistically awesome.

We have come to accept a view that sees individuals acting out their search for personal identity through politics. Perhaps the more common model in America is closer to Thoreau's experience. A self that is in a constant state of crisis cannot provide more than a series of judgments concerning politics. The Thoreauvian failure—perhaps the failure of all of us—may be traced not to some colossal, imperial self but to a self that is so fragile that it is in danger of collapse.

The inability to travel (both theoretically and psychologically) from moral outrage to a commitment to institutional change is evident in all of Thoreau's journeys. Thoreau's attacks on reform appear in all these works. Frequently they are sharply accurate, often they are simply cranky, occasionally they have a mean cast to them.

In *Cape Cod,* Thoreau reports coming upon a shack on the beach. He learned that it was called a "humane house," a temporary shelter for shipwrecked sailors built by a "benevolent person who promised to inspect it annually." Thoreau seemed fascinated by this practice. He learned that such huts dotted the Cape Cod shoreline. Standing near a humane house on the beach Thoreau could hear an "imaginary guide thus marshalling, cheering, directing the dripping, shivering, freezing troop" of shipwrecked sailors along. Then he reports that he peeked into the shack where, after adjusting his eyes to the darkness, he saw a nearly empty interior: "We discovered that there were some stones and some loose wads of wool on the floor, and an empty fireplace at the further end; but it *was not* supplied with matches, or straw, or hay, that we could see, nor 'accommodated with a bench.'" By looking through the knothole into the humane house Thoreau had looked "into the very bowels of mercy . . . for bread we found a stone." He thought "how cold is charity; how inhumane humanity! This, then is what charity hides! Virtues antique and far away, with ever a rusty nail over the latch; and very difficult to keep in repair, withal, it is so uncertain whether any will ever gain the bench near you."[54]

The entire passage is poignant. Thoreau's general negative attitude toward charity is momentarily altered, only to be reinforced by further observation. The image of the empty shack, neglected, forgotten, and nearly useless, a remnant of some antique virtue, is a powerful critique of institutional welfare. This is mixed with Thoreau's own psychological estrangement from society. He is unable to enter this hut, miserable as it is, "shivering round about, not being able to get into it, ever and anon looking through the knothole into the night without a star. . . ."[55] In *A Week* Thoreau had argued that institutional reform was a pale and even a grotesque imitation of friendship, but the very presentation of this alternative dissipated as he was forced to confront his personal crisis.

The portrayal of charity and reform in *Walden* is not so ambivalent. When Thoreau searches for his strongest metaphor of evil it is always meat, decayed and rotten. For instance, he applies it to the philanthropist: "There is no odor so bad as that which arises from goodness tainted. It is human, it is divine, carrion. If I knew for a certainty that a man was coming to my house with the conscious design of doing me good, I should run for my life . . . for fear that I should get . . . some of its virus mingled with my blood." [56]

The moral virtues of empathy and charity are not tied to the metaphors of decay through some theory of history or economics. To Thoreau "do-gooders" are themselves "diseased," "dyspeptic," and "contagious." The images are truly literal ones. In his *Journal* Thoreau wrote of the "slimy benignity of reformers" who "rubbed you continually with the greasy cheeks of their kindness" and "lay their sweaty hand on your shoulder, or your knee, to magnetize you." [57] William Penn and the English prison reformers, John Howard and Elizabeth Fey, are so diagnosed. They are not England's "best" people, "only, perhaps, her best philanthropists." "Doing good" is a contagious disease and Thoreau, pursuing the gastronomic metaphor, diagnoses reform as dyspeptic. "If any thing ail a man, so that he does not perform his functions, if he have a pain in his bowels even,—for that is the seat of sympathy,—he forthwith sets about reforming—the world." [58]

It is clear that acts of charity and organized reform are for Thoreau, at best, spent in wasted time, and are not unlike the wasted labor that he saw in the economic system in general. One must cure oneself first; then presumably the impulse for doing good will disappear. It is not necessary to discuss in any detail what the cultural impact of Thoreau's position is on welfare. At its best, it legitimizes a principled privatism; at its worst, it provides a cultural atmosphere of political callousness. Often Thoreau's attitudes on this point are traced to his own individualism, but this explanation is at once too partial and general. At one level, Thoreau's critique is a critique of a smug bourgeois paternalism. Most of his arguments are ad hominum ones that thinly disguise his alienation from bourgeois society. Thoreau's opposition to reformers is the other side of his opposition to commerce. Yet the arguments against reformers are so intense and so cranky that a further explanation is necessary. The metaphors of disease and decay are overstated even in the context of Thoreauvian polemics, yet they seem to fit into another pattern. The description of reformers in terms of dyspepsia and carrion is related to Thoreau's horror at watching Therien lumbering through the wood with a pail of woodchuck meat strapped over his shoulder or to Thoreau's disgust at his own desire to pounce on one of those wood-chucks. Meat ("dead," "decaying," "over-ripe," "slimy," "beastly," "filthy") is concrete evidence of a sensuous existence. For Thoreau this aspect of ourselves cannot be "wholly expelled," it is "like the worms which, even in life and health, occupy our bodies." The reformers, for all their feigned "purity," represent an attempt to take us toward this animallike life. They demand a psychological closeness (those "greasy cheeks" and "sweaty hand"); they pry and peep at people's needs; they exhort us to be more cooperative. Thoreau's fragile command of his own sense of self cannot permit these invasions: "The only cooperation which is commonly possible is exceedingly partial and superficial; and what little true cooperation there is, is as if it were not, being a har-mony inaudible to men." Thoreau has no doubt that "the gradual im-provement" in the human race requires us to "leave off eating animals" just as "savage tribes have left off eating each other."[59] The effort to help others, whether governmental or individual, is an animal instinct that must be overcome. What is so intriguing about Thoreau on this point is that the metaphor, while hyperbolic, is so concrete. Diet, self-identity, and charity are all part of an applied ethics.[60]

Nonetheless, one cannot say that Thoreau had no utopian vision. His attempts to rediscover a state of nature, on the Concord and Mer-rimack, at Walden and on Cape Cod, were noble and personally coura-geous efforts. None of them, however, could provide him with the kind of commitment that he insisted was necessary. Of course, that commit-ment could never be forthcoming because he never had sufficient hold of his own identity to make it. Perry Miller, one of Thoreau's more se-vere critics, referred to Thoreau's life as a "perverse pilgrimage." He complained that the transcendental fascination with friendship was constructed on a model that was so demanding that it seemed to be designed to destruct.[61] The same point can be made—albeit in a more sympathetic manner—about Thoreau's political thought. Thoreau de-manded the most severe moral commitment in the political sphere, a commitment that he knew his fellow citizens could not make. The same great demands that provided a rationale for his own political iso-lation also provided a rationale for his social isolation. Few, if any, friends could offer him anything but the "cheap civility" he despised.

As a consequence Thoreau dreamed about a conversion, a conversion of himself and his fellow citizens. Needless to say, that sense of grace never fell upon Thoreau nor, for that matter, on America itself. Ironically, the individual estrangement and moral outbursts that prevent a revitalized American political theory may be the only characteristics that sustain the cultural basis for such a reformulation.

J U D G I N G

WHITTAKER CHAMBERS AND
LILLIAN HELLMAN

Consider the testimony of these two witnesses before the House of Representatives' Un-American Activities Committee.

"Almost exactly nine years ago—that is, two days after Hitler and Stalin signed their pact—I went to Washington and reported to the authorities what I knew about the infiltration of the United States Government by Communists. For years, international Communism, of which the United States Communist Party is an integral part, had been in a state of undeclared war with this Republic. With the Hitler-Stalin pact that war reached a new stage. I regarded my action in going to the Government as a simple act of war, like the shooting of an armed enemy in combat.

"At that moment in history, I was one of the few men on this side of the battle who could perform this service. I had joined the Communist Party in 1924. No one recruited me. I had become convinced that the society in which we live, Western civilization, had reached a crisis, of which the First World War was the military expression, and that it was doomed to collapse or revert to barbarism. I did not understand the causes of the crisis or know what to do about it. But I felt that, as an intelligent man, I must do something. In the writings of Karl Marx, I thought that I had found the explanation of the historical and economic causes [of the crisis]. In the writings of Lenin, I thought I had found the answer to the question: what to do?

"In 1937, I repudiated Marx's doctrines and Lenin's tactics. Experience and the record had convinced me that Communism is a form of totalitarianism, that its triumph means slavery to men wherever they fall under its sway and spiritual night to the human mind and soul. I resolved to break with the Communist Party at whatever risk to my life or other tragedy to myself or my family. Yet, so strong is the hold which the insidious evil of Communism secures upon its disciples, that I could still say to someone at that time: 'I know that I am leaving the winning side for the losing side, but it is better to die on the losing side than to live under Communism. . . .

"For a year I lived in hiding, sleeping by day and watching through the night with gun or revolver within easy reach. That was what underground Communism could do to one man in the peaceful United States in the year 1938.

"I had sound reasons for supposing that the Communists might try to kill me. For a number of years, I had myself served in the underground, chiefly in Washington, D.C. The heart of my report to the United States Government consisted of a description of the apparatus to which I was attached. It was an underground organization of the United States Communist Party developed, to the best of my knowledge, by Harold Ware, one of the sons of the Communist leader known as Mother Bloor. I knew it at its top level, a group of seven or so men, from among whom in later years certain members of Miss Bentley's organization were apparently recruited. The head of the underground group at the time I knew it was Nathan Witt, an attorney for the National Labor Relations Board. Later, John Abt became the leader. Lee Pressman was also a member of this group, as was Alger Hiss, who, as a member of the State Department, later organized the conferences at Dumbarton Oaks, San Francisco and the United States side of the Yalta Conference.

"The purpose of this group at that time was not primarily espionage. Its original purpose was the Communist infiltration of the American Government. But espionage was certainly one of its eventual objectives. Let no one be surprised at this statement. Disloyalty is a matter of principle with every member of the Communist Party. The Communist Party exists for the specific purpose of overthrowing the Government, at the opportune time, by any and all means; and each of its members, by the fact that he is a member, is dedicated to this purpose.

"It is ten years since I broke away from the Communist Party. During that decade, I have sought to live an industrious and God fearing life. At the same time, I have fought Communism constantly by act and written word. I am proud to appear before this Committee. The publicity, inseparable from such testimony, has darkened and no doubt will continue to darken my effort to integrate myself in the community of free men. But that is a small price to pay if my testimony helps to make Americans recognize at last that they are at grips with a secret, sinister and enormously powerful force whose tireless purpose is their enslavement.

"At the same time, I should like, thus publicly, to call upon all ex-Communists who have not yet disclosed themselves, and all men within the Communist Party whose better instincts have not yet been corrupted and crushed by it, to aid in the struggle while there is still time."[1]

"I am most willing to answer all questions about myself. I have nothing to hide from your Committee and there is nothing in my life of which I am ashamed. I have been advised by counsel that under the Fifth Amendment I have a constitutional privilege to decline to answer any questions about my political opinions, activities and associations, on the grounds of self-incrimination. I do not wish to claim this privilege. I am ready and willing to testify before the representatives of our Government as to my own opinions and my own actions, regardless of any risks or consequences to myself.

"But I am advised by counsel that if I answer the Committee's questions about myself, I must also answer questions about other people and that if I refuse to do so, I can be cited for contempt. My counsel tells me that if I answer questions about myself, I will have waived my rights under the Fifth Amendment and could be forced legally to answer questions about others. This is very difficult for a layman to understand. But there is one principle that I do understand: I am not willing, now or in the future, to bring bad trouble to people who, in my past association with them, were completely innocent of any talk or any action that was disloyal or subversive. I do not like subversion or disloyalty in any form and if I had ever seen any I would have considered it my duty to have reported it to the proper authorities. But to hurt innocent people whom I knew many years ago in order to save myself is, to me, inhuman and indecent and dishonorable. I cannot and will not cut my conscience to fit this year's fashions, even though I long ago came to the conclusion that I was not a political person and could have no comfortable place in any political group.

"I was raised in an old-fashioned American tradition and there were certain homely things that were taught to me: to try to tell the truth, not to bear false witness, not to harm my neighbor, to be loyal to my country, and so on. In general, I respected these ideals of Christian honor and did as well with them as I knew how. It is my belief that you will agree with these simple rules of human decency and will not expect me to violate the good American tradition from which they spring. I would, therefore, like to come before you and speak of myself.

"I am prepared to waive the privilege against self-incrimination and to tell you anything you wish to know about my views or actions if your Committee will agree to refrain from asking me to name other people. If the Committee is unwilling to give me this assurance, I will be forced to plead the privilege of the Fifth Amendment at the hearing."[2]

The first statement was made by Whittaker Chambers in 1948, the second by Lillian Hellman in 1952. Chambers was an informer, what was called a "friendly witness." Hellman refused to testify. Chambers's testimony became known as "The Case," Hellman's as the "Great Refusal." Chambers and Hellman became heroes and villains of the American Left and Right. Their autobiographies are attempts to justify these two acts of witness, to tell the truth about "a whole generation on trial" (Chambers), to tell the truth about "this sad, comic, miserable time in our history" (Hellman). Was Chambers a psychotic liar? Was Hellman a clever fellow traveler? Was Chambers a man of courage who bore witness to the Communist conspiracy? Was Hellman a woman of "guts" in a generation that "swallowed any nonsense that was repeated often enough"?[3] What were the consequences of these testimonies? Did Chambers give the West one last chance "to write the next several chapters of history"?[4] Did Hellman prophesy the war in Vietnam and Watergate?

Above all else, Chamber's *Witness* and Hellman's *Scoundrel Time* involve questions of political judgment. Political theory is generally thought to revolve around the formulation of concepts like justice and freedom. But in a sense political theory is not simply a body of knowledge about "perennial questions" and "contested concepts." The "great theories of politics" are tools to help us make political judgments. For Chambers, Marxism summoned mankind "to turn its vision into practical reality." Chambers, of course, found communism to be a false guide. He had asked, "What if we were wrong?" The Communist finally hears "screams": "They come from husbands torn forever from their wives in midnight arrests . . . from the execution cellars of the secret police, from the torture chambers of Lubianka, from the citadels of terror now stretching from Berlin to Canton." Chambers concluded that twenty years of judgments had been wrong, that he must bear witness to how he "committed the characteristic crimes of my century."[5] For Hellman the Communists were "people who wanted to make a better world." They may have "justified murder, prison camps, torture" but they were "honest and thoughtful men." She would not clear herself "by jumping on people in trouble." Hellman offered a different kind of witness, a witness against "scoundrels," "spitballing whatever and whoever came into view."[6]

Which judgment was correct? Which witness ought we to follow? For me, Chambers was, on the whole, right and Hellman, on the whole, wrong. But the more fundamental question that these autobiographies raise is "How does one make political judgments?" There is much to be learned about this question in both *Witness* and *Scoundrel Time*. Yet curiously, both these autobiographies fail from the standpoint of political theory, despite the fact that all the complexity of political judgment (one's own motivations and those of others, the consequences of actions taken and not taken) is examined by both Chambers and Hellman.

Let me use as the starting point in my examination of this failure two reviews, one by Irving Howe and another by Nathan Glazer. Howe declares his own judgment at the outset of the essay: "That Whittaker Chambers told the truth and Alger Hiss did not, seems to me highly probable." What did it matter that Hiss was a pleasant fellow and Chambers an overwrought one, when "at stake was the commitment of those popular-front liberals who had persisted in treating Stalinism as an accepted part of 'the Left'?" But *Witness* troubles Howe. He is amazed that as a work of ideas it should be so "ragged and patchy." "In a work of over 800 pages there is hardly a sustained passage of, say, five thousand words devoted to a serious development of thought, everything breaks down into a sermon, reminiscence, self-mortification, and self-justification." That Stalinism is an evil Howe takes as self-evident. What appalls him is that "nowhere in his 800 pages does Chambers attempt sustained definition or description, nowhere does he bound the shape of the evil." Howe's is a serious charge, especially since Chambers regards his witness to be against "terrible," "evil" men. The source of the failure of *Witness* for Howe lies in Chambers's rejection, not of communism, but of the entire Enlightenment. Everyone is guilty, at least since the eighteenth century: "Voltaire, Jefferson, Lenin, Roosevelt, Hitler, Stalin; not equally evil, but all, apparently, 'indifferent to God.'"[7] Chambers has no social theory, only a Manichean demonology.

Glazer's own political judgments are that Hiss was guilty, that communism was a more serious threat to liberty than HUAC. Naturally, Hellman's autobiography angers him. But Glazer raises a point independent of this reaction. He complains that Hellman insists that the Communists *she knew* were not the enemy. But there was Czechoslovakia and the Gulag and at home the intractability of Communist organizers in NAACP chapters and in CIO locals. On these and other questions Hellman was silent; "she is remarkably coy now."[8]

Both of these reviews suggest that in *Witness* and *Scoundrel Time* there is a gap between the political judgment exercised and defended and the theoretical explanation of these acts of witness. Chambers is able to portray his conversion from Communist functionary to anti-Communist informer in great detail. Every action he undertakes—from his attendance at his first cell meeting, to his acceptance of an underground assignment, to his decision to leave the Party, to his meeting with Berle, to his testimony before HUAC, to his lie before a grand jury, to his decision to accuse Hiss of espionage and to turn over the "pumpkin papers"—is subjected to careful, even minute analysis. But, as Howe notes, Chambers sees not only his own life in terms wildly apocalyptic but the last three centuries of Western civilization as well. It is not enough for Chambers to say that the Hiss case was more than a contest between two men or even between New Deal liberals and conservatives or even the "two faiths" of communism and Christianity. The case was a battle between Good and Evil. Evil itelf was "not something that can be condescended to, waved aside or smiled away." It was not an "uninvited guest" but rather it lay "coiled *in foro interno* at home with good within ourselves."[9] Tocqueville's complaint that Americans as theorists jumped in one huge step from personal observation to cosmic speculation is given another elaboration by Chambers. Chambers leaps from existential to Manichean philosophy, and the flight is so swift and soaring that he rests at a cosmic level for but a second. Personal sin becomes a "tragedy of history" which becomes a battle of faiths only to swiftly become once again a problem for the human heart. Social and political theory cannot compete with a soul that leaps to heaven and falls back again. Chambers could have been an American DeMaistre or Dostoyevski, but his angst is too great to even consider an American version of the hangman or Grand Inquisitor. He suffers too much for himself to assume these roles. Chambers was not crazy, as so many of his opponents insist, but the central problem that his political judgment raises is not the construction of a political theory (Christocentric or otherwise) but the construction of his own self.

Chambers's preoccupations really remain personal ones. The same is true for Hellman's although in a very different way. For Hellman the crimes of Stalinism are remote. They are not distanced by a reactionary cosmology that justifies the acts of witness but by a different kind of fixation on personal experience. "About foreign gunmen I know only what I have read, but the American radicals I met were not violent men."[10] She thought that Dashiell Hammett probably joined the Party as an act of redemption for his past in the Pinkerton agency. That is a good enough reason for her. In fact, all the Communists she knew— and refused to testify about—were simply ordinary people. Communism is for her almost a personal eccentricity. Here were some "silly" or "stubborn" or "boring" people, some were even "genuine nuts," who never really did any harm. Her characterizations of the Communist party border on how one might describe vegetarian activists. If *Scoundrel Time* can be said to have any political theory at all, it is a self-consciously personalist theory, as Manichean as Chambers's in its own way. There are those gentle creatures who in their own complicated ways "seemed to me people who wanted a better world" and there were the "McCarthy boys," the "cheap badies," the scoundrels. Political theory is political judgment is personal loyalty. E. M. Forster had once said that if he were faced with the choice of loyalty to a friend or loyalty to his country he hoped he would have the courage to choose the former.[11] But Forster's statement has no meaning to Hellman. Countries and institutions, even movements, have no meaning; there is no conflict of loyalties. Hers is only a world peopled by "rebels" and "scoundrels." If she and the Communist party had made "mistakes," so what? That they had kept their own personal witness was their own business and no excuse for the "disgraceful conduct of intellectuals no matter how much they disagreed."[12]

Chambers and Hellman then offer two styles of political judgment. There is a distinct moral system in each, but the moralities upon which their acts of witness are based are not the stuff from which a full account of politics can be made, despite the fact that both Whittaker Chambers and Lillian Hellman possess a great deal of political knowledge. The best way to appreciate this problem is to look in detail at their respective moralities in order to see precisely how they affect not only their judgment but their inability to learn from their acts of witness in a theoretical sense. Chambers's model we can call a "Saul/Paul" morality after the first conversion. Hellman's we can call a "tough-guy" morality. Apologies are due to Hellman. I do not suggest that she was so hypnotized by Hammett that she assumed the role of the private dick. But it is she who reflects a particular morality that represents an accommodation of sorts with American life.

"What I had been fell from me like rags . . ."

Saul had been stricken blind on the road to Damascus. A voice said to him: "I have appeared to you for a purpose: to appoint you my servant and witness, to testify both to what you have seen and to what you shall yet see of me" (Acts 26:16). Thus began the Great Conversion, the first ministry of the Christian Church, the witness of the Gospels to the Gentiles—all led by a former persecutor of the new religion. Paul suffered. He was stoned and left for dead in Lystra, beaten with rods in Philippi, driven out of Berea, imprisoned in Rome. His churches were divided by factions and heresies, his flocks subject to constant backsliding and misinterpretation of the Gospels. Yet through it all, Paul kept his witness, offering an eschatological vision of the Kingdom of God. There is but one Church; the Jews have the Law as their guide, for the Gentiles "their conscience is called as witness." All would be held accountable when "God judges the secrets of human hearts."

The Great Conversion is the model for all conversions. At its center there is a tremendous personality change. Saul/Paul is an account of a persecutor of Christianity and its first minister, of a Jew and a universal man, of a backwater colonial and a world traveler. But the Pauline conversion has its special lessons. Paul's suffering is, of course, a mirror of Christ's agony, but more generally the Pauline witness emphasizes self-sacrifice, withstanding ridicule, the almost constant threat of death. There is a description of the beauty of a life touched by grace in Romans but even here Paul dwells upon the pain: "the whole universe groans in all its parts as if in the pangs of childbirth." Paul's witness is above all an act of teaching. He must teach the Gentiles faith without the Law and the Jews faith in addition to the Law. The consequences for rejecting the teachings are awful. Without God people are left to "their own depraved reason." They will break "all rules of conduct": "They are filled with every kind of injustice, mischief, rapacity, and malice; they are one mass of envy, murder, rivalry, treachery, and malevolence; whisperers and scandal-mongers, hateful to God, insolent, arrogant, and boastful; they invent new kinds of mischief, they show no loyalty to parents, no conscience, no fidelity to their plighted word; they are without natural affection and without pity" (Rom. 1:29–31). But when "God's just judgment will be revealed," every man "will pay for what he has done."

On these principles—conversion, living martyrdom, teaching, and eschatological vision—Whittaker Chambers conceived his life. All of these elements appear at the opening of *Witness*. Chambers imagines that someday his children will ask, "What was my father?"

> I will give you an answer: I was a witness. I do not mean a witness for the Government or against Alger Hiss and the others. Nor do I mean the short, squat, solitary figure, trudging through the impersonal halls of public buildings to testify before Congressional committees, grand juries, loyalty boards, courts of law. A man is not primarily a witness *against* something. That is only incidental to the fact that he is a witness *for* something. A witness, in the sense that I am using the word, is a man whose life and faith are so com-

pletely one that when the challenge comes to step out and testify for his faith, he does so, disregarding all risks, accepting all consequences.[13]

It is this kind of language that drove Chambers's opponents so wild that they accused him of psychosis. When he said that he suffered more than those whom he accused, they saw mental imbalance. When he timed his revelations like a long agony, they saw revenge. When he declared himself a representative of one of two faiths locked in a death struggle, they saw political opportunism. And most of all when as Carl he testified to a great friendship with Alger Hiss, they saw a liar. No other figure in American history has been subject to more disbelief in regard to conversion than Whittaker Chambers. Even HUAC was slow to believe him. But these doubts, these denials only served to heighten Chambers's conception of his own witness.

Did Chambers consciously attempt to live his life as a Pauline figure? Certainly not before 1939 and perhaps not fully so until he set out to write his autobiography. Even before the acts of witness, however, there are objective signs of a personality awaiting grace. Change of name is a common outward sign of transformation. Chambers adopted well over a dozen names, many of them before his career in the Communist party. Born Vivian Chambers, he used the name Charles Adams when he left home, Charles Whittaker when he returned, and Whittaker Chambers when he registered at Columbia. George Crosley was the name by which Hiss said he knew Chambers and became part of the eventual dichotomy that characterized his conversion.

The famous Commodore Hotel confrontation was for a generation the incident that linked Crosley/Chambers and Hiss. Chambers clearly saw the dramatics of the moment as well. For here was the ghost of Crosley, the old personality, appearing to accuse Hiss. Hiss had asked Chambers to speak, then read aloud, then he examined his teeth. Very reluctantly he admitted that his accuser was indeed a man he had known over ten years ago as George Crosley. Of course, for him the identification of Crosley was simply the admission that he had befriended a "deadbeat." Chambers, however, saw the "horrible" confrontation in very different terms. He had expected that the meeting would be like an "interrupted conversation, to be taken up where it was dropped." Instead he saw Hiss not just as a "memory and a name" but as a "trapped man." Hiss was trapped by the converted Chambers and Chambers insists that throughout the session he had hoped that Hiss too would disclose the truth about his past. That, of course, was not to happen. Hiss insisted on "acting." When he cross-examined Chambers and seemed puzzled by the inconsistencies in Chambers's responses (yes, he spent time at the apartment on Twenty-ninth street; no, he did not sublet an apartment on Twenty-ninth street), the full force of the witness of the life of the "old" Chambers appeared. "How do you reconcile these responses?" Hiss asked. "Very easily, Alger," replied Chambers. "I was a Communist and you were a Communist." [14]

It was the meeting at the Hotel Commodore that so dramatically began Chambers's witness. But the conversion had occurred much earlier. It began less on the model of Paul's experience at Damascus than in the subtleties of the Puritan tradition of conversion. Chambers was a doting father. His infant daughter was "the most miraculous thing that had ever happened in my life." Chambers's eye "came to rest on the delicate convolutions of her ear—those intricate, delicate, perfect ears." There is a real beauty in the memory invoked of this experience. As is generally the case, the reasoning that follows is stilted in comparison:

> The thought passed through my mind: "No, those ears were not created by chance coming together of atoms in nature (the Communist view). They could have been created only by immense design." The thought was involuntary and unwanted. I crowded it out of my mind. But I never wholly forgot the occasion. I had to crowd it out of my mind. If I had completed it, I should have had to say: Design presupposes God. I did not then know that, at that moment, the finger of God was first laid upon my forehead.

Later Chambers learns to pray. He joins the Quaker church of his grandmother. He studies the Quaker conception of witness and concludes the original Quaker witnesses were so important, not because "it is desirable that the world should be convinced by them" but because the Quaker makes "his own person a living testimony against the world." [15] Chambers takes to plain dress, avoids gossip, gives up swearing and heavy drinking. He becomes an informal confessor for blocked and troubled writers at *Time*.

These acts of personal religiosity all occur before Chambers decides to undertake his witness against Hiss and communism. But Chambers was a man twice saved and it is important to an understanding of his political thought to appreciate his first conversion. The confession, particularly the confession as a work of political art, is most vulnerable to self-deception in its depiction of a life before conversion. Sometimes personal sins are exaggerated to illustrate the impact of the conversion to come. Every judgment, every act is hopelessly mistaken. The confessor tries to tell us about two completely different beings in the life told. Curiously, Chambers's account is very far removed from the problem of the convert's treatment of his or her earlier life. The story of the religious conversion we have just discussed is real enough. And there are plenty of rogues in the Communist party. There are some finely drawn portraits of Colonel Bykov's cowardice, of Hiss ("He was as American as ham and eggs . . ."), of Scott Nearing ("women always flocked around him"). But throughout all of these twelve years, Chambers's memories are highly rational ones. The spy activities seem almost biographical. Chambers could have written them in the third person. The work that so influenced his entrance into the Communist party was Lenin's *A Soviet At Work,* an account of a day in the life of a local soviet. "The reek of life was on it. This was not theory or statistics. This was socialism in practice. This was the thing in itself. This was how it worked."[16] Few of the Communists in his first cell hold any interest for Chambers. He is remarkably indifferent to Marxist theory. The factional disputes do not interest him. He sides with neither the Lovestonites nor the Forster-Browder group. The purges of the Lovestonites and later the Trotskyists bring no reaction. He attends the Nearing study group but finds the discussions "extremely dull and rambling" and never writes up his research on the Hungarian revolution that was to be part of the group's book. Through a Party oversight Chambers was never assigned to a unit and he was delighted with his good fortune. Party meetings were "unbearable." When he was to leave the Party the book that helped him to do so was Tchernavin's *I Speak for the Silent,* an eyewitness account of the Soviet labor camps. As a Communist, then, Chambers was not motivated by the rigor and vision of Marxist theory.

Nor was he very taken with the commitment of his comrades. In truth I think Chambers did not like people in general, but the Party members he remembers are an ordinary lot, not too bright, not very courageous as individuals, not especially evil for that matter. Chambers doesn't really like practical politics, even Communist party style. Elizabeth Bentley conveyed the thrill and danger of underground work.[17] Chambers always described his activities with the Ware group in bureaucratic terms: "I came to Washington as a Communist functionary. . . ."

How then can one understand Chambers's twelve years as a Communist from the first trips around New York City as a collector for the *Worker* to the clandestine meetings with the Soviet secret police? The answer to this question, the key to an understanding of Chambers's judgments on politics and his second conversion, is that a sense of personal self-sacrifice is the only basis for the justification of action. Chambers saw his uniqueness in the fact that "he was a witness to the two great faiths of our time." But what did Chambers witness? The message of the autobiography is a message of the loss of a personal faith and the gaining of another. Most of all, it is a message of the suffering entailed in following each. When Chambers was asked by a juror, "What does it mean to be a Communist?" he replied by telling of three of his revolutionary heroes. One, a Polish Communist named Djerjinsky, who had been head of the Tcheka and organizer of the Red Terror, was captured and jailed in Warsaw. He was "ascetic, highly sensitive and intelligent" (characteristics Chambers often used to describe himself and Hiss). Djerjinsky insisted upon being given the job of cleaning latrines on the grounds that it was the "most developed member of any community" who must take upon himself the lowliest tasks as an example for the others. "This is one thing it meant to be a Communist." Another was a Communist named Eugen Levine who had been captured when the Bavarian Soviet Republic was crushed. When he was told that his sentence was death, Levine replied, "We Communists are always under the sentence of death." "That," said Chambers, "is another thing that it meant to be a Communist." The third example haunted Chambers throughout his life. It is the story of a pre-Communist revolutionist named Kalyaev who had been exiled to Siberia because of his part in an assassination attempt on a tsarist minister. When his fellow prisoners were flogged, Kalyaev "sought some way to protest this outrage to the world." He drenched himself in kerosene and set himself on fire. "That also is what it meant to be a Communist" and here Chambers adds, "that also is what it means to be a witness." [18]

When Chambers temporarily left the Party for two years he wrote four short stories that were so successful that they caught the attention of Moscow and prepared the way for his reentry into the Party. Each was a story of self-sacrifice. Chambers had wanted to write "not political polemics, which few people ever wanted to read, but stories that anybody might want to read—stories in which the correct conduct of the Communist would be shown in action and without political comment." The stories are moral guides, "stories of four basic commitments—in suffering, under discipline, in defeat, in death." By far the most dramatic and most prescient in view of Chambers's later conversion is an account of a Christ-like figure who is about to be shot. It was reported through the eyes of a "cynical fellow prisoner" (not unlike Barrabas) who, "only when the execution was over, sensed that he had been touched by something new in his experience—the moral force of men who were prepared to die for what they believed." [19]

After Chambers's second conversion, the theme of sacrifice is redefined as Pauline living martyrdom although the suffering is directed inward. His new heroes are Dostoyevski, Karl Barth, and Kierkegaard. Each represents a conservative theology that is quite different from the Arminian and social gospel trends in American religion. But even more important, each offers an intensely existentialist conception of God, one that emphasizes a personal qualitative leap in religious faith to a God who is in Barth's words, *ganz anders* ("wholly different"). Chambers insisted that the "plain men" of the grand jury of the Southern District of New York knew "exactly what I was talking about" when he paraphrased these men.

During this period Chambers wrote an essay on Reinhold Niebuhr for *Time*. In *Witness* he announces that it was "at that time my most personal statement about religious faith:"

Christian faith is a paradox which is the sum of paradoxes. Its passion mounts, like a surge of music, insubstantial and sustaining, between two great cries of the spirit—the paradoxic sadness of "Lord, I believe; help Thou mine unbelief" and the paradoxic triumph of Tertullian's "Credo quia impossible" (I believe because it is impossible). Religiously, its logic, human beyond rationality, is the expression of a need epitomized in the paradox of Solon weeping for his dead son. "Why do you weep," asked a friend, "since it cannot help?" Said Solon: "That is why I weep—because it cannot help."

This, says Chambers, is the answer to anyone who "seeks to know what the mind, the mood and character of Whittaker Chambers was like on the eve of the Hiss Case." He remembers appreciatively Niebuhr's comment on the article, quoting his brother: "Only a man who has deeply suffered could have written it." [20]

Chambers's stories of martyrdom, those both before and after his second conversion, were to become the basis for his own actions. He writes: "In the end, the only memorable stories, like the only memorable experiences, are religious and moral. . . . If my story is worth telling, it is because I rejected in turn each of the characteristic endings of our time—the revolutionary ending and the success ending. I chose a third ending." The years with *Time* are described in the autobiography as "the tranquil years." The designation, I suppose, is a relative one because the angst described above hardly appears to suggest peace of mind. There was the farm, of course. Chambers described his work there as an act of witness. But even the life of the cosmopolitan bourgeois becomes an ending not taken, as he denies it to himself: "By deliberately choosing his life of hardship and immense satisfaction, we say in effect: The modern world has nothing better than this to give us. Its vision of comfort without effort, pleasure without the pain of creation, life sterilized against even the thought of death, rationalized so that every intrusion of mystery is felt as a betrayal of the mind. Life mechanized and standardized—that is not for us." [21]

Under subpoena by HUAC, Chambers concludes that the "time of the witness of words was over and the time of acts had begun. . . . Acts were also required of a man if there was something in him that enabled him to act." [22] Again and again throughout the case, Chambers would push himself to what he saw as the necessary conclusion to this "witness of acts." When he considered destroying the microfilm he asked whether he should bear a witness of justice against Hiss or a witness of mercy. He went to the woods to pray and the image of Kalyaev appeared from the "depths of memory." In one sense, of course, he rejects the model of the Russian revolutionary's martyrdom. He must not destroy the film; he must be a "living witness." But in Chambers's mind he had also followed Kalyaev's example, for the witness "would only mean my destruction by slower means." That was to be Chambers's life ending, "that was my penalty."

The flaw in Chambers's judgment and the inability to present a more complete account of politics lay not in his belief that he saw God everywhere (even the contention that the appointment of Thomas Murphy as government prosecutor "pleased God"). The flaw did not in itself even lie with the self-centered character of Chambers's world. That a preoccupation with self-sacrifice can lead to a complicated kind of selfishness is certainly demonstrated by Chambers. What, above all, is the negative lesson of *Witness* is that judgments cannot be justified as simple acts of faith whether one's faith is in the Party or in God. Chambers, the critic of the naivete of American liberalism, presents us with his own kind of political hyperindividualism. It is certainly true that an enemy of the Enlightenment can find few institutions with which to ally. If the belief that man's rationality is divine is a heresy of American Protestantism, then where does an American Dostoyevski turn? Every major institution in America is a product of the Enlightenment. Chambers as conservative is left only with his personal faith. Was HUAC to be America's agency of redemption, a collection of Grand Inquisitors? Certainly its opponents drew pictures of this sort. For Chambers, however, HUAC was simply a collection of politicians with average intelligence and shrewdness. There are a few scattered populist references to the intuitive capacities of the people, mostly jurors. Most of all, however, one feels in *Witness* a strong implication that American society itself is corrupt at its core, that the corruption is deeper than the "revolution by bookkeeping and lawmaking of the New Deal," that America and the Soviet Union are on the same side as nations "indifferent to God," that the insistence of the American people that the dispute between Hiss and Chambers was a "personal grudge" on both sides was evidence of willful disregard for national salvation.

Chambers was not the first conservative, nor will he be the last, to experience estrangement from American society. Chambers's acts of witness only exacerbated the alienation, for he knew that he was an informer: "Men shrink from that word and what it stands for as something lurking and poisonous." In what is surely one of the most moving and perceptive passages in *Witness,* Chambers outlines the moral costs of the decision to inform on others. The informer "uses his special knowledge to destroy others." It is the "special information" he has to give "because he knows those others' faces, voices and lives, because he once lived within their confidence, in a shared faith, trusted by them as one of themselves, accepting their friendship, feeling their pleasures and griefs, sitting in their houses, eating at their tables, accepting their kindness, knowing their wives and children" that makes him so useful to the state. The police protect him but now "he is their creature." "When they whistle, he fetches a soiled bone of information." "The informer is a slave. He is no longer a man. He is free only to the degree in which he knows what he is doing and why he must do it." Still, he must deal with his captors, "men of many orders of intelligence, of many motives of self-interest or malice, men sometimes infiltrated or tainted by the enemy, in an immensely complex pattern of politics and history." [23] To be effective, the informer must exercise the "shrewdest judgment."

Chambers's sketch of the informer is one of a man alone. He has broken a basic moral law, "an honorable and valid one," which enjoins men to keep confidences among intimates. Chambers had betrayed a friend, but for him this betrayal was the penalty he must pay for his complicity in "the crimes of politics and history." The only real freedom he felt that remained to him as he traveled on a road that "is always night" was his own political judgment. But the basis for judgment was so restricted by the act of witness itself that Chambers had only to rely upon his own sense of self-sacrifice and faith. These were not totally insignificant braces. He could certainly be shrewd (his opponents knew this well) but shrewdness is only a limited aspect of judgment. For the most part he saw himself as the "fat man" who was hated by the Left, used by the Right, and treated as part of a "sporting event" by the citizenry as a whole. Chambers was the archetypal outsider. His model may have been Paul, but, I think, he could never quite reject the contention that he resembled Cain more. That is why Chambers, unlike Paul, could not build a Church in America.

Paul suffered, but through his witness he taught the West to accept Christianity. The teachings of Chambers leave no legacy. There is suffering all right, and there is a witness and even an apocalyptic vision, but Chambers offers communion without a church. In his later writings the same enormous swings reappear. *Cold Friday* is a stilted collection of Chambers, the witness, whose own revelations predict the inevitable destruction of both superpowers. The series of letters to William Buckley shows the other side of Chambers: "Those who remain in the world, if they will not surrender on its terms, must maneuver within its terms. That is what conservatives must decide: how much to give in order to survive at all; how much to give in order not to give up basic principles. And of course that results in a dance along a precipice." [24] Here is Chambers, the informer, the man whose special knowledge makes him a captive who can only "maneuver." He did judge correctly but never with certainty could he answer his own question, "Who appointed me judge?" More than anything else, Chambers wanted to be a witness "for something," but he could never tell us what it was.

"Life had changed and there were many people who did not call me"

Lillian Hellman's witness appears very different from Whittaker Chambers's. Hellman was a woman who, at considerable personal risk, "refused to cut [her] conscience to fit this year's fashions." The image she offers, and the one that is accepted by her admirers, is of a person who made a political judgment based upon a simple morality: "I was raised in an old-fashioned American tradition and there were certain homely things that were taught to me: to try to tell the truth, not to bear false witness, not to harm my neighbor, to be loyal to my country, and so on." The listing of these "homely things" is great theater. Hellman, Broadway playwright, Hollywood screenwriter, and world traveler, did not forget the lessons of McGuffey's *Reader.* She indignantly reminds the HUAC committeemen, small-town Americans all, of what are "the simple rules of human decency" derived from the "good American tradition." In fact, Hellman's own childhood owed more to Tennessee Williams than to Booth Tarkington. Her mother's rich family had ripped off poor blacks and the beloved aunts mentioned in all her memoirs are frequently portrayed as victims of small-town morality. There is, none-theless, an element of truthfulness in Hellman's devotion to a homely American morality, even if in terms different from those offered before HUAC. In *Scoundrel Time* she saw herself (and the Communists) in the tradition of southern eccentrics. When Dashiell Hammett warned her that the punishment for radical beliefs was jail, she insisted that her dissent was a simple exercise of her "inherited rights" as an American. In fact, most of the indictments of *Scoundrel Time* are directed against the financially comfortable American intelligentsia who were too complacent to make simple moral judgments. In fact even nativist explanations are offered: "The children of timid immigrants are often remarkable people: energetic, intelligent, hard-working; and often they make it so good that they are determined to keep it at all costs." [25] Most convincing of all in terms of the veracity of Hellman's persona as a woman acting upon simple American moral precepts and exercising inherited rights is her intense feeling of betrayal and anger. "In every civilized country people have always come forward to defend those in political trouble." But few helped her on Hammett. She had believed that "the educated, the intellectual, lived by what they claimed to believe." But this was not so. When after the publication of *Scoundrel Time,* a woman she met at a party chided her by saying, "You must learn to be more toler-ant," Hellman's anger assumed volcanic proportions. *Scoundrel Time* was too restrained. Now she would really take her moral stand: "I never want again to watch people turn into liars and cowards and others into frightened, silent collaborators. And to hell with the fancy reasons they give for what they did." [26]

But what so angers Hellman's opponents is not her refusal to cut her conscience to fit fashion; what drives her detractors to frenzy (much in the same way as Chambers's critics are angered) is their belief that Hellman was not a woman of independent judgment at all. She had not come forward when American Trotskyites had been persecuted under the Smith Act. She had not criticized the monumental crimes of Stalin. She had not publicly opposed the Communist take-over of the Henry Wallace campaign. In short, she had not helped people in political trouble. The woman of conscience who had exercised political judg-ment is regarded as a hypocrite. In truth, Hellman's defense against this charge is weak. She contended that she did take "too long to see what was going on in the Soviet Union." But the confession is immediately retracted as she attacks "anti-Communist writers and intellectuals": "I do not believe that we did our country any harm. And I think they did."[27] Leaving aside how forthright opposition from the Left might have saved some individuals from the Gulag, one still must ask important questions. Had the positive relish with which the Communist party supported persecution of a small splinter group not provided conditions for McCarthyism? Had the failure to criticize the Soviet Union actually discredited the entire American Left for a generation? Even these concerns do not reach the core of Hellman's failure in political judgment, for she had not simply made simple errors of judgment on selected political issues. For years she had forfeited her political judgment. If that much-abused term, "fellow traveler," has any objective meaning, it fits the political career of Lillian Hellman. She states that despite overtures from Earl Browder and V. J. Jerome she never joined the Party. "In any case," she continues, "whether I signed a Party card or didn't was of little importance to me." She defended the Moscow trials. She attacked Dewey's Commission of Inquiry. She attacked a relief committee for Finns during the Soviet invasion. Where, her critics justly ask, was her conscience during last year's fashions?[28]

I think that in her own mind Hellman was totally innocent of the charge of hypocrisy, that she thought that she had always exercised her political judgment, certainly not flawlessly but without guile and deceit. That she felt this way despite the overwhelmingly powerful charges of her critics can only be explained by her adoption of an ethical system that she herself never fully understood. Can one live by a "simple," "homely" morality *and* the Party line? Hellman did, but the costs were high. They make her witness much more complicated than either she or her critics thought.

There is no conversion experience at the center of Hellman's memoirs, but there is in her narratives a set of remembrances that speaks to the conversion experience. It constitutes what can be called an anti-conversion ethic or perhaps, more accurately, a "dry conversion." In *Scoundrel Time* her HUAC experience is expressed in these terms. Her life had changed: "My belief in liberalism was mostly gone. I think I have substituted for it something private called, for want of something that is more accurate, decency." The American intelligentsia failed to provide leadership; it has "written no words of new theory in a country that cries out for belief. . . ." There were other "penalties" as well: her income falls from $140,000 to $10,000 as a result of the blacklist, she must sell her farm ("corrupt and unjust men made me sell the only place that was ever right for me"); she must write screen plays for B movie directors at only a fraction of her market value; she has passport problems and believes that she has been harassed by the CIA; she has an affair with a "bastard" (recalling it as a punishment self-inflicted). Hellman's account has all the features of a conversion experience. She undergoes momentous, traumatic psychological change in a brief period of time. Her past life appears mistaken and misunderstood. But the new personality that emerges is not like Thoreau's metaphor of the cocoon and the butterfly. In fact it is quite the opposite. Her account is of a loss of faith, a disintegration of old beliefs without a corresponding emergence of new ones.[29]

But what the convert reveals he/she also hides. *Scoundrel Time* still maintains the myth of a woman upholding the homely principles of the "good American tradition." Here, she writes, are the consequences suffered from the exercise of "inherited rights"—loss of friends, livelihood and, most of all, belief in the reliability of friends. She has, of course, "recovered": "I tell myself that was then, and there is now, and the years between then and now, and the then and now are one."[30] But Hellman suffered and, unlike Paul, her witness is only a witness to scoundrels and cowards. But the "dry" conversion, the loss of faith, has already occurred at another level long before her "punishment" by scoundrels. In fact, it is the earlier outlook that accounts for her peculiar approach to politics and determines the kind of witness she offers as well as her reaction to the scoundrels.

The autobiographical form is an ideal structure for the exposition of Hellman's moral theory. All of her narratives are composed of moral portraits. This format is an ideal didactic device; we learn about Hellman from the models she sketches; we are also taught by Hellman about right and wrong by the moral lessons these lives offer. Thus she is able to avoid what can often become insufferable for the reader of autobiography. The seemingly endless alternation between self-deprecation

and self-justification that one finds in Chambers, the moralist, is softened by the indirect character of Hellman's teaching. But what does
Hellman teach?

The now famous Julia is a woman who paid for her moral convictions with her life. Julia, daughter of a wealthy family, is Hellman's
childhood friend. The two continue to correspond after Julia goes to
Vienna to study medicine. Julia's letters warn of the dangers of Nazism
but, although Hellman is concerned, she is busy writing *The Children's
Hour* and drinking with Hammett and their friends. Hellman knows
that Julia "had become, maybe always was, a Socialist" and that she
now lived in a one-room apartment in a slum district in Vienna, "sharing her great fortune with whoever needed it." But Hellman is shocked
to learn that Julia has been injured in a battle between workers and Fas-
cist troops. Bewildered, she sees Julia in a hospital in Vienna. In 1937
she is approached by a member of the resistance and asked to smuggle
money into Germany. Hellman is naturally terribly frightened but she
undertakes the mission and again briefly meets Julia in Berlin. The
scene is powerfully recalled: the already distraught Hellman cries at
Julia's physical condition, Julia quietly urges calm and explains her
cause. Later Hellman learns that Julia has been killed. She goes to London to make funeral arrangements, but is never able to keep her last
promise to her friend. She is not able to find Julia's infant daughter.
Throughout all these years, Hellman is enraged by the cruel indifference of Julia's family. She contrasts Julia's life (and death) to her other
friends. The Fitzgeralds, Dorothy Parker, the Murphys had only played
at radicalism, choosing instead to live their lives based only on "style."
They were unknowingly bought off by the rich. Others, like Hellman
and Julia's mutual friends, Ann-Marie and Sammy, have sunk to a level
of decadence only the rich can reach. There is boasting of incest and
the malevolent accusation of lesbianism against Hellman and Julia.

Bethe is another of Hellman's heroes. She is Hellman's cousin, a
German immigrant who is deserted by her husband and who later lives
with an Italian gangster. Bethe's lover is killed and parts of his body are
found buried in the garden behind their apartment. Bethe is a counter-
part to Julia. She is an uneducated woman who is never able to grasp
English. She is a woman of physical passions. The central scene of the
portrait takes place in an Italian restaurant. Bethe had invited the young

Lillian for lunch. Bethe sees her lover across the room: I "found her staring at the man, her lips compressed as if to hold the mouth from doing something else, her shoulders rigid against the chair." Hellman realizes that she was "seeing what I had never seen before. . . ." But Bethe pays for sexual desire as Julia paid for her radicalism. She is rejected by Hellman's family. She lives a life of danger and poverty. Like Julia, she is a teacher to Hellman. "Do not sadden, Liebchen," she assures the young Lillian. "No longer am I a German. No longer the Bowmans. Now I am a woman and woman does not need help." Bethe dies in a shack hidden in a Louisiana swamp.[31]

There are many other moral portraits all designed to illustrate lessons to be derived from the ambiguities of life; there is Uncle Willy, Hellman's first love, who flouts middle-class convention as a swashbuckling entrepreneur. Willy directs a Latin American company which hires mercenaries to keep "the peons quiet." But Hellman is more disturbed by her Aunt Lil's pretenses, although she is a morphine addict and has had a string of lovers. Hellman now knows that it was childish romanticism to think that money earned from a bank was different from money earned from international speculation. Nevertheless, she is tempted to accept Uncle Willy's invitation to go adventuring in South America. There are Hellman's two aunts, Jenny and Hannah, unmarried women slighted by society, who suffer the indignity of running a boarding house and devote their lives to their brother. There is wildly eccentric, enigmatic Arthur W. A. Cowan who talks like a reactionary but quietly gives huge sums of money to radical causes.

But the most compelling portrait of all is that of Dashiell Hammett, Hellman's central moral teacher. Hammett was Hellman's lover. On Hellman's admission, both had innumerable affairs, both drank far too much, both squandered their money, both quarreled a great deal. Nonetheless, it is the moral lessons that Hammett taught that form the core of Hellman's remembrances. For Hellman, Hammett was the most "interesting man" she had ever met. She admired his presence before other people, his reading habits, his physique, his writing craft. Most of all, she admired his morality: his decision to join the Communist party; his decision to refuse to cooperate with the government despite the penalty of a jail sentence; his unwillingness to ask friends for help after he had been blacklisted; his decision to join the army when he was forty-five. In an addendum to her elegy to Hammett in *Unfinished Woman*, Hellman reports a conversation that suggests the nature of her admiration of Hammett as moral teacher:

> One night . . . I said, "Did you read Kant when you were young?"
> "When I could stand him. Why?"
> "Is that where you got a lie is 'an annihilation of dignity'?"
> He laughed. "I don't think so. I just think lies are boring." [32]

Hammett had a moral code; he may not have lied. But neither Hammett nor Hellman was a Kantian. There are some similarities, of course. Both rejected the calculation of consequences as the basis of morality. Both rejected prudence as an acceptable basis for action. But the similarities end there and the key to the difference is Hammett's answer to the morality of truth-telling: "I just think lies are boring." Hellman's repeated questions about morality all receive a standard reply from Hammett which says in effect, "my decisions cannot form the basis for any objective form of generalization; to even discuss my motivations is a futile enterprise." Hellman nevertheless keeps asking. But all she receives in return is a joke, exasperation, and finally an admonition to stop the queries. All of the Hammett-Hellman conversations have a staccato quality about them. When Hellman tells Hammett that Abe Fortas suggested that it was time for someone to take a "moral position," Hammett, "halfway through dinner . . . pushed the plate away and said, 'that's shit. Plain liberal shit.'" When Hellman asks Hammett about his commitment to communism, he replies, "Now please don't let's ever argue about it again because we're doing each other harm." Hellman is never sure if Hammett is a Party member.

This kind of moral silence characterizes their personal relationship. Hellman is on the verge of a nervous breakdown over concerns about her sexual attractiveness. She is obsessed with the belief that she "smells" and confesses to Hammett her neurosis: "I think I smell and so you wouldn't like me." Hammett replies: "And you're crying. Go to sleep now and tell me about it when you're ready." No further discussion takes place. Hellman leaves for a trip and sleeps with a stranger in order to test her fears. Years later, after Hellman refused Hammett's drunken advances, he never sleeps with her again. No discussion is permitted. Hellman concludes in her memoirs that Hammett did not believe in the words "right" and "wrong," but that he "had formed a set of principles . . . by which he stood in eccentric isolation." This is just what Hellman "needed":

> His rules were not my rules, but sometimes mine met his and we agreed, although that mattered less to me than Hammett's refusal to deviate from his, whatever the dangers or the temptations. For many people that would not be much to find: for me, even when I disagreed, it came at a time when I was going under.[34]

Garry Wills, in his introduction to *Scoundrel Time,* perceptively compares Hellman to Hammett's Nora Charles. She is "one tough lady." Hellman did indeed adopt a "tough-guy" morality. But Wills's belief that the tough guy is a person "armed with no ideological weapons, just with a personal code, with undefended decency" is as much a myth as Hellman's justification for refusing to testify on the basis of "good American tradition."[35] Wills argues for a distinction between the ideologue and the radical. The latter does not possess the cold hatred derived from a commitment to a philosophy (ironically, Chambers is Wills's example) but rather acts on the basis of a personal code. The radical hates only "vicious and harmful people." How then can Hellman, the "radical," so consistently support the "ideologues" of the Communist party? Hellman's answer to this would have been immensely instructive, but of course she can give no answer, save for the confession of personal "mistakes," just as Hammett could not tell Hellman why he joined the Party.

The tough-guy morality is a defective morality and this explains why Hellman's own witness is so unsatisfactory. Her moral portraits all reveal a focus upon moral decision as the center of life. But although these decisions always exhibit acts of courage (Julia's antifascism, Bethe's selection of a gangster as a lover, Hammett's refusal), all of them deemphasize the justification for the actions taken. Often Hellman has us believe that the right course is so obvious that no justification is necessary. Who would not be an anti-Fascist? Who would not be devoted to one's lover? Who would not keep the confidences of friends? Moral philosophy, on Hellman's view, is for cowards, for those who must explain why they failed to do right. But the underlying reason for the absence of justification in the lives of Hellman's mentors is that there are no standards of right. Morality is a ruse to excuse cowardice, to hide hypocrisy, to justify ambition. The world of the tough guy is a corrupt society in which nearly everyone is beyond redemption. Morality is a trick, a game for the predators, a trap for the sap. Without hope of change the tough guy adopts a code of personal honor. A loss of faith in the social order forces the tough guy to approach the world only as a set of personal relationships. The tough guy does have a set of rules that governs his behavior, and it may include telling the truth or helping others, but he decides when to apply the rules and how. Thus Sam Spade has an affair with his partner's wife but later concludes that he must avenge his partner's death. The latter is not an act of redemption for the former. The two actions are unrelated. He doesn't have to fully explain his actions because no one deserves an explanation. They're all scoundrels anyway.

Albert Camus saw the implications of the tough-guy morality and concluded that its defects lay not in its existential character but rather in its total abandonment of hope. The tough guy refuses to linger to examine motivation. Instead his is a world seen only from the outside, a world of "wretched automatons in a machine-ridden universe." [36] Camus contends that the tough-guy novelist ultimately renders a "heart-rending but sterile protest" because by abandoning hope he abandons the very idea of rebellion.

The tough guy then is not the radical that Wills describes. He may attach himself to the causes of the Left but his commitment rests only upon a decision that his personal honor requires a set of actions. He may appear to base his decision on personal relationships, but his is a debased conception of persons. He cannot really know them except as occasions for the exercise of his personal honor. As the holder of a tough-guy morality Hellman was able to summon the courage to resist the scoundrels of HUAC. But as a tough guy she was also able to follow the Party line without ever fully seeing the chain of her actions. Two more of Hellman's portraits can help make this point. One is an account of V. J. Jerome, Communist party theoretician, the other Frank Costello, gangster. Jerome and several other Communist officials were in the same jail as Hammett. Hammett and Jerome had been playing ping-pong with a convicted murderer. Jerome questions a call. When

Hammett suggests not to expect honesty from criminals, Jerome insists upon the "socialist necessity" to reform all men. A moment later the inmate cheats again and Jerome directly accuses him. The inmate charges Jerome with a knife in hand. Hammett is able to intervene and promises an apology from Jerome. But the Communist official refuses to retract his charge: "I do not wish to apologize. You should be ashamed of yourself for cheating a jailed comrade. . . ."[37] Hammett is able to avoid violence by offering packs of cigarettes as reparations for the insult.

Frank Costello was introduced to Hellman by a nightclub comic. The two began to have dinner together at least once a month. Conversation was quite limited. Hellman recalls speaking only a few minutes and not again for a half hour. One evening Hellman complained about her difficulties in collecting money for the Spanish republicans trapped on the International Bridge from Spain to France. Costello reached into his pocket and handed Hellman $5,000. He had said, "Friends of yours are friends of mine." When Hellman tried to explain the civil war and fascism, Costello interrupted her: "None of that, please. Don't tell me about it. I don't get mixed up in politics and when you hand over the money, you forget my name, kid."[38]

Neither Jerome nor Costello were tough guys. Both lived lives "outside of society" but both in their own ways were organization men. But their gestures did appeal to Hellman's own tough-guy morality. Jerome had risked his life for principle. The principle was applied absurdly. The context called for prudence (as Hammett had indeed exercised). But the fact that Jerome's behavior was "silly" is proof to Hellman that the communists were not "dangerous." It was also proof that those who had left the Party were overreacting when the "faithful" used "extraordinary language" to attack them. "Only literary people can confuse shouts of 'renegade' or 'traitor' with the damage of a gun or a bomb." In her line of reasoning Hellman admired Jerome because his action was so reckless and so inappropriate. The Communists were for Hellman practitioners of the old-fashioned American homely principles she understood. Just as Jerome had acted so quirkily before the murderer, the Party had misapplied their principles in its imitation of the Russians. The American Communists had embraced Russian theory and practice "with the enthusiasm of a lover whose mistress cannot complain because she speaks few words of the language." [39] But Costello was a dangerous man. Part of the reason Hellman went to dinner with him was because she hoped that she might hear some "small piece of information about a murder." But what forms Hellman's moral judgment is always an appreciation of a gesture in itself. Costello could just as easily have given money to Franco. The complete absence of political judgment on his part is what Hellman finds so attractive. That someone gave $5,000 to a cause of which he had no knowledge is an admirable moral act. Where Costello's money came from, protection rackets, prostitution, drug dealing, is a question Hellman is simply not interested in pursuing, just as she was unwilling to consider the question of Stalinism. In a world peopled by scoundrels and badies, the gestures of Jerome and Costello complete the possibilities for moral life. When Hellman finds a book for Costello he attempts to give her $500 for her trouble. Hellman refuses. Costello thinks for a moment and concludes, "I guess I wouldn't take it, either, but then you and I are a lot alike." [40] There is a categorical imperative in that statement, but it is a tough guy's Kantianism, implemented on whim and subject only to personal interpretation.

The fascination with the gesture as a moral act reveals a paradox in the tough-guy morality. Robert Edelbaum has described the tough guy in "daemonic" terms. [41] He/she is an individual free of memory, free of convention, free of attachments to the social order. As such, the tough guy is free of the kinds of temptations that afflict the rest of us. The tough guy is not afraid of death, is free from the lures of money (Julia, Uncle Harry, and Hammett all are unconcerned about money) and romance. This estrangement from society is the source of the tough guy's power. In the detective novel it is a power to solve mysteries. The tough guy is so immune to the temptations of ordinary life that he can "see through" people. Only one free from the temptations of money, power, and romance can see how they drive others. Thus Julia can see the dangers of fascism because she has forfeited her inheritance. Bethe needs no help because she is no longer a German or a Bowman. Hammett does not need anyone's friendship. "As you came toward Hammett to shake his hand, you wanted him to approve of you because he had reserves so deep that we know we cannot hope to touch him with jokes or favors." [42] Even prison guards called him "Sir."

It was the kind of power that Hellman thought she exercised over the Committee and it was its absence that in Hellman's mind led so many others to fail to act. These timid comfortable people were too tied to status or money to judge. When Elia Kazan tries to explain why he will testify Hellman doesn't understand until he blurts out, "It's OK for you to do what you want, I guess. You've probably spent whatever you've earned." [43]

But the same perspective that permits the tough guy to "see" the motivations of others severely restricts his ability to create social bonds. Hellman can only understand others as types, the scoundrels, the timid, and the comfortable. Those who are free like she is she can only understand at moments of moral gesture. Camus had said that the tough guy observes the world behind a pane of glass. Only in her last memoir, *Maybe*, does Hellman consider the consequences of the tough-guy morality. *Maybe* is Hellman's only real confessional. It does have all the elements of the detective story: incest, murder, drugs, insanity, betrayal. The role of the tough guy in this genre of fiction is to uncover instances of corruption beneath the facade of social order. In *Pentimento* and *Scoundrel Time* Hellman had been able to summon up her power to draw moral portraits and witness against the scoundrels, but in *Maybe* she is a lost person. The central memory that Hellman attempts to capture is of Sarah. She meets Sarah sporadically throughout her account but she is unable to draw her usual moral portrait, perhaps because in a sense it is Sarah whom Camus would have seen as the tough guy, as a symbol of a despairing world. Sarah is truly a person without memory and without hope. "It's not a question of life or people with Sarah. She has no interest in tomorrow because she has no interest in yesterday. It comes down to hours." [44] Sarah has a child by Carter Cameron (later Hellman's lover as well) but she insists upon naming him Som for "son of many." Sarah's aimless promiscuity is only part of the consequence of her estrangement from others. She is a pathological liar. She masquerades at various points in the narrative as German and then Italian royalty. Sarah is involved in a shooting incident, and apparently she dies ignominiously in Italy.

There are elements in this biography of Sarah that suggest Hellman's conventional moral didactics. Sarah is indeed a free spirit; she simply ignores rather than flouts social convention and of course she must pay a price for her freedom. She is divorced, loses custody of her child, is rejected by the "respectable" rich, and roams through Europe. Hellman can never quite find the kind of moral certainty at Sarah's core that she has discovered in her other portraits. She cannot quite even present a picture of Sarah as a "good" scoundrel like Uncle Willy. The search for the real Sarah becomes the quest of this memoir. The attempt to "remember" Sarah in some moral sense takes major significance because Sarah's life (as well as Hellman can reconstruct it) bears striking parallels to her own. Both women are moderately promiscuous (at least compared to the men in their lives). In fact they share two of the same lovers. One of them is responsible for Hellman's nervous breakdown. Alex had told Hellman that she "smelled." Hellman becomes obsessed with the belief that she has a "strange but interesting odor." She takes four baths a day and queries anyone who will listen (no one does) about her smells. Hammett tells her that Freud had said that one cannot remember a smell. A befuddled farmer is even quizzed after he casually notes that he likes the smell of a barn.

Hellman is temporarily relieved when Sarah tells her that Alex had also complained about her in the same way. It may not be too presumptuous to suggest that Hellman's concern about her "smell," now shared with Sarah, is a reflection of Hellman's suspicion about her own moral integrity. Both women travel with gangsters and when Hellman hears of a shooting scandal involving Sarah she hires a researcher to provide her details. Later Sarah gives Hellman a version of the incident. For Hellman her racketeer lover must have been "very handsome and interesting." Sarah had testified that the shooting was in self-defense. Was this a moral gesture worth remembering? Was it a lie as an act of love? Was Sarah another Bethe, this time a society girl who willingly moves into the world of gangsters? Hellman asks her own gangster. Frank Costello checks the information Hellman gives him and finds that Sarah's lover was a "third-rate runner" in his seventies. Costello concludes, "And I ain't no authority on what society girls think is handsome, but he was five feet six maybe, had a slashed nose and his face was all over slashed from prison fights he'd been in all his life."[45]

Hellman is never able to completely demystify Sarah because neither she nor Sarah is able to remember individuals and events except in hazy and jumbled ways. When Sarah tells a story it always lacks coherence. Because Sarah has no reasons for her actions, memory of a "vulgar" raincoat is mixed with witnessing a murder. All of Hellman's memories of Sarah have this surreal quality. She can never quite remember when she first met Sarah; Sarah cannot remember at all. Sometimes when she meets Sarah, she is not Sarah but Signora Pinelli or Melaniess. Sometimes Hellman cannot recognize Sarah and sometimes Sarah cannot recognize Hellman. Attempts to verify incidents through third parties meet with the same kind of confusion. Reflecting on memories of Sarah, Hellman begins to question whether she had told the truth in her other memoirs: "I tried very hard for the truth. I did try, but I don't know much of what really happened and never tried to find out. In addition to the ordinary deceptions that you and others make in life, time itself makes time fuzzy and meshes truth with half truth. But I can't seem to say it right. . . ." [46]

Maybe, a memoir about puzzles and mysteries, itself ends on a puzzling note. Hellman, the tough guy with the freedom and hence the power to see through others ends her narrative without solving the mystery. She learns that Sarah is not dead, that her death was a ruse to collect insurance. The woman cast out from society for her eccentricities had not died in poverty. A few months later Hellman goes for a midnight swim at Martha's Vineyard: "The water was the right temperature, everything was better; there was even the possibility that there could be some answer to the future and that it wouldn't be as bad as I thought." But this moment of contentment is brief. Hellman finds that she cannot see the shore. She remembers that "frightened" is not the right word to describe her feelings: "Something else was happening to me: I was collapsing in a way that had never happened before." Hellman manages somehow to swim ashore. She races from the beach, cuts herself on a rugosa bush, and staggers back to her cottage. After falling asleep, she awakens, having lost track of time. "I was in the kind of temper that has no name because it is not temper but was some monumental despair that makes crazy people kill cats or stifle crying babies." She telegrams Cameron, Sarah's exhusband and her own exlover. The message says: "*There are missing parts everyplace and everywhere and they are not my business unless they touch me. But when they touch me, I do not wish them to be black. My instinct repeat instinct repeat instinct repeat instinct is that yours are black. Lillian.*" [47]

The closing of *Maybe* manages to stay within the boundaries of the tough-guy morality. Hellman's crisis is resolved by an act of will that requires no explanation. The outside world is one of moral chaos "(there are missing parts everyplace and everywhere") but she does not have to solve these puzzles or even discover moral gestures in others to make a judgment. Hellman need only rely upon instinct. Yet barely beneath this final defense of the tough guy is a realization of its consequences. Sarah is the tough guy without the capacity or the inclination for moral judgment. Her estrangement from society is so complete that she does not even lash out in bursts of moral judgment. She is vaguely troubled by the murder and her complicity in it, but she is so cut off from human relationships that she cannot piece together its significance. The most she can manage is, "I've always thought that's the real wages of sin: you never get to know much." [48] Hellman searches repeatedly and vainly for some moral aura around Sarah, but the more she looks, the more the mindless and despairing aspects of Sarah's rebellion come into focus. Hellman sees a Sarah in herself: the drug taking, the compulsive drinking, the unpleasant affairs, and, most of all, the almost complete absence of fellowship and community in her life. Hellman's despair turns inward in a moment of crisis; she was "collapsing in a way that had never happened before." *Maybe* does end with a great effort at moral assessment, but the exposure of the underside of the tough-guy morality is too vivid, too sustained to be pushed aside, despite (or perhaps because of) the strength required for that final moral gesture.

In *Scoundrel Time* Hellman frequently complains about the inability of American intellectuals to remember their political judgments: "We are a people who do not want to keep much of the past in our heads." [49] But the tough guy, as Camus said, is a person without memory. Hellman, the autobiographer and the radical, cannot really remember herself, at least in a moral sense. In a world of scoundrels and tough guys, respect is so occasional and intuitive that no history is possible. There are only missing parts every place and every where. How strange and how sad that Whittaker Chambers and Lillian Hellman, the two great opposing witnesses of our age, should fail so completely in presenting a theory of their acts of witness.

R E M E M B E R I N G

HENRY ADAMS

LINCOLN STEFFENS

RICHARD WRIGHT

Despite a certain amount of self-deception, the American autobiographer confronts the self in a way that no liberal political thinker does. Chambers had to make and remake his own identity. Only then could he assume the role as "a witness to the two great faiths of our time."[1] Hellman struggles to live where there are "missing parts everyplace and everywhere."[2] For the liberal the individual is offered axiomatically. The task of political philosophy is to fashion a society on the basis of competing conceptions of the good life selected by autonomous selves.

Part of this assessment is based upon an analysis of the special conditions of American political development, but in a broader sense liberalism as a political philosophy assumes a unique burden. Liberals insist that a single conception of the good life cannot be the basis for a political philosophy.[3] Under this condition, standards of political conduct must be derived from principles accepted by all. Only by positing a "State of Perfect Freedom" can one imagine the inconveniences of life without common rules and so derive standards of conduct that all can agree upon.

John Locke is, of course, the exemplar of this state-of-nature tradition. In America this liberal resolution has always been especially attractive. Covenant theology, liberal revolution, the founding, the frontier, even the immigrant experience, have given a historical plausibility to the concept. The belief that political principles could be derived from free and equal beings has confirmed the liberal consensus. Contemporary American liberals continue this tradition. John Rawls's veil of ignorance, Ronald Dworkin's auction, and Bruce Ackerman's imaginary societies are all designed to function as states of nature. Each structure represents an attempt to discover some compelling "moral settlement," one that advances principles that one would agree to regardless of life plan or position in the "natural lottery."[4]

One of the great costs of this Lockean resolution, however, is that in the effort to find common political principles individuals are stripped of all those characteristics deemed inessential to the settlement. Thus, the liberal as a defender of individualism offers an image of truncated beings, decision makers driven to maximize their position in society. Contemporary American liberals, in their efforts to reframe a new settlement, have carried this tendency to extremes. Locke had envisioned his individuals as holders of property and religious vision. Recent theorists deprive the inhabitants of their states of nature of personality itself. Family, talent, ambition, life plan are all portrayed as biases that could undermine the moral settlement. Bertrand de Jouvenal's characterization of the traditional state-of-nature theorists seems an even more apt description today: here are "childless men who must have forgotten their own childhood."[5]

"There everything may grow and spread as it pleases"

The autobiography as a genre of political writing in America can be studied, nonetheless, as an attempt to evaluate independently the moral settlement of liberal society without creating the abstracted individualism of conventional American political thought, because, in addition to the historical and formal functions, there is an individual and psychological function of the state of nature that is not generally fully presented. As an act of liberal imagination, the state of nature is a description of unregulated desire. Norman Jacobson's analysis of Thomas Hobbes emphasizes this aspect of the concept: "I am persuaded that the state of nature Hobbes divined is instead perpetual, a metaphorical description of what moves us all as creatures. The manifestations of the state of perpetual nature within are ordinary fancies, dreams, and idle thoughts. Its outward expression is found in . . . society."[6]

Psychoanalytic theory speaks to this aspect of a state of nature. Freud discussed one of the functions of fantasy as an attempt to recapture pleasure renounced by the adoption of the reality principle:

In phantasy . . . man can continue to enjoy a freedom from the grip of the external world, one which he has long relinquished in actuality. The creation of the mental domain of phantasy has a complete counter-part in the establishment of "reservations" and "nature-parks" in places where the inroads of agriculture, traffic, or industry threaten to change the original face of the earth rapidly into something unrecognizable. The "reservation" is to maintain the old condition of things which has been regretfully sacrificed to necessity everywhere else; there everything may grow and spread as it pleases, including what is useless and even what is harmful. . . .[7]

On these terms the state of nature as a description of desire that can lead to terror or contentment is always recoverable in our imagination. Rousseau and Hobbes portrayed the poles of these sets of fancies. Locke examined both. The American autobiographer recalls these "dreams" in order to understand the moral settlement of which he/she is a party.

A study of American autobiography discloses a belief that one's childhood is a state of nature which one has left. Writer after writer show us the dual images of the Lockean state of nature in their own childhood: the pastoral element described by Locke as full of "peace, goodwill and mutual assistance" along with the terroristic undertones of "enmity, malice, violence and mutual destruction." In Lockean theory, the former must be abandoned because of the need for political settlement. Childhood too must give way to acceptance of common rules of conduct. Childhood as a state of nature is seen on the one hand as a state of perfect freedom. The child is still in many ways "outside of society," without full responsibilities, a creature of innocent desire. On the other hand, the child is exposed to the uncertainties of which Locke spoke. The family is a source of protection and love, but it is also a source of unexpected violence and disappointment. Thus, childhood as a source of both solace and terror, a dimly remembered pastoral with gothic undertones, is a state of nature that does not appear historically intermittently or in moments of rarified reasoning in the mind of the philosophically inclined liberal citizen. The state of nature is *replicated each generation individually,* in childhood. The autobiographer's recollection of childhood then becomes a pilgrimage, a return to his state of nature as a way of clarifying his position in society.

This recollection of the "reservation," this Lockean world of "peace, good will and mutual assistance," assumes a special temporal location for the autobiographer as childhood experience. But the autobiographer also remembers his childhood in the spatial sense of the pastoral. The pastoral as a form has traditionally served a different function from the state of nature. It is a state of repose, an escape from both city and wild (Tityrus's farm is bounded by marshland and Rome in Vergil's poem).[8] In America the "middle landscape" of the European pastoral is noticeably expanded in the American mind:[9] sometimes it is the small town itself, sometimes a quiet backyard or a treehouse. In urban America, the vacant lot, suitably gauzed through memory, will do. When the town is regarded as too "civilized," a pastoral is literally re-created, just as Thoreau did at Walden. The American state of nature so perfectly described by Mark Twain's Tom Sawyer as a "delectable land, reposeful and inviting" is indeed a model of childhood freedom where "everything may grow as it pleases" and where the profusion and harmony of color and sound and smell and taste make it an alternate society (even with its gothic threats), which remains in memory as a basis for evaluating one's place in the liberal world.

The pastoral, like memories of childhood in general, always dissipates from both within and without. Early pastoral paintings regularly contained a representation of Death with the motto "Et in Arcadia Ego" as a reminder that the scene of repose was temporary. The *First Eclogue* of Vergil concludes with Melibus's realization that his participation in the pastoral was only a day's postponement of his exile. Childhood recollected exhibits the same quality of lost Arcadia. Memory is experience only temporarily felt and the mind of the child himself is only briefly recaptured. More important, the memories of repose are shattered not by Roman soldiers but by families and peers, and most significantly by the assumption of adulthood in a liberal society, for the values of the pastoral—wonder, abundance, and abandon—stand inversely to the principles of the liberal order.[10] The pilgrimage to the pastoral of childhood becomes on these terms a rejection of the American success story that forms the basic structure of the larger autobiography.

This dreamlike character of the pastoral childhood can, of course, utilimately confirm liberal thought all over again, but this pilgrimage to the past is still an attempt to find or reclaim a different conception of a self than that outlined by the liberal settlement. The state-of-nature theorist shows us the consequences of lives lived as "fancy," where everything may grow and spread as it pleases. He constructs a society in which individuals are protected from his dreams and the dreams of others. The autobiographer uses remembrance to produce a different kind of political act. He uses his state of nature in a way that is the opposite of its function in conventional liberal theory. His act of remembrance seeks to discover a lost self, a self discarded as he accepted the burdens and advantages of a life in a liberal society. Could, the autobiographer asks, these pastoral moments have formed the basis for a different self than I became? The question is never answered completely. After all, the general task of the autobiographer is to understand the life that was lived. But the journey itself reveals the nature of the real base of American liberalism (fragile and fissured as it is), doing more than just formally confirming its existence.

Of course, childhoods vary historically and by class. Moreover, life bestows failures and triumphs specific to each individual. Let me illustrate the points above by introducing these complexities in a discussion of autobiographers from different generations: Henry Adams, grandson of presidents, public servant, and writer; Lincoln Steffens, upper-middle-class journalist, progressive reformer, and ultimately self-styled revolutionary; Richard Wright, poor black, novelist, Communist, and Pan-Africanist.

"The memory was all that mattered"

Henry Adams's life is a failure. Despite his novel and history writing and his record of public service, he could not understand the significance of public events, his place in American history, his place in the Adams family. Life is a series of shocks—not reversals in any economic sense (the ones that fill Franklin's autobiography) or mistakes (Rousseau)—but buffets to Adams's ability to understand both his public persona and his personal mission. Because he can grasp no religious principles, Adams does not wait like Jonathan Edwards for conversion. He is, however, a seeker in a Christian sense. He craves salvation. "Education" is the term Adams uses to describe his quest. But "education" always eludes him. Harvard has a vague negative influence; Lowell's Concord transcendentalism puzzles him; German philosophy is incomprehensible (Adams cannot even bring himself to learn the language); diplomacy is a series of half-kept secrets whose significance he cannot quite understand. Adams is a confused man and the *Education* is a chronicle of the confusion he experienced, despite his efforts to understand his society and his place in it.

In a sense, Adams's frequent tours of Europe and its cathedrals represented a return to a preliberal state of nature antecedent to his confusion. Mont-Saint-Michel and Chartres and other ancient churches and chapels stood as a "door of escape" back to a world not yet shaped by the Reformation, the Renaissance, and liberal reason. Here was a world that existed before the "eternal truths" of the eighteeth century were discovered, before "Boston had solved the universe." Puritan reformers had not yet abolished Mary, and at Chartres Adams could still feel the spirit of the Virgin, a force so strong that it "embarrassed the Trinity" and made those "utter strangers" like Adams "not far from getting down on our knees and praying to her still." Mary just "never loved bankers." Religion without the corrosive devotions of the bourgeois was "love" not "logic." Chartres taught Adams that God could not be reached except by emotion, "by absorption of our existence in His." [11]

But although "the centuries dropped like autumn leaves" when Adams toured cathedrals, the psychic connection between the thirteenth and twentieth centuries was difficult to maintain. The "Virgin's pilgrim" would have his doubts ("To what purpose had she existed, if, after nineteen hundred years, the world was bloodier than when she was born?") [12] and, perhaps more important, Adams's act of identification with a world so foreign to his own experience required a seeking more intellectual than emotional. Adams certainly *felt* like getting down on his knees but he didn't (or at least he doesn't tell us that he did). Whether he did or not (and speculation is almost certain to produce a negative answer) is still less important than that what interested him most was the *idea* of kneeling before the Virgin. [13]

It is in Adams's return to his youth in Quincy as the "boy Henry" that offers the most successful attempt to understand his own failure and confusion. Often the most effective evocations of Our Lady depend upon this autobiographical state of nature. It is Quincy that informs Chartres.

Adams's boyhood memories are complex, perhaps more so than those of any other American autobiographer. The recollection of Quincy brings forth a charming pastoral, a colonial society enclosed in time without the "systematic organization of hatred" and the "telegraphy and railroads" of Boston. Like nearly all American autobiographies, Adams's pastoral involves a psychological connection between boyhood, nature, and freedom. Quincy in the summer is a state of perfect freedom: "Town was restraint, law, unity. Country, only seven miles away, was liberty, diversity, outlawry, the endless delight of mere sense impressions given by nature for nothing and breathed by boys without knowing it." But the man Henry Adams can recover its significance. "To the boy Henry Adams, summer was drunken." Smells are recalled lovingly: the "smell of hot pine woods and sweet fern in the scorching summer noon; of new-mown hay; of ploughed earth; of box hedges; of peaches, lilacs, syringas; of stables, barns, cow-yards; of salt water and the low tide of the marshes. . . ." Taste left memories too ("pennyroyal and flagroot"; the "shell of peanut") as did color ("a peony, with the dew of early morning on its petals"; "the intense blue of the sea"; "the cumuli in a June afternoon sky"). Even schoolbooks rekindle Adams's pastoral longings. The letters of a spelling book—"the taste of A-B, AB, suddenly revived on the boy's tongue sixty years afterwards."[14]

If a Quincy summer was a state of perfect freedom where "boys are wild animals," the Boston winter forbade such "tropical license." November evenings were "cold grays." After January blizzards the sun was "violent," "cold white," and the general atmosphere toneless. Summer was "sensual living," while winter was "always compulsory learning." For Adams these two seasons had immeasurable personal significance. They had given him a "double nature" that ran through his life creating "perplexing, warring, irreconcilable problems."[15]

Adams's gothic is not the terror of unrestricted violence. Forcible restraint there is in the world of Quincy, but it is Tom Sawyer-like. The boy Henry is escorted by his grandfather to school when he refuses to go. There were no lectures from the venerable grandfather; "no syllable of revolting cant about the duty of obedience" was offered perhaps because for a boy in such a state of freedom "a moral education would at that moment have fallen on the stoniest soil." The boy Henry impishly eats his grandfather's prize peaches intended for re-seeding; he only consumed "the less perfect," although he "ate more by way of compensation." (Boys have their own natural laws.) Always the man Adams remembers that "a boy's will is his life," that he seldom met with restraint, that familial authority is a "boy's natural enemy" and thus he "bore no grudge," and that, after all, the Adams tradition itself was "almost Cromwellian."[16]

But there is still a familial terror that invades even the remembrance of Quincy. Once an Irish gardener said to the boy Henry: "You'll be thinkin' you'll be President too!" The man Adams never forgot the remark. "That there should be a doubt of his being President was a new idea."[17] The source of Adams's fear lies in this enormous weight of his patrimony. Certainly, the Adams gothic is a complex one. The Adamses, particularly John Quincy, are frequently evoked affectionately. But in the man Adams's works there is an overbearing sense of resentment, the opposite of that implied by the Irish gardener. For Adams resented not what he didn't have, but what he did have. He resented not what the Adamses did to him but what they were. Sometimes his resentment is Schelerian, like the gardener's. He was not to be president; he was not even to be listened to. More often his resentment was only generalized: he was an Adams.

The famous opening paragraph of *The Education* states Henry's indictment:

> Under the shadow of Boston State House, turning its back on the house of John Hancock, the little passage called Hancock Avenue runs, or ran, from Beacon Street, skirting the State House grounds, to Mount Vernon Street, on the summit of Beacon Hill; and there, in the third house below Mount Vernon Place, February 16, 1838, a child was born, and christened later by his uncle, the minister of the First Church after the tenets of Boston Unitarianism, as Henry Brooks Adams.
>
> Had he been born in Jerusalem under the shadow of the Temple and circumcised in the Synagogue by his uncle the high priest, under the name of Israel Cohen, he would scarcely have been more distinctly branded. . . .[18]

Adams ponders the justice of what contemporary liberal theorists call the "natural lottery." "Probably no child . . . held better cards than he." "Had he been consulted," had he stood behind Rawls's veil of ignorance, "he would have been astounded by his own luck." But Adams wonders had he been consulted would he "have cared to play the game at all." As one most favored in a system in which neither "he nor anyone else back to the beginning of time knew the rules or the risks or the stakes" he had tried to act as Rawls now tells we should. He would "never make the usual plea of irresponsibility. He would accept his situation as though he had been a party to it." He would act as if he were truly free as "a consenting, contracting party and partner from the moment he was born to the moment he died." But Adams could not quite play the Lockean game: "he lost himself in the study of it. . . ."[19]

Here lies Adams's indictment. His lifelong anxieties, his confusion, shocks, and failures were traced to his childhood origins. Of course, his childhood was America's as well. The burden of the natural lottery that made him a third-generation Adams was the burden of every American. If Adams was a child of the seventeenth and eighteenth centuries, how could he "play the game of the twentieth"? Had he seen (or had any American seen) a "New York stock-list of 1900, and had studied the statistics of railways, telegraphs, coal, and steel—would he have quitted his eighteenth century. . .?"[20]

The death of his grandfather in 1848, when the boy Henry was ten years old, is remembered as a personal shock. Adams's "boy-life was fading away." "What was he?—where was he going? Even then he felt that something was wrong." But the death is also presented as a national crisis. "The end of this first, or ancestral and Revolutionary, chapter" had arrived "when the eighteenth century, as an actual and living companion, vanished." Adams, as well as America, "had to pay for Revolutionary patriots."[21]

Actual violence was located in Boston. Adams came to see it as a burden chosen by the Adams family but one that the boy Henry was also forced to bear. Henry's "education" was his inheritance and his own suffering involved more than superfluity in the new industrial America. "His father's business in life was to get past the dangers of the slave-power, or to fix the bounds at least." Charles Adams's antislavery activitiy placed the Adams family at the center of Boston politics. Newspapers "derided or abused" the family. "If violence were a part of complete education, Boston was not incomplete." The boy Henry never witnessed violence, but he knew that "mobs were always possible." As a child, thoughts of violence "wrought frenzy in the brain of a fifteen year old, eighteenth-century boy from Quincy." His "education," after all, had him "living in the atmosphere of the Stamp Act, the Ten Tax and the Boston Massacre." For the man Adams the political duty of his "eighteenth-century" family had its irresponsible and self-serving side. It "mattered little" to his father that others must pay for his politics "with their lives wasted on battlefields or misdirected energies and lost opportunity." He had discovered that abolitionism was, in part, a reflection of class perspective. For men like Charles Adams politics offered no difficulties, for their moral law was their "sure guide." "In New England society was directed by the professions. Lawyers, physicians, professors were classes and acted not as individuals but as though they were clergymen and each profession were a church." The dirty little secret of abolitionism was that it was only part of an upper bourgeois political agenda. These men "required state support and had commonly received it." The man Adams felt "deceived and betrayed"; "he took for granted that Boston had solved the universe."[22]

These resentments are crystallized in *The Education* in another act of remembrance. Adams records that when he was twelve a "slight tie" with the eighteenth century remained. John Quincy Adams's wife had stayed in Washington, D.C. after the president's death. In 1850 she became seriously ill. The boy Henry and his father traveled from Quincy to visit her. What so impressed the boy Henry was not the Senate chamber or the White House but the "special raggedness," the carelessness and disrepair of the Maryland countryside and the city. So this is what slavery had caused: "Slavery struck him in the face; it was a nightmare; a horror; a crime; the sum of all wickedness! Slave States were dirty, unkempt, poverty stricken, ignorant, vicious!" Henry would return to Quincy more "political than ever." His politics "were no longer so modern as the eighteenth century, but took on a strong tone of the seventeenth. Slavery drove the whole Puritan community back on its Puritanism. The boy thought as dogmatically as though he were one of his own ancestors. The Slave power took the place of Stuart kings and Roman popes."[23]

But if the Washington trip had served to reaffirm the boy Henry's education, it still offered moments of doubt. George Washington had been a "Pole Star, . . . amid the endless restless motion of every other visible point in space." But the pilgrimage to Mount Vernon is remembered for its demythologizing impact: "when we got there, Mount Vernon was only Quincy in a Southern setting. No doubt it was much more charming, but it was the same eighteenth century, the same old furniture, the same old patriot, the same old President."[24] Moreover, although the trip South had indeed driven Henry "further into politics" (and what was to be his life-long confusion), it also reawakened his pre-political pastoral. The South had another side:

> The May sunshine and shadow had something to do with it; the thickness of foliage and the heavy smells had more; the sense of atmosphere, almost new, had perhaps as much again; and the brooding indolence of a warm climate and a negro population hung in the atmosphere heavier than the catalpas. The impression was not simple, but the boy liked it: distinctly it remained on his mind as an attraction, almost obscuring Quincy itself. The want of barriers, of pavements, of forms; the looseness, the laziness, the indolent Southern drawl; the pigs in the streets; the negro babies and their mothers with bandanas; the freedom, openness, swagger, of nature and man, soothed his Johnson blood. Most boys would have felt it in the same way, but with him the feeling caught on to an inheritance.[25]

The state of nature is meant to be transcended, but for Adams his state of nature was his problem; his "double nature" could never be reconciled. He remembers and glimpses it in antebellum Washington and it wreaks havoc on his political education. The stained glass at Chartres allows Adams to momentarily recover his childhood awe. He complains that developed societies have lost their sense of color as well as taste and smell. As a tourist in the twelfth century, Adams "sees" again. He is "ashamed" to be "as extravagant as he wants to be" at the sight. The craftsmen sacrificed everything to color: "The French held then the first point in colour decoration was colour, and they never hesitated to put their colour where they wanted it, or cared whether a green camel or a pink lion looked like a dog or a donkey provided they got their harmony or value. . . . So we laugh to see a knight with a blue face, on a green horse, that looks as though drawn by a four-year-old child, and probably the artist laughed too; but he was a colourist, and never sacrificed his colour for a laugh."[26]

But if Chartres allows Adams to reexperience the pleasures of Quincy, no one was more aware than Adams of the distance between his Norman ancestors and Boston. Writing to his brother Brooks, he exclaimed that "our Norman grandpas did great things" but each generation of descendants "kept only the qualities that were useful, with a dull instinct recalling dead associations. So we get Boston." The crowds at Mont-Saint-Michel drive him to a frenzy. There is every kind of repulsiveness: "odious Frenchwomen, gross, shapeless, bare-armed, eating and drinking. . . . dreary Englishwomen . . . American art students, harmless and feeble, sketching from every hole in the walls."[27] Wandering along the streets "in close and intimate conversation with Thibaut of Champagne" he is jarred into the twentieth century by the sight of a newspaper and the confusion begins again: "chaos of time, place, morals, forces and motive—gave him vertigo."[28]

Most of Adams's efforts to reconcile the freedom of the state of nature and the demands of civil society involve a repudiation rather than an affirmation of the pleasures of Quincy. If society cannot be a place where everything may grow, perhaps nothing should. There is, to put the point directly, a preoccupation (even apart from the theory of history) with things dead or inanimate in Adams's thought. In the preface to *The Education* the ego is described as a manikin to be fitted. Although the remarks are initially meant to be a commentary on the purposes of education, the focus of the metaphor turns on the person-thing, not the fitters, and Adams notes that the manikin "must be taken for real; must be treated as though it had life."[29] Had the weight of Adams's patrimony made him a manikin? The questions raised by the preface become even harsher. Does society take boys and make them things? Are there no real people left? Do we now pretend that we are not things, that society only appears to be tailoring energies when its youth are already dead?

Imposing nature, mountains, and oceans, would terrify Thoreau; Adams seems always almost ready to jump. In *Esther* the heroine looks at Niagara Falls and shocks her friend with the energy with which she grasps the thought that the falls are a kind of Nirvana: "the next world is a sort of great reservoir of truth, and that what is true in us pours into it like raindrops."[30] The Adams letters show a habitual use of metaphors of death. Adams had, of course, suffered greatly from his wife's suicide, but the mourning was suited to his temperament. He was a "long established ghost," a "mummy," a mind in 'saline' solution whose "curtain had already dropped." His surroundings were often similarly charac-

terized: Europe was a "senile wreck"; England had a "broken neck";
Russia was "weak and rotten"; France was in "decline"; the United
States was "rotten as punk."[31] The remembrance of the death of his sis-
ter took on an awakening of the sensual that he had reserved for
Quincy summers:

> Death took features altogether new to him, in these rich and sen-
> suous surroundings. Nature enjoyed it, played with it, the horror
> added to her charm, she liked the torture, and smothered her vic-
> tim with caresses. Never had one seen her so winning. The hot
> Italian summer brooded outside, over the marketplace and the
> picturesque peasants, and, in the singular color of the Tuscan at-
> mosphere, the hills and vineyards of the Apennines seemed burst-
> ing with mid-summer blood. The sick-room itself glowed with the
> Italian joy of life; friends filled it; no harsh northern lights pierced
> the soft shadows; even the dying woman shared the sense of the
> Italian summer, the soft velvet air, the humor, the courage, the
> sensual fulness of Nature and man. She faced death, as women
> mostly do, bravely and even gaily, racked slowly to unconscious-
> ness, but yielding only to violence, as a soldier sabred in battle.
> For many thousands of years, on these hills and plains, Nature has
> gone on sabring men and women with the same air of sensual
> pleasure.[32]

Adams, the stylist, had never written a more moving passage. Death
is less counterpoised to summer as life than merged with it. She (for
death is in Adams's mind a feminine figure, an anti-Mary) is a daytime
vampire, a seductress at a summer lawn party. "Horror added to her
charm" and she turned the atmosphere "mid-summer blood." And then
in Adams's remembered "drunken summer" she slew his sister.

In *The Education* Adams admits that he "revelled at will in the ruin of
every society in the past, and rejoiced in proving the prospective over-
throw of every society that seemed possible in the future."[33] The man-
nered self-deprecation of the autobiography generally prevents the dis-
play of the spitefulness of the crank. The Adams letters, however,
abandon this self-restraint. A death wish often appears, as when Adams
tells a correspondent that "hating vindictively as I do, our whole fabric

and conception of society . . . I shall be glad to see the whole thing utterly destroyed and wiped away. . . ."[34] And look how colors and sights and tastes are incorporated in this ugly fantasy:

> I have grown so used to playing the spider, and squatting in silence in the middle of this Washington web, and I have seen so many flies and other insects caught and devoured in its meshes that I have now a little the sense of being a sort of ugly, bloated purplish-blue, and highly venomous hairy tarantula which catches and devours Presidents, senators, diplomats, congressman and cabinet-officers, and knows the flavor of every generation and every country in the civilized world."[35]

Of course, Adams's autobiographical fame rests with his discovery of the dynamic force of history at the Great Exposition of 1900. He had felt like kneeling at Chartres not before a statue as such but because he felt he could feel the Virgin as the twelfth-century supplicant had felt her, as a "real person, whose tastes, wishes, passions were intimately known." Standing before the gallery of machines, Adams felt the same awe, the same desire to kneel, the same sense of infinity but here was a symbol "not so human." Adams's Mary worship was at least ostensibly based upon his perception of her infinite grace. Without Mary, the Christian knew there was no escape. She alone represented Love; "men rushed like sheep to escape the butcher, and were driven to Mary";[36] they pleaded and talked to her and offered excuses. But the dynamo was mindless and Adams knew it, and that is why he thought it was the "most expressive" of symbols. Thus the dynamo became for Adams more than a symbol of the mindless energy of the Gilded Age. It was a repudiation of his eighteenth-century education. It was a repudiation of his twelfth-century education. Our Lady was just a force and it was "the historian's business to follow the track of energy."[37] The Force now rested in the machine and to this extent Adams insisted that he too was a machine, albeit a worn-out one.

Adams himself had once boasted to his brother that he was going to dive and "remain underwater until he came up with an oyster and a pearl." In *Indian Summer* Van Wyck Brooks replied that *The Education*, despite its popularity with the young men to whom it was dedicated, was only the oyster, not the pearl. Only with Chartres had Adams offered any real education to the next generation because Chartres had stood for all "believing communities" of which New England had once been one.[38] But I think that for Henry Adams the pearl was never re-covered except in memory of those "happiest hours" of a childhood summer "lying on a musty heap of Congressional Documents in the old farmhouse at Quincy, reading *Quentin Durward, Ivanhoe,* and *The Talis-man,* and raiding the garden at intervals for peaches and pears." [39]

"The boy on horseback"

Steffens's autobiography parodies rather than imitates the Christian narrative. His chapter headings include "I become a hero," "I get reli-gion," "I become a drunkard," "I inherit a fortune," "I become a capi-talist." But the autobiography as a whole suggests a tyrotic struggle. Like Adams, Steffens recounts his many and varied occupations and travels, but he focuses on his childhood. "The Boy on Horseback," the title of the first part of the autobiography, is an account of Steffens's own personal state of nature, an explanation and defense of his own adult political sensibilities. If the state of nature as a device in conventional political thought is used as a measure of current political practice, Steffens uses his boyhood to reconstruct his own vision of the political world. At one level "The Boy on Horseback" is a conventional boys' adventure story. Steffens's most vivid impressions are of cowboys "shout-ing on bucking bunches of broncoes," teamsters, miners, and steam-boat men "drinking, gambling, girling, fighting." He sees his "infant mind . . . snapping wide-eyed shots of these rough scenes and coloring and completing them with pictures painted on my memory by the con-versations I overheard . . . I played I was a teamster, a gun-playing bronco-busting vaquero or a hearty steamboat man, or a steamboat." [40]

Steffens's childhood was a model for American boyhood. In fact, "A Boy on Horseback" was separated from the complete autobiography and widely used as grammar-school reading. Steffens's childhood was a "happy life—happier and happier"—"free, independent, full of ro-mance, adventure, and learning of a sort." [41]

Yet a sense of dread infects Steffens's state of nature. Steffens had built a tree house ("a wigwam to me") to observe the world below "un-aware that I, a spy, an Indian, an army scout, could see all that they did." But an older boy "saw my hut; he spied my two spying eyes." He climbed up the tree and provided Steffens with his first introduction to sex. The hut suddenly became "dark, tight, hidden" and the young boy sneaked down to the "nice, clean dust of the sunlit ground."[42] The pastoral had been invaded by a marauder, armed with knowledge from adult society. On another occasion Steffens recounts his fear of school and the "Terror," the "mob of wild, contemptuous, cruel strange boys," who formed a gauntlet before him.

For the most part, however, Steffens is able to avoid these threats by creating a solitary pastoral. He plays "steamboat" with a chair and later takes up horseback riding. Steffens remembered himself as a loner, even as a college student: "I was out of the crowd as I had been as a boy." There are occasional encounters with men on Steffens's travels, but they are limited to boy-men, bridge-tenders, and stable boys, marginal people who had also not fully entered society. Boys who had horses that were used in their father's work were disdained as were boys interested in marbles, tops, and knives. Steffens as an adult felt that those games were the first lessons in business and, hence, entrance into society. Far better to stay away from the playground with its "fashions, laws, customs and tyrannies" which were a direct entrance to the "herding habits" of "Main Street."

Steffens was painfully aware that his father had also traversed through this same state of nature. The elder Steffens had traveled to California on horseback confronting danger (he still kept an arrow that had killed a friend), but when the wagon train broke and scattered, Steffens had not sought gold but a start in business. In San Francisco he found it as a bookkeeper in the firm of Fuller and Heather, importers and dealers in paints, oils, and glass.

Lennie Steffens had hoped to remain in his state of nature by becoming a professional jockey. "Being a jockey became what a knight or a poet or a vaquero used to be." Soon he learned, however, about the fix. He quit the track. Anyone now involved in racing was a "sucker"— both those who bet and those who put in the fix. When he later went to the race track with his father and his friends, he didn't tell them that the fix was in (his father had bet on the favorite). He could not explain to the puzzled elder Steffens: "I could not tell . . . because they were suckers and . . . I did not care for suckers, only niggers, horses, and other gentleman, like the bridge-tender."[43]

Boyish energy (charming as it is) extended into adulthood undergoes transformations. And so with Lennie Steffens who became a lout. Steffens was nicknamed "D.S." ("damned stinker") by his classmates but he preferred to see himself as Napoleon. Part bully, part petty criminal, he tried to introduce a fagging system at his boarding school. When the younger boys naturally objected, he blackmailed some students whom he had learned had participated in homosexual activities. "We made fags of the young criminals. It was fun. It was sort of a reign of terror and we tyrants enjoyed our power so much that, like grownups, we rather abused it."[44]

When the basis for the system was discovered, the headmaster, fearing scandal, left Steffens unpunished. Steffens's remark, "My first essay in muck-raking cost me nothing," is peculiar. The comment is meant to be humorous, which it hardly is. Moreover, blackmailing young boys does not seem to fit courageous reporting. What Steffens meant, I think, was that he had stood up to authority. The headmaster knew he was "the head of the whole conspiracy" but Steffens was able to defy him.

When Lennie commandeered a brewery wagon and got half the school drunk, he met his own Waterloo. He was placed in a guard house for twenty-two days (the school record). When his sentence was served he was greeted as a hero on the campus. Temperance books given him during his punishment converted him, however. He saw his drinking as pretentious. When grown men handle it as a pose "the romance went out of it. . . . I was as ashamed of it as I was of being a sucker in the betting-ring."[45]

The "prison" experience had also converted Steffens into an intellectual. He gave up dreaming of Napoleon, but scholar or not, he was still mean, "as a horse is mean." He broke the windows of the president's house, strangled the treasurer's chickens. College also provided another lesson in cheating. Steffens and his classmates often gambled for spending money. Each month the lucky few winners went to the opera and theater while the rest moped around campus. When Steffens learned that some players had been cheating, he went to a professional

gambler who took him to gambling houses to teach him the tricks of
cheating. "Now you won't need never to be suckers again," the old
timer said. Steffens and his roommate practiced several tricks until they
were "cool and sure." After that, Steffens remembers fondly, "our luck
was phenomenal. We had money, more than we needed."

Despite all these episodes, the young Steffens was very much interested in understanding justice and fairness. After college he traveled
through Europe hoping to discover the foundation of ethics, only to
learn that the reasons given by scholars for not lying or stealing were
no better than "the stupidest English gentleman's: 'It isn't done.'" Yet
Steffens had indeed developed his own ethics. It seemed to be based
largely upon his conception of himself in his childhood pastoral. There
were free men (boys) who made promises and kept them and there
were the "suckers." But the suckers as victim and fixer engaged in
wrongful behavior because they had destroyed or threatened to destroy
a carefully constructed and fragile arena of play. This is why Steffens
found the people at the race track to be so reprehensible, both the bet-
tors and the fixers, why he invented fagging (he had read *Tom Brown*
and thought the system would be "fun"), why he did feel guilt at cards
only because he was playing (and cheating) for money and not "sport."
One could still cheat and steal, however, in an unsuckerlike fashion if
one upset the (corrupted) rules. This cheating and lying made an activity fun again and hence was acceptable, even laudable. Thus Lennie
Steffens could make suckers out of his father, school officials, and even
fellow students. All of them were already suckers or had tried to make
him into one.

Locke had insisted that promise keeping belonged to men as men,
and not as members of society. Steffens lived by this belief and came to
regard the agreements between two bosses (the vaqueros of his childhood pastoral) as the only true form of keeping faith. Business had corrupted the institution of promise keeping between men in the state of
nature by converting it into the "bargain, the bribe, the con, the contract." In this sense the old political machine boss always received
a peculiarly sympathetic treatment by Steffens. These "open" or "honest" crooks—"conscious crooks" was Steffens's most preferred term—
deeply challenged his own sense of his self. Convinced that these men
stood outside society making promises to men as men, Steffens found

he must show himself that he was not "good" or respectable, that he was neither liberal reformer nor businessman. Once he locked himself into a railroad car to meditate and "convince myself that I'm a crook." He concluded that although he did not take bribes he did trim his writings for his readers and editors.[46] Steffens could now in good conscience continue on horseback viewing American city after city steeped in corruption. Eventually he would embrace communism. But, as Louis Hartz notes, few American liberals drift toward socialism and Steffens really was no exception. His sympathy with communism as a peculiar and eccentric one. Steffens never joined the Party. When a Party official pressed him to run as a Communist candidate from California for the United States Senate in 1934, he replied:

> We liberals must not have power, not ever; we must not be leaders, we must not be allowed to be parties in the leadership. Too much to lose, besides our chains, which we are used to.
>
> The liberals, all privileged persons, and all the associates of the privileged, belong in the second line,—when their eyes are opened. And this goes for me. See? I am not doubting others; I am doubting me.[47]

Sometimes Steffens would not be so antiliberal a liberal. He was a "broken liberal" who believed "a *little* in majorities, in democracy, in liberty." Sometimes he seemed to call himself a liberal out of enervation. But, oh, how he loved dictators! They were able to give him tremendous boosts of enthusiasm. As an eye witness to the Russian revolution, he wholeheartedly approved of Bolshevik dictatorship. The soviets were a chaotic organization, a "herd of wild cattle, restless, troubled, sensing danger." Delegates would "mill and mill, round and round, looking for a direction in which to stampede." What they needed—and what they got—was a leader, a boy on horseback. Lenin had been, after all, a "liberal by instinct" but as the Russian leader explained to him, "We have to . . . get rid of the bourgeoisie. . . . I don't see, myself, why we can't scare them away without killing them."[48]

For Steffens, Henry Ford could be an American Lenin—"a prophet without words, a reformer without politics, a legislator, statesman, a radical." He had already "freed" himself by his repurchase of stock and could now take "risks and adventure." He could centralize industry and, as the Russians were doing, destroy Main Street and the middle class. Theodore Roosevelt had disappointed Steffens as he had Adams. Wilson never had a plan. Mussolini, however, receives an entire chapter of the *Autobiography* and he is described ecstatically. He was a "romantic figure," a "blazing thunderstorm" made by God "out of a rib of Italy." El Duce sneered and berated reporters as he did parliaments. Steffens loved it. He told him that "there is an empty throne in every country and that, given the emergency, the bold man can seize it—and hold it." Steffens loved this kind of posturing. Both Mussolini and Lenin were totalitarians, and Steffens loved them for it. Italy and Russia were in the midst of two great "experiments": they had "abandoned the democratic method and were using dictatorship supported by a small, instructed, disciplined, armed minority of rebellious but really romantic, obedient youth."[49]

Ironically, Steffens's continued identification with his pastoral state of perfect freedom led him to recommend a regimented society. He could support anyone on horseback as long as he promised to get rid of the "suckers."

"I'm a rootless man"

Like nearly all black autobiographers, Richard Wright's adult life shows an obsession with the dream of escape. Wright's pilgrimage to his own childhood was itself an attempt to escape. He recalled that writing *Black Boy* was "the hardest thing on earth, harder than fighting in a war, harder than taking part in a revolution . . . the clean, strong feeling that sweeps you when you've done it makes you know that."[50] The second part of Wright's autobiography, his account of his experience in the Communist party, reveals a truth that is well known to anyone who has lived or even studied the American black experience: the state of nature can never really be left behind in some troubled portion of the unconscious, because the black in America lives in a state of nature all his life. He may find a way to escape its immediate gothic dimension, but in a sense he is always outside society. Wright's accommodation with his childhood state of nature is reached through an appreciation derived from literature. He had overcome his "chronic distrust" by reading Mencken, Dreiser, Masters, Anderson, and Lewis. It was because of these writers that he "felt touching my face a tinge of warmth from an unseen light." The autobiography closes with an account of his flight from the South (a place of "despair and violence"): "With ever watchful eyes and bearing scars, visible and invisible, I headed North, full of a hazy notion that life could be lived with dignity, that the personality of others should not be violated, that men should be able to confront other men without fear or shame. . . ."[51] There is then, at the end of *Black Boy,* the hope for a liberal moral settlement, a hope that agreement to common rules of conduct might overcome the enmity of the state of nature. That hope was never fulfilled for Wright. "Defensive living" always seemed rational.

Richard Wright's depiction of his state of nature far exceeds a Lockean gothic. His childhood is one of almost unrelieved brutality, yet all the themes of Steffens's early life are replicated. Wright too became a drunkard, but he takes to drink at age six. He is not the temporarily dissolute adolescent who, like Steffens, "really hated the taste" of liquor and became a drunkard as he became "a knight, a trapper, and a preacher"—"not for long and exactly with my whole heart, but with a larger part of my imagination." Wright's childhood alcoholism was precocious but truly obsessive and degrading. For the amusement of men he would receive drinks in exchange for repeating obscenities to women.

Early in Steffens's autobiography there is a report of a spanking administered by his mother. Steffens was understandably resentful. *Black Boy* begins with an account of punishment as well. Wright was beaten unconscious and still remembers that "my mother had come close to killing me." In place of vaqueros and steamboat men and steamboats are neighborhoods that "swarmed with rats, cats, dogs, fortunetellers, cripples, blind men, whores, salesmen, rent collectors, and children." Steffens lived near a railroad repair shop and remembered it to be a "place of mystery and adventure." Wright has a different recollection:

In front of our flat was a huge roadhouse where locomotives were cleaned and repaired. There was an eternal hissing of steam, the deep grunting of steel engines, and the tolling of bells. Smoke obscured the vision and cinders drifted into the house, into our beds, into our kitchen, into our food; and a tarlike smell was always in the air.[52]

Thus in the episodic character of childhood memories, Wright recalls events with a sense of clarity and realism that both Steffens's and
Adams's memories of boyhood lack. Steffens's account is suffused with
an imaginative light. In fact, it is the imagination of Steffens, the boy,
that is so prized. The "real" aspects of his childhood, his confrontations
with parents and the San Francisco bourgeoisie are pushed aside as in-
trusions into his pastoral. Wright, on the other hand, constantly fights
to keep his realistic recollection in the forefront. Every episode of his
early life is stripped of mystification. His anger at his father and mother,
at school teachers and whites is described in detailed reportorial fashion. The boy Wright is never clever or bright, he rarely understands the
motives of others; his existence is defined totally in gothic terms—anger, fright, dread, terror. Yet the pastoral aspect of his state of nature
appears, nevertheless. It is not integrated into the gothic and is never
used to soften any particular incident. Sandwiched between his account of two punishments administered by his mother (one brutally
physical, the other psychological), Wright lists two pages of pastoral
musings from the recollection of his childhood. Each deals with an individual interaction with nature. Here are a few examples:

> Each event spoke with a cryptic tongue. And moments of liv-
> ing slowly revealed their coded meanings. There was the wonder I
> felt when I first saw a brace of mountainlike, spotted, black-and-
> white horses clopping down a dusty road through clouds of pow-
> dered clay.
> There was the languor I felt when I heard green leaves rustling
> with a rainlike sound.
> There was the love I had for the mute regality of tall, moss-
> clad oaks.
> And there was the quiet terror that suffused my senses when
> vast hazes of gold washed earthward from star-heavy skies in si-
> lent nights. . . .[53]

Wright's childhood state of nature offers a dual lesson. There is the
lesson of distrust and anger and fear, which led to an ethic of survival.
"Defensive living," Wright called it, and his experience produced an
individuality "which life had seared into my blood and bones." There
were even conventional Lockean overtones to Wright's individualism.

He too believed that "he had to work and redeem himself through his own acts."[54] Wright's pastoral is so much in the imagination, so overwhelmed by his gothic, that it assumes the character of simple longing only barely remembered and sporadically experienced. In a way, Wright's own sense of self is dependent upon a nurturing of this despair, both as an exercise in survival (he must remember or he would perish) and as an advancement in a Lockean sense.

Thus Wright's novels are nearly always concerned with defensive living and with the importance of remembrance for survival. They are stories of men cut off from society, alternately ignored and maltreated, occasionally befriended. These men invariably misunderstand acts of kindness and acts of violence result. Often personal destruction comes from simple bad luck. Wright's masterpiece, *Native Son,* creates a moral monster in the character of Bigger Thomas. Thomas is a killer simply because he is "scared and mad." He barely can convey his motivations and not even Wright's Marxist lawyer can defend his acts. In *Savage Holiday,* a white man experiences accidental violence. He too goes on a murderous rampage. In "Big Boy Leaves Home," an early short story, a charming pastoral is drawn. A group of boys sing songs, tell jokes, go swimming. A white woman appears. The boys are frightened and frighten her. Her boyfriend arrives with a rifle. Big Boy wrestles the weapon away, but it discharges and kills the white man. The boys flee but Big Boy's friend is caught by a lynch mob and tortured, mutilated, and burned. Big Boy flees North. In "The Man Who Lived Underground," a black who is forced to confess to a crime that he did not commit flees and sets up his own solitary life in a sewer. At night he makes brief trips to stores, entering through the basements. The sewer is a horrific world; there are rats and dead babies. The underground man steals a typewriter and starts to write his name without capitals and spacing, "freddaniels." He soon forgets his own identity, however, and when he later tries to leave the world of the sewer to tell police of his innocence, he is unable to communicate: " 'It was a long time ago,' he spoke like a child relating a dimly remembered dream."[55] The police shoot him.

Defensive living, Wright's fiction tells us, is ultimately pathological. The black American lives as best he can, but the ethic of survival requires a self-restraint that is inhuman. He constantly seeks escape, by traveling North, going underground, and most ominously of all, by violence. In fact, the world of Wright's imagination is peopled by men so angry, so alienated, so unlucky, so marked by society for oblivion that it is difficult for the reader to imagine any *other* world for these men.

But Wright himself was not a violent man, save in his thoughts. How had he lived after leaving the South? *American Hunger,* the second part of Wright's autobiography, describes his life in Chicago from 1927 to the outbreak of World War II. In many ways, the account is a suppressed success story. Wright undertakes a variety of menial jobs. As he works as a porter, dishwasher, clerk, janitor, he prepares for a civilservice examination and eventually becomes a mail clerk. The Depression arrives and he suffers setbacks. He sells burial insurance but then acquires a series of positions, each reflecting slightly higher status, with the Federal Writers Project. At the account's end, Wright is a published writer, halfway through completing his first novel.

But Wright's Lockean success is overshadowed by a sense of failure. Wright, arriving in Chicago and finding a strange "mechanical city" with "no curves, no trees, only angles, lines, spaces, bricks and copper wires," asserts that he had not been able to have "a single, satisfying, sustained relationship with another human being." The narrative ends after Wright has been forcefully removed from participating in a May Day parade by his former comrades. The "renegade" and "class traitor" watches the banners flutter by in the May breeze. Sitting alone on a curb, he asks, "Well, what had I got out of living in the city? What had I got out of living in the South? What had I got out of living in America?" His country had shown him "no examples of how to live a human life." "All my life I had been full of a hunger for a new way to live. . . ."[56]

Thus Wright concludes that success is finding a way to live with others. Without a sense of belonging he is a failure. He had fled the southern terror of his childhood. *American Hunger* recounts a terror without Jim Crow. Everywhere he looks he finds fear. Everywhere there are "striken, frightened black faces trying to cope with a civilization that they did not understand." Wright, as had other immigrants, hoped to take a part of the South and transplant it in "alien soil to see if it could grow differently . . . perhaps to bloom. . . ." Instead, he had "fled one insecurity and had embraced another."[57]

The great disappointment of the autobiography is the Communist party. The Party had indeed helped Wright with his writing career, perhaps much more than the autobiographer is willing to admit. It found outlets for his stories and poems, introduced him to other writers and editors, and with the John Reed Club provided a forum for his work. But according to Wright, the Party could never provide "the vaulting dream of achieving a vast unity" that it had promised. Black Communists were all really outsiders, "illiterate peasants" used by the Party. Some were able to hide their origins by copying speech patterns of Polish Communist immigrants, some found comfortable minor bureaucratic positions, others would be "bought off" with trips to Europe and the Soviet Union. But most of all, black Communist party members were scared—scared of reading the wrong book, taking the wrong position, talking to the wrong person.

Wright was ready to accept this fear to the extent that it was the precondition for the community. He was genuinely impressed with the Party's "trial" of a black member for deviation. Confession is what the Party wanted and that is what it got. The defendant's voice broke in a sob. "No one prodded him. No one tortured him. No one threatened him. He was free to go out of the hall and never see another Communist. But he did not want to. He could not. The vision of a communal world had sunk down into his soul and it would never leave him until life left him. He talked on, outlining how he had erred, how he would reform." Here was a man who was one "with the members there, regardless of race or color; his heart was theirs and their hearts were his. . . ."[58]

But Wright's experience in Mississippi had taught him about the terror that can rest behind community. He left the meeting before it was over. The trance was broken by the realization that "if they held state power I would have been declared guilty of treason and my execution would have followed." Although Wright does not say so, the Party had been an ally in his own quest for Lockean individualism as well as a focus for his longing for pastoral community. But his own ethic of survival, his own sense of the terror (no doubt rationally awakened by what the Party represented as well) forced him to reject such a "commitment of faith." Wright's original title for the second part of his autobiography had been "The Horror and the Glory," an apt description not only of what the Party had represented for him, but of Wright's own conception of himself as well.

After his disappointment with the Communist party, Wright retreated again to a state of nature, this time to embrace it. His quest eventually ended in a permanent escape, one more permanent, more desolate, than that of the most anguished émigré:

> I'm a rootless man, but I'm neither psychologically distraught nor in any wise particularly perturbed because of it. Personally, I do not hanker after, and seem not to need, as many emotional attachments, sustaining roots, or idealistic allegiances as most people. I declare unabashedly that I like and even cherish the state of abandonment, of aloneness; it does not bother me; indeed, to me it seems the natural, inevitable condition of man, and I welcome it. I can make myself at home almost anywhere on this earth, if I've a mind to when I'm attracted to a landscape or a mood of life, easily sink myself into the most alien and wildly differing environments. I must confess that this is no personal achievement of mine; this attitude was never striven. . . . I've been shaped to this mental stance by the kind of experience that I've fallen heir to.[59]

His travels to Africa and commitments to national liberation were ultimately made from the vantage point of an outsider. New countries required a "military organization" of society in order to sweep out the tribal cobwebs of the people and rid them of "parasitic chiefs."[60] His novels continued to explore acts of individual violence. Only with his trip to Spain were his early powers rediscovered. In *Pagan Spain* he described a society that reminded him of Mississippi. At a religious festival the penitents in white robes gave him the "creepy feeling" of watching a Klan rally. The march to the statue of the Virgin produced emotions far different from Adams's. Were these white-clad marchers protecting the "purity of white womanhood"? Everywhere he found terror and backwardness. Here was a society of "white niggers."[61] Wright was at home again describing a topography of oppression.

Ironically, Wright's confession of "rootlessness" neatly fits the model of the contemporary state-of-nature theorists. Of course, for Rawls, Dworkin, and Ackerman, Wright's condition is presented as an analytic given, even implicitly as part of the achievement of liberalism, without the awareness that the kind of experience he "fell heir to" is obtained from knowledge of personal alienation, autobiographically derived.

"There was something wrong with the ends as well as the beginnings"

We have examined only one aspect of American autobiography as a form of political theory in this chapter. But if the examples of Adams, Steffens, and Wright are representative, they illustrate the promise of the study of autobiography as a way of understanding America as a liberal society. These autobiographies replicate a basic structure in liberal political theory. Each writer's exploration of his childhood as a state of nature shows us how Americans come to think of themselves as individuals described by Locke and his present-day followers. Each writer explains how he found it necessary to shear away features of his personality. For Adams it involved the rejection of his place in the natural lottery. For Steffens it involved the rejection of bourgeois respectability. For Wright it involved rejecting first "his place" in the South and then in America altogether. Each writer had taken part in the liberal moral settlement and had been more or less liberated from his own origins. Each had experienced the Lockean "inconveniences" of the state of nature. Each, often reluctantly, had become a party to the social contract.

What these autobiographies do reveal, however, are the ways in which the liberal consensus is not fully replicated. Locke's state of perfect freedom or Rawls's veil of ignorance, or Dworkin's auctioneers assume aggressively self-reliant individuals. The examples of Adams, Steffens, and Wright show that individual autonomy is agonizingly incomplete, in part because everyone must traverse a state of nature that forces a denial of a more richly conceived individualism. The selves described by Adams, Steffens, and Wright may look like stable individuals from the vantage points of the Lockean state or Rawls's well-ordered society, but the autobiographical self suggests a tortured and often tragic individualism.

Adams stands generationally alienated from the eighteenth-century liberal world. The "education" provided by his forefathers is exposed under inspection like the worn furniture at Mount Vernon in daylight. The patrimony he finally uncovers, which is America's as well, is one of both unexamined moral smugness and venality. But the twentieth-century liberal alternative is also uncompelling. Who would, if one could, contract to live in a world ruled by railroads, telegraphs, coal, and steel? Steffens is a reformer who finds he has more sympathy for the agents of corruption than for the victimized citizenry he initially defends. Somehow corruption is dependent upon liberal elites and liberal morality. He challenges not only the liberal settlement but liberalism itself: "There was something wrong with the ends as well as the beginnings." And, of course, Wright lives the paradox of the marginal man in a liberal society. His life story is one of victimization and success hopelessly intertwined, for the greater his personal achievements the more his conception of himself is dependent upon his remembrance of personal injustice.

When these American autobiographers are able to reconstruct a self with some degree of confidence, they reach for pastoral memories of a preliberal self, one that was not guaranteed but destroyed by the liberal settlement. Adams's "drunken" summers in Quincy, Steffens's boyhood role-playing, Wright's sense of awe and wonder, all of these, even when remembered with the "inconveniences" of which Locke darkly spoke, suggest an individual happiness unexplored in liberal theory. Of course, it is possible to contend that the autobiographical pastoral is politically irrelevant, even as a critique of the liberal consensus in America, because its focus is so individualistic (all of these pastorals are largely solitary environments), the feelings evoked are little more than a simple yearning for the pleasure principle, the political implications for each autobiographer are problematic and frequently unpleasant.

But even if one accepts these rejoinders, it can be noted that the nature of the autobiography as a form is in an important sense a corrective to liberal theory, because the autobiography is foremost an act of remembrance. Despite all the deceptions (unconscious and conscious) of the autobiographer, remembrance holds out the possibility of developing real measures of the costs and advantages of life in liberal society. It serves as an act of witness to the complexity and variety of actual individuals. Adams, Steffens, and Wright never could retrieve their pastorals except in reminiscences of childhood, but their acts of remembrance suggest that alternatives could be conceived and recorded for other generations. The autobiographical state of nature, with all its unfulfilled longings, does, after all, take place within a liberal society.

CHAPTER SIX

REFORMING

CHARLOTTE PERKINS GILMAN AND
JANE ADDAMS

The autobiography would seem to be the ideal structure for feminist political theory. The historical subjection of women has taken the form of what John Stuart Mill called "bonds of affection."[1] When a woman looks to identify the sources of her oppression she looks not only at the factory and its boss but also at the family and its bosses, the father and husband. For the feminist, the personal is political in a way that is fundamentally different from the experience of other writers.

This perspective can permit an understanding of the origin of politics and liberal society that the male writer can never appreciate in an autobiographical sense. For the feminist, childhood is not an escape from the demands of liberal society but rather a source of her subjection. A woman's remembrance of childhood as a state of nature is gothic but it is not its anarchic violence that she remembers. Rather it is an ordered subjection. There are, of course, many variations in this theme of childhood as a memory of bondage, as a world of "free" boys and "captured" women and girls. The autobiography can reveal the range of human experience in a way that conventional political theory cannot. There are permissive as well as overbearing fathers, homes without fathers, homes run on matriarchal principles, homes with brother and sister treated alike. But the weight of both female experience and tradition teaches the autobiographer to come to the conclusion that childhood remembered as "idylls of innocence and redemption" is a male "idealization."[2]

But what are the consequences of this view of childhood as a state of bondage, of the effort to demythologize the origins of one's self? One result, I think, is that the autobiography, despite its penetrating analysis of social institutions, suffers from a fundamental confusion of the personal and the political, of the public and the private. In part this confusion is the consequence of patriarchy in the context of a liberal society. The autobiography simply reflects in refracted ways the burdens of social structure. The burdens here can be heavy indeed. If the self of a woman is in part the result of these institutions of bondage, then she must fashion a new identity. But a liberal society takes autonomy as, if not a given, at least the responsibility of each self. Once patricide has been committed in a psychological sense, where does a woman find her new identity? Certainly not in relation to a husband and children; that choice would involve the kind of generational reconstruction of patriarchy that the feminist wishes to break. In general, the answer to this problem lies in the feminist conception of reform. In fact, the autobiography as a positive act involves the attempt to find a new self through political action. New communities must be built, so says the feminist autobiographer, and her life is offered as an exemplar of reform. But if the recognition of sisterhood is a revolutionary act requiring devotion and commitment, what precisely is the nature of the feminist's obligation? If the construction of a new identity is the duty one sister has toward another, then is personal self-improvement an act of service and community building? Is self-aggrandizement selflessness? Is egoism an act of altruism? Is reform of the self political reform? Not all feminists have conflated the personal with the political in such a way, but the problem always remains ready to be answered in this fashion. There are ways out; there are ways in which it is possible to convert personal troubles into new and genuinely collaborative visions, and the autobiography is indeed the structure that can permit that kind of self-consciousness. That road is suggested by Jane Addams. The other and more traveled route is taken by Charlotte Perkins Gilman and many others. The source of the confusion of the personal with the political may rest with the injustice of patriarchy itself but it also lies with the confusion that bonds of affection are really bondages.

"My mother was a baby-worshiper"

Are fathers the concealed enemies of daughters? Does family structure determine consciousness? The memories of Charlotte Perkins Gilman and Jane Addams reveal how complex an affirmative response to this question can be. Gilman's father abandoned his family; Addams's mother died when she was two years old. For Gilman "the word Father, in a sense of love, care, one to go to in trouble, means nothing to me." Her father was only "an occasional visitor, writer of infrequent but always funny drawings, a sender of books, catalogues of books, lists of books to read, and also a purchaser of books with the money sadly needed by his family."[3] Addams, on the other hand, cannot recall many experiences apart from her father. Her memories form a "single cord" of "supreme affection" and a "clue" to which she clung in the "intricacy of the mazes" of "the moral concerns of life." Much of her childhood involves memories of attempts, "so emotional, so irrational, so tangled with the affairs of the imagination," to express her "doglike affection" for her father.[4]

A fatherless childhood, for Gilman, did not create a childhood independent of the consequences of paternal power. The Perkins' matriarchal family moved nineteen times in eighteen years, fourteen of them from one city to another. Gilman's memories of childhood are "thick with railroad journeys, mostly on the Hartford, Providence and Springfield; with occasional steamboats; with the smell of 'hacks' and the funny noise the wheels made when little fingers were stuck in little ears and withdrawn again, alternately." She resented bitterly the sets of clothes she had to wear on these trips so that the number of suitcases could be kept to a minimum. Her mother refused to give up waiting for the return of her husband. She longed to see him before she died: "As long as she was able to sit up, she sat always at the same window watching for the beloved face. He never came."[5]

The father who deserts his family exacts economic punishment through his absence. But for Gilman this exercise of paternal power affected all familial relationships. Mary Perkins avoided showing any sign of affection toward Charlotte so that her daughter would not later suffer from the same kind of bond that she had. When nursing, her mother would push aside the infant's hands. Charlotte was never hugged or kissed. Later she discovered that her mother would wait until she was asleep and then quietly caress her. The young daughter would use pins to keep herself awake, carefully pretending to be asleep until her mother would arrive, "and how rapturously I enjoyed being gathered into her arms, held close and kissed."[6]

Charlotte was a victim of her father, and she was further victimized by the withdrawal of maternal affection, itself the result of her mother's victimization. What was the source of Charlotte's mother's suffering? Her life was "one of the most thwarted" Gilman had ever known. The young Mary Westcott was the "darling of an elderly father and a juvenile mother." She was "petted, cossetted, and indulged." She was "delicate and beautiful, well educated, musical . . . femininely attractive in the highest degree." There were always lovers, "various and successive." One man proposed to her at first sight. But Mary Westcott was a "childlike" woman. Even at seventeen she would excuse herself from gentleman callers to go upstairs to put her dolls to bed. Finally, after many engagements broken, renewed, and rebroken, Mary married at the age of twenty-nine. From this point, her life was lived in tragic contradiction: "After her idolized youth, she was left neglected. After her flood of lovers, she became a deserted wife." The "most passionately domestic of home-worshiping housewifes," she was forced to live with a succession of relatives. After a "long and thorough musical education," she was forced to sell her piano when Charlotte was two. Mary was a "baby-worshiper"; two of her four children died in infancy.[7]

Through all these ordeals, Charlotte's mother remained absolutely loyal and as "loving as a spaniel." She was devoted to her children and "in her starved life her two little children were literally all; all of her duty, hope, ambition, love and joy." But there was to be no consolation even here. Mary could only really care for babies. As her children grew older, "she increasingly lost touch with them, wider and wider grew the gulf between. . . ."[8]

Biblical injunction ("the sins of the fathers . . .") and psychiatric theory both confirm what all of us, including Charlotte Perkins Gilman, know autobiographically: families replicate themselves. But the young Gilman was determined not to become another victim. She must reconstruct a personality that avoided her mother's errors, a personality that would be beyond the reach of paternal power.

Charlotte Perkins Gilman's critique of her mother becomes the basis for her self-measurement and the basis of feminist reform. Mary Perkins was dependent first upon her husband, then upon the good will of relatives. She was a devoted mother but "love, devotion, sublime self-sacrifice" were not enough even in a "child-culture." Mary Perkins lacked knowledge. The descendant of Lyman Beecher and subsequent generations of "world-servers" could only serve and then would lose touch with them because of her limited knowledge of the world. She would embrace Swedenborgianism. But Charlotte regarded these meetings of coreligionists as proof of her mother's intellectual inadequacy. The Swedenborgians would sit around a table "floating and wallowing about in endless discussion of proofless themes and theories of their own . . . interminably talking on matters of religion and ethics."[9]

Charlotte Perkins Gilman's formal education is limited largely as a result of her mother's position. She attended seven different schools and estimated that she had received only about four years of education. But she ferociously initiated her own system for self-education, which has all the earmarks of Franklin's plan. First there is the attempt, undertaken with great enthusiasm, to develop a philosophy of everything, which became the central characteristic of her later writings. The young Charlotte wrote her father for a list of books, "saying that I wished to help humanity . . . and where shall I begin." She read widely in history and anthropology and joined the Society for the Encouragement of Studies at Home. Armed with "the story of life on earth," Charlotte set out to "build her own religion." The result, achieved after consideration of God, evil, death, and pain was stated in a single maxim: "The first duty of a human being is to assume right functional relations to society '—more briefly, to find your real job, and do it.'" God had a plan for the human race that was revealed in some evolutionary "telic force," and Gilman's task was to discover her role in this process. For that she needed her own plan: "And I set to work, with my reliable system of development, to 'do the will' as far as I could see it."[10]

Charlotte Perkins Gilman described herself as a "philosophic steam engine." She believed that she had invented her own praxis. "My method was to approach a difficulty as if it was a problem of physics, trying to invent the best solution." In order to develop the energy necessary to carry out her plan, she invented her own system of "physical culture." She adopted her own style of dress (short, light garments), which included inventing a new kind of bra. She walked five miles a day and started an exercise class for women. She redecorated her stuffy room by taking a window out of its casing and installing a leaf from a dining-room table to keep out snow. On some mornings, Gilman proudly recalls, her wash bowl had ice so thick that she could not even break it with her heel. As a result, her health was "splendid": "I never tired. . . . When asked, 'How do you do it?' it was my custom to reply, 'as well as a fish, as busy as a bee, as strong as a horse, as proud as a peacock, as happy as a clam.'"[11]

But the plan included more than a regimen for physical fitness. She worked on methods of "the turning of consciousness from self to others." She began with "minor self-denials." "I would gaze at some caller of mother's and consider what, if anything, I could do for that person; get a footstool, a glass of water, change a window-shade, any definitely conceived benefit." These efforts, however, were "too slow, too restricted." Charlotte "devised a larger scheme." She discovered a crippled and blind young girl and arranged to meet her. The girl laughed bitterly when young Charlotte asked, "Will you do me a service?" But Charlotte explained: "You see, I don't think about other people, and I'm trying to learn. Now I don't care anything about you, yet, but I'd like to. Will you let me come and practice on you?" The practicing included reading to the "unhappy creature," bringing her flowers, buying a small present. When Charlotte learned second-hand that the girl had said that Charlotte Perkins was "so thoughtful of other people," she recalls exclaiming, "Hurrah!, another game won!"[12] With the victory over selfishness assured did Charlotte continue her visits to the young girl? Here the autobiographer is silent. We do not know if she moved on to other projects to acquire new virtues.

Like Franklin before her, Charlotte Perkins Gilman had created a new personality as an act of will. And like Franklin's, this new person entailed political implications. All of the newly acquired freedoms of both individuals were replicable. Franklin had avoided the narrow horizons of a tradesman as well as the dissipated life of a journeyman. Charlotte Perkins Gilman, at least up to this point, had not become like her mother. She was independent, educated, and primed to dedicate her life to service beyond the confines of the family. But when it had become time to marry, she could not simply find a "helpmate."

After many delays, she married Charles Walter Stetson in 1884. A year later Katherine was born. She was "angelic," "the best," "a heavenly baby." Charlotte Stetson had a "charming home; a loving and devoted husband; an exquisite baby, healthy, intelligent and good; a highly competent mother to run things; a wholly satisfactory servant— and I lay on the lounge all day and cried." "That baby-worshipping grandmother" had to come to take care of the baby because Charlotte has become a "mental wreck." No plan, no amount of will, could bring Charlotte Stetson out of her "growing melancholia." She, "the ceaselessly industrious, could not mop a floor, paint, sew, read, even hold a knife without suffering from sheer exhaustion." But worse than the inexplicable weariness was a sense of shame: "You did it yourself! You had health and strength and hope and glorious work before you—and you threw it away! You were called to serve humanity and you cannot serve yourself."[13]

On a doctor's advice, Charlotte Stetson went West to Utah to visit her brother and from there to California to visit friends. As soon as the train moved she felt better. A month later she went home and the symptoms returned almost immediately. In 1887 she and her husband were divorced and Charlotte Gilman went to California. "After I was finally free . . . there was a surprising output of work, some of my best."[14] Later she returned the young Katherine to her father.[15]

In San Francisco, Charlotte Gilman begins the second reconstruction of her personality. She starts another plan with the realization that at thirty-five she is "a failure, a repeated, cumulative failure." She had published a collection of poems, worked on a small newspaper which had folded in twenty weeks. But the basis of Gilman's livelihood and of her new personality as well was the public lecture. She would speak before women's groups, church gatherings, and Nationalist Clubs. *The Living of Charlotte Perkins Gilman* is filled with accounts of the reactions to her lectures, including records of the donations that followed the talk: "lectured in Brooklyn . . . $20.25"; "spoke" in Kansas City on "'The New Motherhood.' Successful. Stayed to dinner. Stupid evening—the men afraid of me. $10.00"; "I spoke in a little church in Madison, Kansas, and on Thursday, . . . went to Eureka. . . . Friday I spoke twice, $17.00; again visiting the Addisons, and preaching the next day in the Congregational church—$4.00"; "in Bedford, Iowa, with a friend's friend, and an address—$5.45, and so back to Chicago."[16]

This constant movement provided the structure for her new self. Gilman described herself as "propertyless and desireless as a Buddhist priest." She replicated the endless travels of her childhood, not as a mother dependent upon the charity of relatives but as a free independent woman who was dedicated to the emancipation of mothers. She had freed herself of "the home." In a visitors' book in Los Angeles she proudly signed, "Charlotte Perkins Stetson. At Large." The airy, belligerent confidence achieved by the first plan had returned: "'Don't you feel very much at sea?' someone asked. 'I do. Like a sea gull at sea.' And when inquiring friends would ask, 'Where do you live now?' my reply was, 'Here.'" Charlotte Gilman was again "as happy as a clam."

But there were, on Gilman's own admission, two selves, her "outside life" in which there was "a woman undergoing many hardships and losses" and an "inside" self that was a "social inventor, trying to advance human happiness by the introduction of better psychic machinery."[17]

Gilman is not the first reformer whose activity was impelled by psychic needs. What is instructive here in terms of American political thought is that her conception of her "real" self, the self that holds together her personality, is understood by her to be her social self. The "outside" self, the self that is existential and finite, the self that suffers and has longings, is epiphenomenal. Seen in light of Gilman's political theory, feminism promises to "free" women by abolishing those institutions that are responsible for the maintenance of this outer self.

One of the most puzzling aspects of feminism is its formation as sets of small local groups and its political agenda that promotes bureaucratic organization. Gilman's autobiography reveals how this happens and as such provides us with a complete feminist political theory. Let me recapitulate the theory as autobiographically presented thus far. Gilman's growing up is influenced by the consequences of patriarchy. With great effort she is able to conceive, and to a limited extent live, a life independent of male control. Marriage and motherhood, however, threaten this effort, an effort made at considerable psychic cost. After all, Gilman had had to deny first her father and then her mother, and this brings about a breakdown. She recovers, however, by denying her husband and her daughter and traveling to California, that land of "swift enthusiasms." Her new personality, now twice reconstructed, is formed through an identification of the only nonpatriarchal communities she can find, voluntary associations composed in part by like-minded women. Service to these groups is her "real" self, the other self becomes a recurring ghost of doubts about her independence. Thus Gilman can never really identify with the suffrage movement or socialism. "My main interest was in the position of women . . . . economic independence" was "far more important than the ballot."[18]

But how does one translate the transient nature of the voluntary association to a firmer basis? Must Gilman travel forever, like Thoreau had considered, to maintain her real self? One alternative, offered by Addams, would be to give the voluntary association some structural permanence by linking it to traditional institutions and presumably transforming both in the process. But Gilman could not take that path. She turned down an offer to direct a settlement. When she finally did give up her "at-large" identity, by renting a flat late in life, she notes the "insidious drugging effect" of a home. She still attempted to avoid the insidious effects of "spending one's time waiting on one's own tastes and appetites, and those of dear ones" by recurrent lecture trips. Her sense of a "real" self depended upon continual contact with these groups as if her personality was strewn across the country in clubs and associations, which in a sense it was. There was also the possibility that the groups who paid her to present visions of new structures might become like her mother's Swedenborgian groups, "floating and wallowing about in endless discussion. . . ."

Thus Gilman's life work—her service, her fame, and her livelihood—is devoted to the presentation of structures that will abolish the home and the "outer" self and replace it with surer nonpatriarchal institutions than voluntary associations. Gilman's feminism, and that of others who followed her, seeks to destroy the very kind of relationships that have really made women's emancipation possible. Sisterhood is, above all, a set of personal relations, relations built upon a personal community of common experience and common goals. Can this vision be realized in sets of bureaucratic institutions? Gilman says they must.

This paradox in feminist thought can be illustrated by briefly comparing Gilman's autobiographical short story, "The Yellow Wallpaper" to her The Home. "The Yellow Wallpaper," written during her first years in California, is a moving fictional account of her own breakdown. It tells the story of a young middle-class wife and mother who suffers so from the bonds of affection that her personality disintegrates before the eyes of the reader. The story concludes with a doctor's prescription that the woman cease all intellectual efforts and focus what little energy she has on her family. Of course this regimen only serves to sink the young woman to deeper levels of depression; the swirls she sees on the wallpaper of her bedroom begin to float and undulate uncontrollably, as does her conception of her self. The story suggests the woman's need to experience a community of equals beyond her family. But then look at Gilman's solution to the yearning for sisterhood. In The Home she insists that she offers no "iconoclastic frenzy of destruction" but only a "pruning" of a "most precious tree," but she portrays the home in what is actually a much more negative light. She looks at it as an institution that has thus far resisted "social evolution." The sentimental attachment to the home is traced to two ancient twin gothics, a sexual contract (bodily submission in exchange for protection) and religion. Today our conception of religion is monotheist, we no longer need household gods. Harems have been abolished in civilized societies, but for the man the home is still his "private harem—be it ever so monogamous—the secret place where he keeps his most private possession."[19]

Division of labor characterizes modern work but women still labor like their ancestors. They cook, clean, nurse, educate. Women must rise to the "higher plane" of evolution for which they are fit. Water and sewage used to be taken care of on an individual household basis but now there is "an insidious new system of common supply of domestic necessities." If water and sewage have come to be "fully socialized," why not food, housekeeping, nursing, and education? The endless repetition of kitchens could be replaced by cooked-food supply companies. In anticipation of modern children's rights theorists, Gilman asserts that children must be recognized as a "class" with "rights guaranteed by the state." Every baby is better off with a "good trained nurse." The housewife ought to enter the world of productive work, pay her substitute and contribute to the "world's wealth."[20]

Of course, in a sense, The Home perceived changes in the structure of families and family life that were in process and Gilman simply carried them to what she saw as a logical conclusion. The language that chronicles the development of the new home of the future is that of the progressive's interpretation of evolution. The present structure of families is "irrational" in the sense that performance of its functions is wasteful and erratic. Both good wholesome food and babies are produced by families almost by happenstance. Gilman's assertion that bakers' bread is always better than homemade captures the spirit of the entire essay. But what is most important is that the new home constructed by Gilman is modeled on her conception of her "real" self. Life is service but service abstractly conceived. And who can fail to detect the element of retribution and scorn for women behind the measured arguments of progressive reform? In fact, the home conceived by Gilman has all the characteristics of Marx's description of crude communism.

Marx had warned that in the first stage of revolution the workers seek to "destroy everything which is not capable of being possessed by all as private property." "The category of laborer is not done away with but extended to all men."[21] The community becomes the universal capitalist; private property becomes "universal private property." Transpose women for proletariat, service for universal private property, and one sees Gilman's recommendations as a feminist version of crude communism. A woman must become a "free cook, a trained cook, a scientific cook."[22] "For profit and for love—to do her duty and to gain her ends—in all ways, the home cook is forced to do her cooking to please John. It is no wonder John clings so ardently to the custom." Notice the depiction of the future: "Never again on earth will he have a whole live private cook to himself, to consider, before anything else, his special tastes and preferences. He will get better food, and he will like it." What brings Gilman to advocate this "thoughtless" communism is certainly in part what she calls the "sexuo-economic" structure of the family. But instead of attacking a gender-based system in which acts of personal sacrifice, love, and service are a perversion of the ideal of personal relationships, to be replaced perhaps by mutual acts, she seeks to destroy personal relations themselves. Who can adequately serve, she asks, under "direct pressure of personal affection?" "It is very, very hard to resist the daily . . . demands of those we love."[23] That "outer self" is finally destroyed by Gilman in her home of the future, and only the real self remains. The personal is indeed political for Gilman and she transcends the latter by destroying the former.

"Sweet dessert in the morning"

If Charlotte Perkins Gilman's conception of self and political theory was the result of efforts to overcome patriarchal power asserted through the denial of bonds of affection, Jane Addams's struggle is centered around the consequences of the benevolent father. Addams's devotion is complete, so complete that she seeks to be her father. She was obsessed by the disparity in their physical appearances. She remembers herself as an awkward, homely child who so dreaded the thought that "strangers" would see the incongruity between her and the dignified man in the great frock coat that she would walk to church with her uncle. She longed to attain some physical likeness, even if it meant acquiring burns on her hands similar to those that her father had suffered during his early work as a miller.

Father Addams (he is never named in the autobiography) was also the major employer in Cedarville (he owned two mills) and the Addams house was the largest in the town. In antebellum Cedarville paternal authority was complete. The young Jane associated the mill with her father's activities and "centered upon him all that careful imitation which a little girl ordinarily gives to her mother's ways and habits." [24] Of course, Jane Addams would learn that she could never completely imitate her father. We can even leave the Freudian implications of this observation aside. Jane Addams could not become the "self-made man" that her father was; she could not be a member of the legislature; she could not be a soldier in the "Addams Guard." But her sense of estrangement was even greater. She was born too late to be a member of even the last postwar generation of middle-class, small-town Protestant elites. America was turning away from men of "entrepreneural appetites and republican zeal," men who admired Lincoln and Mazzini and in coalition with the Protestant clergy would work for a genteel reform. [25] New elites, robber barons and city bosses, would serve the people and be models of "careful imitation."

Jane Addams was thus doubly estranged, first as a result of her gender and second as a result of her class. Paternal authority was, of course, generally responsible for her predicament. She was a daughter and she was a daughter of the outdated middle class. Later in life, Addams was to understand an aspect of her dilemma. The liberated women of her day were liberated from the home, but then they were also liberated from the positive elements of their class and gender. They had "departed too quickly from the active emotional life led by their grandmothers and great-grandmothers. . . . somewhere in the process of 'being educated' they had lost that simple and automatic response to the human appeal, that old healthful reaction resulting in activity from the mere presence of suffering or of helplessness." They could not imitate their mothers. Nor could they imitate their fathers. A vague desire for service in the world has no outlet. "The girl loses something vital out of her life to which she is entitled. She is restricted and unhappy;

her elders, meanwhile, are unconscious of her situation and we have all the elements of a tragedy."[26]

These truths, this awareness of estrangement, are autobiographically learned. Addams had entered college but it took her eight years after her graduation "to formulate my convictions in at least a satisfactory manner. . . ." During that time she had been "absolutely at sea so far as my moral purpose was concerned."[27] She had suffered through two major crises during this period. In 1881 her father died. Addams experienced the kind of estrangement that no political theory can ever remedy.

She does not directly discuss the loss but she gives an account of the grief she had felt at the death of the family nurse many years before: "As I was driven home in the winter storm, the wind through the trees seemed laden with a passing soul and the riddle of life and death pressed hard; once to be young, to grow old and to die, everything came to that, and then a mysterious journey out to the Unknown. Did she mind faring forth alone?" The father was dead but the daughter was alive and in imitation of him. Addams herself tried to fare forth alone in life. She enrolled at the Women's Medical College in Philadelphia but developed a severe spinal condition that left her "literally bound" to bed for six months. An operation helped but the procedure made it impossible to have children. Jane Addams had a nervous breakdown, "traces" of which haunted her long after her work had begun at Hull House. She attempted to find solace in religion. Theological speculation only worsened her depression. Baptism into the Presbyterian church helped somewhat. She "longed for an outward symbol of fellowship." She visited some farms in the West where she had invested some of her inheritance in mortgages. The expectation had been pastoral but instead she witnessed "starved hogs," "despair" and children "not to be compared to anything so joyous as satyrs, although they appeared but half-human."[28] She immediately sold her shares. In the summers Addams lectured to women's groups and took courses in European art history. She wintered in Europe although the trips always failed to raise her spirit.

In 1887 she finally did undergo a conversion. She witnessed a bull-fight. The entertainment does not horrify her and, on the contrary, "the sense that this was the last survival of all glories of the amphitheater, the illusion that the riders on the caparsoned horses might have been knights of a tournament, or the matador a slightly armed gladiator facing his martyrdom, and all the rest of the obscure yet vivid associations of historic survival, had carried me beyond the endurance of any of the party." Later that evening she came to see the reality of this "disgusting experience and the entire moral situation which it revealed." The next day she made up her mind to carry out her plan for a settlement for the poor, "whatever happened." No longer would she be tied to the "oxcart of self-seeking," her "passive receptivity" had come to an end; she was finished with the "ever-lasting 'preparation for life.'"[29]

The account of the bullfight, at first reading, offers a puzzling conversion. In the months preceding the occasion Addams had witnessed far more horrifying sights. She had seen children that looked only "halfhuman," the poor fighting for food "which was already unfit to eat." What the bullfight had achieved and the sights of urban poverty had not was a realization that her search for culture was a futile quest. She had attempted to find personal meaning in sight-seeing and collecting objets d'art. The application of this cultural knowledge to the bullfight so disgusted her that it produced a conversion and sense of commitment that church membership or the medical profession could not. But, most important, Addams told a whole generation of middle-class women that "somewhere in the process of 'being educated' they had lost that old healthful reaction resulting in activity from the mere presence of suffering or of helplessness." Their lives were incomplete because the pursuit of education had only added to their class ennui. Their lives were unsatisfactory because they were "smothered and sickened" with social advantages. It was like eating a "sweet dessert the first thing in the morning."[30] Jane Addams knew these assertions were true because she had lived them. Likewise she knew the truth of the solution. After the bullfight experience, Addams's life became a totally public one. Service had been justified as an alternative to class boredom, as a kind of relief from personal problems.

Up to this point the autobiographical lessons of Addams and Gilman are fundamentally the same. Both women's identity had been determined by paternal authority. Both suffered as a consequence. Both fought bravely to discover an independent self. Both failed, only to finally succeed in reconstructing a personality beyond paternal power through dedication to service. But Addams's solution is different from Gilman's in very basic ways. Her life of service, her leadership in the settlement movement, her political theory, are not based upon an abolition of the "outer self" but upon a recognition of the personal as the basis for human community, however stunted and tortured this aspect of people's lives has become.

The central focus of Addams's teaching is based upon her image of immigrants as a "household of children whose mother is dead."[31] Addams saw in the immigrant what she saw in herself, for she too was an immigrant, herself adrift from parental power, from the security of her class and the sorority of her forebears. In nearly all her analyses of political and social life she was able to capture the nature of the immigrant's estrangement and at the same time to discover aspects of her life that deserved to be preserved, even treasured, as that estrangement was overcome. In a sense, Addams had developed a praxis of social life, an achievement that Gilman, or for that matter, American liberal reform in general, never attained.

Addams included her essay "The Subjective Necessity of Social Settlements" in her autobiography. She had openly promoted the settlement house as a solution to personal problems. Youth, "so sincere in its emotion and good phrase and yet so undirected, seems to me as pitiful as the other great mass of destitute lives."[32]

Christopher Lasch has argued that the essay exposes Addams's motives as a reformer.[33] Addams's efforts to help the poor were motivated not by the outrageous conditions of the city and still less by feelings of class guilt. What animated Addams's entry to public life was her desire to avoid a sense of ennui. But to this, Addams readily admits. It becomes the central thesis of her autobiography. The important question here is how Addams sought to overcome her personal problems and what she saw as the same problems that troubled middle-class women.

The early stages of Hull House did exhibit an attempt to simply enlarge the audience of middle-class women. There were teas, discussion groups, and art appreciation classes. But the young volunteers soon provided the sorts of services that the residents needed. They washed new-born babies, prepared the dead for burial, nursed the sick, minded the children, provided shelter for battered wives. Hull House was a dynamo of invention. Some efforts were, of course, unsuccessful. Addams confessed that she was never able to find a social alternative to the saloon. One of these attempts deserves special attention because it illustrates Addams's concern with estrangement and its transcendence through the expansion of social life. Addams had been concerned over the estrangement between immigrants and their children. Why, she asked, "should that chasm between fathers and sons, yawning at the feet of each generation, be made so unnecessarily cruel and impassable to these bewildered immigrants?" The Italian mothers who came to Hull House despaired over the "loss" of their "Americanized children." Walking down the street she had noticed "an old Italian woman, her distaff against her homesick face, patiently spinning a thread by the simple stick spindle so reminiscent of all southern Europe." The woman's face brightened as Addams passed by and she held up her spindle for her to see and yelled that after she had spun out some more yarn she was going to knit a pair of stockings for her goddaughter. Addams was so struck by the moment that she decided to set up a labor museum at Hull House. She invited immigrant women to demonstrate their crafts. Lectures were arranged to illustrate the industrial history. The museum afforded parents the opportunity to be teachers, "a pleasant change from the tutelage in which all Americans, including their own children, are so apt to hold them." [34]

The museum also had its impact on Addams herself:

> In some such ways as these have the Labor Museum and the shops pointed out the possibilities which Hull-House has scarcely begun to develop, of demonstrating that culture is an understanding of the long-established occupations and thoughts of men, of the arts with which they have solaced their toil. A yearning to recover for the household arts something of their early sanctity and meaning arose strongly within me one evening when I was attending a Passover Feast to which I had been invited by a Jewish family in the neighborhood, where the traditional and religious significance of the woman's daily activity was still retained. The kosher food the Jewish mother spread before her family had been prepared according to traditional knowledge and with constant care in the use of utensils; upon her had fallen the responsibility to

make all ready according to Mosaic instructions that the great crisis in a religious history might be fittingly set forth by her husband and son. Aside from the grave religious significance in the ceremony, my mind was filled with shifting pictures of woman's labor with which travel makes one familiar; the Indian women grinding grain outside of their huts as they sing praises to the sun and rain; a file of white-clad Moorish women whom I had once seen waiting their turn at a well in Tangiers; south Italian women kneeling in a row along the stream and beating their wet clothes against the smooth white stones; the milking, the gardening, the marketing in thousands of hamlets, which are such direct expressions of the solicitude and affection at the basis of all family life.[35]

Addams was no narodnik. *Twenty Years at Hull House* contains its share of comments on what Marx had complained of as the "idiocy" of village life. But it is precisely these liberal antipathies toward the premodern world that make Addams's sentiments so important. She knew the value of literacy, hygiene, and economic mobility as much as any American but she would not forsake these peasant women nor cut their children adrift from their own autobiographical past in the name of liberal emancipation.

In all of her essays Addams strove to find the element of sociability beneath the disintegrative aspects of immigrant life. She was willing to search for social functions in institutions she abhorred. She noted that the city machine, for all its corruption and systematic greed, provided important personal relationships for displaced urban people. The aldermen gave presents at weddings and christenings, bought "tickets galore" for benefits for widows, distributed turkeys at Christmas. Addams asked, "Indeed what headway can the notion of civic purity, of honesty of administration, make against this big manifestation of human friendliness, this stalking survival of village kindness?"[36] These were not the "corrupt and illiterate voters" of which the reformers complained. But neither was Addams prepared to defend a system that ultimately must be judged as one that exploits a "primitive" people. If men of "low ideals and corrupt practice" win the hearts of the people because they stand by them in basic ways, then "nothing remains but to obtain a like sense of identification before we can hope to modify ethical standards."[37]

No institution could agitate Addams's middle-class progressive morality more than the "gin palaces" of Chicago. These huge dance halls were places where youth gathered in which "alcohol was dispensed, not to allay thirst" but to "empty pockets." The places confused "joy with lust, and gaiety with debauchery." But Addams knew that these "lurid places" were a reflection of the modern city. Daily labor had become "continually more monotonous and subdivided." Children had been gathered "from all the quarters of the earth as a labor supply for the countless factories and workshops." Young girls were valued for the products they manufactured. Society did not care for "their immemorial ability to affirm the charm of existence."[38]

Progressive reformers had been able to see two cities in Chicago, one that was represented by the old class of wealth and status and one that was represented by the poor immigrant. But Addams was able to see two cities from the vantage point of the settlement. The new economic structure had convulsively produced a new class ripped from traditional culture. The young people who walked through the city streets after a day in the factories would have attended a dance on the village green or a peasant festival had they not been gathered from across the country and the world to "work under alien roofs." The city "sees in these girls only two possibilities, both of them commercial: first, a chance to utilize by day their new and tender labor power in its factories and shops, and then another chance in the evening to extract from them their petty wages by pandering to their love of pleasure." But Addams saw another city among the poor and displaced which was not economic in character although it had been perverted by the commercial hegemony over all aspects of urban life. The gin palace was meeting, albeit in a "pathetic" way, basic social needs. Addams's description captures this second, and submerged feature of the city:

> As these overworked girls stream along the street, the rest of us only see the self-conscious walk, the giggling speech, the preposterous clothing. And yet through the huge hat, with its wilderness of bedraggled feathers, the girl announces to the world that she is here. She demands attention to the fact of her existence, she

states that she is ready to live, to take her place in the world. The most precious moment in human development is the young creature's assertion that he is unlike any other human being, and has an individual contribution to make to the world.

She continues her story of the girl as she enters the palace and young men "stand about vainly hoping to make the acquaintance of some 'nice girl.'" "They look eagerly up and down the rows of girls, many of whom are drawn to the hall by the same keen desire for pleasure and social intercourse which the lonely young men themselves feel." Of course, Addams knows well that these desires may conclude in only a one-night stand but she is able to see that closing of the palaces without providing some substitute only destroys an outlet, however imperfect, for social life. "Even the most loutish tenement-house youth vaguely feels this, and at least at rare intervals reveals it in his talk to his 'girl.'" [39]

It is, I believe, Addams's discovery of this social aspect of the new city that permitted her to make a connection between the personal and the political quite different from that made by Charlotte Perkins Gilman. For Addams affirmed herself (her "outer self"), fractured and threatened as it had become in her own youth, through an appreciation of the struggles of the displaced. Their estrangement was also hers, but more positively, their victories over anomie and economic exploitation were hers as well. Two incidents, minor in themselves, illustrate Addams's development in this regard. She had been called to come quickly to the house of an old German woman who was resisting re-settlement to the county infirmary. She found a "poor old creature" who had "thrown herself bodily upon a small and battered chest of drawers and clung there, clutching it so firmly that it would have been impossible to remove her without also taking the piece of furniture." She looked like "a frightened animal caught in a trap" and despite the assurances of Addams and a group of neighborhood women, she would not move. Addams concluded:

To take away from an old woman whose life had been spent in household cares all the foolish belongings to which her affections cling and to which her very fingers have become accustomed is to take away her last incentive to activity, almost to life itself. To give an old woman only a chair and a bed, to leave her no cupboard in which her treasures may be stowed, not only that she may take them out when she desires occupation, but that her mind may dwell on them in moments of revery, is to reduce living almost beyond the limit of human endurance.[40]

There is in Addams a frank assessment of the intrinsic value of possessions; these were after all "foolish belongings."[41] But the utility of things owned is not the standard of measurement. This old woman saw the dresser and its contents as a means by which she could retain a conception of herself. From that realization on, Addams found that the old women whom she began to invite to Hull House as a vacation from the poor house had many "shrewd comments on life" and made "delightful companions."

A second incident occurred shortly after Addams had started her settlement. It is not mentioned in *Twenty Years at Hull House* but is reported autobiographically in an essay. A "delicate little child" had been deserted in the Hull House nursery. Addams had been able to find that the infant had been born ten days before in the Cook County Hospital but she could not locate the "unfortunate Mother." After a few weeks the child died and Addams made arrangements for burial by the county. A wagon was scheduled to arrive at eleven o'clock. At nine, Hull House was the scene of protest by neighborhood women. They had taken up a collection "out of their poverty" to pay the costs of a funeral. Addams is able to see two moralities encapsuled in the situation. Her first reaction was defensive. After all, "we instanced the care and tenderness which had been expended upon the poor creature when it was alive." The infant had received the attention of a skilled physician and trained nurse. Where, Addams asked "the excited members of the group," were you when the baby was alive? "It now lay with us to decide that the child should be buried, as it had been born, at the county's expense." Unstated in Addams's defense is the accusation that the community had abandoned an illegitimate child and that the "professional" thus has assumed proprietary interests over those whom it serves. But her remarks are prefaced by confession of the "crudeness" of her position: "We did not realize that we were really shocking a genuine moral sentiment of the community. . . . We were only forgiven by the most indulgent on the ground that we were spinsters and could not know a mother's heart." There is certainly a note of self-deprecation in the concluding response, but Addams is more concerned that sentiments in "the mother's heart" were a collective overlay of biological function. "No one," she insists, "born and reared in the community could have possibly made a mistake like that."[42]

Addams's development of a praxis between the personal and political achieves the status of political theory in her analysis of the Pullman strike. Her essays and the autobiography are always focused upon the problems of women. Men never receive the same empathetic efforts that characterize her accounts of children, young women, mothers, and widows. There is certainly an appreciation for "the sorry men" who "for one reason or other" have "failed in the struggle of life." But the emphasis is on "heroic women" who must deal with drunkards, domestic violence, and deserting husbands. The Pullman strike provided Addams with the opportunity to examine the nature of paternal authority.

George Pullman represented an alternative to the rapacious capitalist of the post–Civil War era. He had created a model company town for his workers. Successive wage reductions led to workers' pleas for arbitration. This Pullman refused. When railway employees would not work on Pullman cars, there were dismissals and then a massive strike which was broken by President Cleveland's deployment of federal troops to Illinois. The strike was broken. Many historians regard the strikers' defeat as a setback that would require labor generations to overcome. The Pullman strike had briefly showed the power of the labor movement (the railways west of Chicago had been shut down) and the American middle class was badly frightened. After all, had not Pullman spent large sums of money to provide his workers with modern plumbing and even a park, a theater, and a church? Is this, they asked, the reward for benevolent paternalism?

Addams, who was clearly sympathetic to the workers but also skeptical of the value of strikes, used Shakespeare's story of King Lear as the basis for her analysis of the incident. Pullman was a modern Lear and the strikers Cordelias. Shakespeare had described a domestic tragedy; Pullman had created an industrial one. Addams was struck by the "similarity of ingratitude suffered by the indulgent employer and an indulgent parent."[43] The lesson of Lear had "modified and softened her judgment" of the workers.

"A Modern Lear" is a neglected masterpiece because it shows how the connection between the personal and political can be made. This, after all is said, is the goal of all American political thought. Addams never tells us that Pullman like Addams is an example of paternal authority: "The minds of all of us reach back to our early struggles. . . ." We all know what it might be like to kill our father: "We have all had glimpses of what it might be like to blaspheme family ties. . . ." We all have suffered from the bonds of paternal will: "The virtues of one generation are not sufficient for the next. . . ." The Lear analogy enabled Addams to see the character of her own struggles as a woman, but it also allowed her to appreciate the struggles of men against paternalism in the industrial sphere. The Pullman strikers may not have agreed that their position was analogous to daughters, but Addams saw a resemblance between them and the workers who first petitioned and then struck out against paternal authority and risked the charge of "ingratitude." Here were for Addams the counterparts to the "heroic women" of Halsted Street. These men were "self-controlled and destroyed no property." They were "sober and exhibited no drunkenness even though obliged to hold meetings in the saloon hall of a neighboring town."[44]

This is not to say that the rejection of paternal authority presents no moral ambiguities. "Cordelia does not escape our censure. Her first words are cold, and we are shocked by her lack of tenderness. Why should she ignore her father's need for indulgence, and be so unwilling to give him what he so obviously craved?" So too the claims of the workers will consist of "many failures, cruelties and reactions." But Addams insisted that paternal authority, those bonds of bondage, must eventually be accommodated. Pullman and Lear were "tragic" examples of paternal authority. They had forgotten the nature of their trust. Lear had "ignored the common ancestry of Cordelia and himself." He could see Cordelia only in terms of signs of fidelity that he demanded. Likewise, Pullman's town became only "a source of pride and an exponent of power": "We can imagine the founder of the town slowly darkening his glints of memory and forgetting the common stock of experience which he held with these men."[45]

Bonds of affection need not always be arbitrary exercises of power. The "family claim" (which Addams had also herself overcome autobiographically) must be "tested" by a commitment to a larger life. The daughter must pass this test by asserting her individuality and so must the father by realizing that the child can fulfill the family claim in all "its sweetness and strength" by enlarging it. The "adjustment of the lesser and larger implies no conflict." In all the affairs of society consent must eventually temper paternal power:

> The man who insists upon consent, who moves with the people, is bound to consult the feasible right as well as the absolute right. He is often obliged to attain only Mr. Lincoln's "best possible," and often have the sickening sense of compromising with his best convictions. He has to move along with those whom he rules toward a goal that neither he nor they see very clearly till they come to it. He has to discover what people really want, and then "provide the channels in which the growing moral force of their lives shall flow." What he does attain, however, is not the result of his individual striving, as a solitary mountain climber beyond the sight of the valley multitude, but it is underpinned and upheld by the sentiments and aspirations of many others. Progress has been slower perpendicularly, but incomparably greater because it is lateral.[46]

Unlike Gilmans, Addams taught that there must always be parents, that the "outside self" is the "real self," and that the realization of the one depends upon the affirmation of the other.

C H A P T E R   S E V E N

CONCLUSION

What could be more irrelevant to American political thought than Hegel and Marx? What nation could be more ignorant of the World Spirit, more unable to grasp *der Gang der Sache selbst* than America? What theorist could write that the state is the march of God on earth? Yet, although Franklin would never say that "the special interest of passion is thus inseparable from the actualization of the universal," his autobiography is an attempt to describe just such a process. To continue, who can deny that America is not one of the great "world historical nations" of which Hegel spoke? What American socialist has not felt the iron grip of his country's Geist?

The importance of Hegel for an understanding of American political thought lies not simply in recognizing that there is a strong, even overpowering, nationalism that lurks through the history of a liberal, individualist culture, one that in the form of what Louis Hartz called the "irrational Locke" periodically makes appearances. Malcolm X, Abbie Hoffman, Lincoln Steffens, Lillian Hellman, and Jane Addams have all seen that specter. Nor is nationalism's importance limited to a realization, advanced by Tocqueville and others, that there is beneath the swirl of competition and conflict in America, a working out of a grand idea. Nor is it Hegel's discovery, to pursue other aspects, that the world historical cultures play out their roles, only to flounder and hopelessly struggle as they are dragged off the stage of world history. So imply Leslie Fiedler and Christopher Lasch; Addams, Steffens, and Whittaker Chambers said as much.

The foremost importance of Hegel is that self-realization is part of the process of a culture's realization. Only the American autobiography begins to appreciate that truth. When the autobiographer succeeds, and he or she rarely does (although Addams's efforts suggest that the demand for the realization of the self can be met in the context of American society), the personal and the political illuminate each other. When the autobiographer fails, when the effort at self-realization is blocked and entangled, the single failure compounds. Others repeat the errors and they, of course, fail as well. The errors copied become patterns of thought, then practices and institutions.

"Something which lies completely hidden in the future"

Whatever the outcome, the autobiography performs two crucial functions in American political thought. First, as we mentioned in chapter one, the autobiographer provides the missing praxis of the sermonic tradition. The great legitimizing texts of American political thought, from *The Federalist Papers* to presidential exhortations to modern classics, by their very nature refuse to examine the claims of sermonic political thought. The seeds of conflict are simply sown in the nature of man, asserts James Madison. Or, as Rawls says: "We are to suppose then that each individual has a rational plan of life drawn up subject to the conditions that confront him."[1] For the theorist of the legitimizing tradition, the sermonic claim of justice or equality is in itself irrelevant. Of course the legitimizers are anything but Whiggish trimers. Madison's is a Newton-like system, each individual, each institution of government balance one another. Nor is the legitimizer always committed to debunking moral claims. He insists, however, that each claim remain unexamined. The claim itself need only be incorporated into the theory. Thus writes Dworkin: "Government must treat those whom it governs with concern, that is, as human beings who are capable of suffering and frustration, and with respect, that is, as human beings who are capable of forming and acting on intelligent conceptions of how their lives should be lived."[2] What are peoples' "suffering and frustration"? Dworkin cannot stop to consider. His task is broader, his search wider. He just continues: "Government must not only treat people with concern and respect, but with equal concern and respect."[3]

From the perspective of the legitimizing theorist, the sermonic claims are pretheoretical. He insists that the question is not "How ought I live?" but what conditions can be created that best permit a resolution to those that ask the question. In Dworkin's words, "a metric" is what is needed. But of course that metric does not accommodate every answer to the question, "How ought I live?" The task of sermonic theorists is to claim that the liberal consensus in force cannot accommodate new answers. If the answer to the personal question is, as Franklin asserted, material success and upward mobility, some metric must be offered that recasts social and political structure. A model that permits hustling$_1$, that permits the necessary fluidity and ethics, is demanded. If, as

Charlotte Perkins Gilman argued, hustling women cannot be happy in the home, the home must be reconstituted. Not all claims can of course be accommodated. How does a political system respond to the assertion that all whites are devils? How can a political theory be constructed in a bourgeois society that demands "Simplify, Simplify, Simplify"? Or "Turn On, Drop Out"? There would be no black independent nor Woodstock nation in America, but there would be affirmative action and a "new morality." Hoffman's observation ("The opportunities that existed were among the most inventive contradictions any capitalist society ever contrived") illustrates the productive relationship between sermonic and legitimizing political thought.

In this sense all sermonic political thought, from Franklin and even Addams to present writers, exhibits the character of hustling we described in chapter two. Each theorist must "hustle" his idea. He must show that the current consensus is unjust, that it ignores in basic ways legitimate answers to the question, "How ought I live?" He must establish that we are unhappy, that we lead lives of "quiet desperation," that we are "indifferent to God," that we are all "crooks," that women are relegated to a "lower plane" of evolution. And what surer way is there to demonstrate our unhappiness and to establish an alternative as well than to write autobiography? That the autobiography, to use Franklin's words, as an account of a life "fit to be imitated" is itself part of the hustle is part of its function in Americn political thought. For the autobiography is designed to establish the practicality of a political idea that had been ignored as utopian by the legitimizing theory.

This is why the conversion, the structural feature common to all American autobiography, is so essential to its role in American political thought. The conversion demonstrates that the new way of life is possible. The personal becomes the method of justification for a new political theory. "New" persons abound in the American autobiography. Always there is the "old" person who suffers with his brothers and sisters under the current liberal consensus. Franklin, struggling for economic independence, fights off abusive employers, vixens, and predators from the upper classes. Many of his friends succumb to alcoholism. Malcolm X is nearly crushed by white men. The black bourgeoisie disgusts him, as do his customers who rip at his drugs "like chicken on corn." Abbie Hoffman works on the frayed edges of bourgeois society as a salesman, mental hospital orderly, movie theater manager: "I started to believe that nobody with a suit and tie worked in America." Thoreau must endure smug New England villagers. Chambers hears screams from Lubianka. Hellman lives in an age of scoundrels. Who would, asks Henry Adams, choose to live in the twentieth century had he known of telegraphs, railways, coal, and steel? Steffens indicts the men of "Main Street," Richard Wright the white terror behind the magnolias, Gilman absent fathers, and Addams the new capitalist class.

For each of these autobiographers, the obstacles to their individual emancipation represent the embodiments of the spirit of the prevailing liberal consensus: aristocrats without titles (Franklin), the sons and daughters of slaveowners (Malcolm X), corporate capitalists (Hoffman), New England reformers (Thoreau), indifferent New Dealers (Chambers), "badies" and cowards (Hellman), New England men of republican virtue (Adams), the "good and respectable" (Steffens), the southern white power structure (Wright), men (Gilman), factory owners (Addams). But the creation of a new person proves that these forces are not natural and that new institutions can be formed in the name of emancipation.

In a sense, the conversion is the American equivalent to revolution. All the basic features of revolutionary activity are present in the conversion experience at an individual level. An entirely new person must be formed at great sacrifice. Discipline and vigilance are always necessary. The convulsions that an entire society undergoes in revolution occur for the single individual. The old society (person) breaks down; the autobiographer has a breakdown. As is the case with revolution, radical change occurs unexpectedly. Like the incident at Concord or the bread riots in Petrograd, the signs of transformation are there but the timing and magnitude of the event are unpredictable. Chambers's life was changed when he contemplated his daughter's ear; Addams began Hull House and left her life of cultural pursuit behind when she saw a bullfight; Steffens changed his perspective when he locked himself in a railway car; Malcolm X when he was locked in prison. Family deaths caused the Big Change for three of the autobiographers we have studied (Thoreau's brother, Adams's grandfather, Addams's father). If private tragedy unloosens the old life from moorings already shaken, so do public events. Hoffman was born "psychologically" in 1960, Hellman saw that her life would never be the same again after her testimony before the House Un-American Affairs Committee.

If the destruction of the old personality is a revolutionary act, the new person (society) has all the characteristics of infancy. On the positive side, everything is seen with new eyes. Both Marx and Tocqueville had described the Paris Commune as a new society in which "everything is possible." For the new person whose old personality has "slid away . . . like snow off a roof" the previous life appears to be like that of "another person." Projects that the old person would never have imagined or had the courage to implement are now enthusiastically undertaken. Addams reports after the bullfight: "I made up my mind the next day, whatever happened, I would begin to carry out the plan. . . ." In Marxist terms qualitative changes can only occur through a revolution. The old society simply cannot absorb the sort of change now possible. Thus so also for the autobiographer. Gilman could not reach accommodation between herself and her family. Franklin had to leave Boston, Malcolm X, Lansing. Thoreau had to go down the Concord and Merrimack and then to Walden; Hellman and Chambers to their farms; Wright and Addams to Chicago; Hoffman to the East Side. In all the accounts of these journeys begun by new people, the world has opened up, life begins anew.

Richard Wright wrote: "I was leaving the South to fling myself into the unknown. . . ." He captures another aspect of the autobiographer's conception of himself as a revolution in miniature. Rosa Luxemburg had insisted in her criticism of the Bolsheviks that the revolution could not be realized through "ready-made prescriptions." The new society is "something which lies completely hidden in the future." All revolutionaries have to guide them are a "few main signposts which indicate a general direction . . . and the indications are mainly negative in character, at that."[4] The American autobiographer feels this same sense of the unknown. Often like Franklin, he does not know how he will live. Gilman would live "at large," "like a sea gull at sea." No one calls Hellman anymore and her sources of income shrink daily. Thoreau must learn to live on his own in the woods. It is no wonder then that the autobiographer struggles so to create "the plan." There are, after all, enemies of the revolution everywhere. Revolutionary societies by their nature have burned their bridges behind them. They cannot fail. For the autobiographer, the old self is dead. What would happen if the new self failed is a frightening thought. It is common then for the autobiographer to rely upon "ready-made prescriptions" like the Bolsheviks, good for all women, blacks, reformers, anti-Communists. With the revolution under constant threat of betrayal who would not rely on the plan?

The autobiography then is the evidence presented in support of changes in the liberal consensus. Although we cannot minimize the revolutionary character of the autobiography, we can begin to see how readily the legitimizing aspect of American political thought can absorb demands that are always presented as impossible to achieve without revolutionary transformation. The very achievement of the autobiographer, his ability to recount the significance of his life and his record of his conversion, establishes the feasibility of altering the consensus within the boundaries of liberal thought. Certainly, as we indicated above, if Ford was to be an American Lenin, or if Americans fled to the woods, or if America prayed before Chartres, a radical transformation of American society would occur. But the autobiographer, however much he writes to support the claims of his political thought, writes of his life as lived. After all is set down, the autobiographer tells a life of success. That, of course, has to be the strategical basis of his project. He must show in Thoreau's words, how "very natural and pertinent" his claims are by living them out. But that very success also occurs within liberal society. No matter what cruelties Wright suffered, he became a famous writer. Malcolm X became a world figure. All eleven of the autobiographers we have discussed became free. Certainly their lives show the tremendous obstacles placed before them. But the incontrovertible fact remains that these people are successes, living examples of the fulfillment of American dreams. In fact the more people that are helped by their plans, the more truth is given to the assertion that the system is adaptable and incipiently capable of providing a wider range of answers to the question, "How ought I live?"

In this respect, American political thought is a Hegelian nightmare. There appears to be no dialectical transcendence, no higher resolution from the challenge to the liberal consensus. Self-realization there is, of course, as well as a minute dissection of American society. But a new consensus is always reformed and the process begins again. Daniel

DeLeon described this process, which was outlined in the first chapter, in regard to radical thought. Critiques are formed with a "powerful immediacy" but nearly always constructed in the context of a world of "immediate sensation." The tradition of sermonic literature, even when its epistemological base in autobiography is made visible, is itself traditionless. Only the legitimizing tradition appears to have a conscious sense of its historical mission. American society lives in a state of permanent revolution and hence never changes in a Hegelian sense.

"And cracked like a plate"

But there is an additional function of the autobiography in American political thought. Ironically it operates in direct opposition to the autobiographer's purpose. The American autobiographer insists that the changes in his life are made possible by conversion. Naturally, as we have already indicated, the more complete the destruction of the old self, the greater the achievement of the new self. But what if all these conversions are less rebirth, the explosion of a "more perfect creature," than a falling apart of the self? What if the new self is not like Thoreau's "airy and fluttery butterfly" but only the same self patched up?

What if the conversions chronicled by the American autobiographers are not conversions at all but instead what F. Scott Fitzgerald called "crack-ups"?

> Of course all life is a process of breaking down, but the blows that do the dramatic side of the work—the big sudden blows that come, or seem to come, from outside—the ones you remember and blame things on and, in moments of weakness, tell your friends about, don't show their effect all at once. There is another sort of blow that comes from within—that you don't feel until it is too late to do anything about it, until you realize with finality that in some regard you will never be as good a man again. The first sort of breakage seems to happen quick—the second kind happens almost without your knowing it but is realized suddenly indeed.

"Ten years this side of forty-nine" Fitzgerald realized that he had "prematurely cracked." The process of cracking-up is described in ways much like the conversion. Fitzgerald whimsically describes himself as "an average mixer, but more than average in a tendency to identify myself, my ideas, my destiny, with those classes that I came in contact with. I was always saving or being saved. . . ." Then suddenly he wished to be alone. Fitzgerald was tired; he couldn't concentrate; he made lists. "And then suddenly I got better." Another conversion story? Fitzgerald adds: "—And cracked like a plate as soon as I heard the news." Like the convert, he had arrived at a moment of great personal discovery. But here the news is different: "Suffice it to say that after an hour of solitary pillow hugging, I began to realize that for two years my life had been drawing on resources that I did not possess, that I had been mortgaging myself physically and spiritually up to the hilt. What was the small gift of life given back in comparison to that?"[5]

Is the autobiographer's account of his or her new life an act of self-deception? Fitzgerald remarked that "a man can crack in many ways." Certainly the American autobiographer confirms this observation. But the evidence suggests that the new person is a cracked person. There are in the American autobiography too many conversions. Counting here is of course speculative but one could argue that Franklin had two, Hoffman, three or four, Malcolm X, four, Thoreau, two, Chambers, two, Hellman, three, Wright, two, Adams, two and Steffens, two. It is certainly possible for a person to undergo several major transformations in his or her life but it is also possible that these repeated conversions are desperate attempts to avoid realization of the crack-up. Moreover, old selves keep reappearing like ghosts. The conversion narrative has standard explanations for this phenomenon. One must always guard against Thermidors. The self is after all only in its infancy. Backsliding is human. But the most telling evidence that a suppressed alternate model better explains the American autobiography is the fact that the new self is never so strong as the old one. It always, despite the bravado of the happy ending of the conversion story, is fragile and threatened. The agony of the conversion to the new person is always more vivid than the description of either the old or the new personality. Thoreau stands before the Merrimack as a bunch of cut flowers or cowers before the Atlantic. Are these remembrances comparable in intensity to his chanticleering? Is Hoffman's loss of identity in underground less vivid than his antics at the Chicago trial? Gilman and Addams fight back the effects of the conversion experience throughout their lives.

Adams and to a lesser extent Hellman seem to come close to recognizing that what they had experienced is a crack-up, that their lives have involved "drawing on resources" they did not possess. And in both of these autobiographies we are able to get the clearest picture of the autobiography's subversive function in American political thought. For Adams insists that his failure is traceable to the failure of America. If Adams cracked up, with all his advantages in the natural lottery, wasn't America cracked up as well? Did America crack when Adams did, when John Quincy Adams died? Hellman briefly sheds her tough-guy persona in *Maybe*. Instead of complaining about scoundrels and cowards and thinkers without memory, she comes to consider if she too can remember anything at all. She had collapsed "in a way that never happened before," "there are missing parts everywhere." Had she too cracked? Maybe, in the words of her last memoir, she was not the new person, the protector of homely virtues, but one who "didn't know much of what really happened and never tried to find out." Maybe the tough guy is more a reflection of American society than a rebellion against it.

For moments in Adams and Hellman we have a Hegelian truth that real self-awareness involves a realization that the cunning of reason may be all that there is of the self. To the extent that the autobiographer recognizes that his life is not a series of conversions but of crack-ups, he pulls himself away from performing his role as the unwitting formulator of another liberal consensus. Whenever he finds a new self, no matter how at odds with the liberal consensus, he again becomes the raw material for the legitimizing tradition. He has succeeded, others too can now succeed. The crack-up illustrates that America produces another kind of individualism, a tragic and fragile individualism, which requires measures beyond the reach of the legitimizing theorist. Thus in an odd way, the failures of Adams, and even the failures of the other ten autobiographers to truly will a new self, are, when fully admitted, the ground for a new kind of American political thought.

Although few autobiographers see their projects in this light, the new personalities they describe reveal (again despite their own efforts) both the reasons for the current failed character of American political thought and also the possible basis for renewal. If one looks at the new selves of the American autobiography, they read like an exile literature: the hustlers (Malcolm X, Franklin, Hoffman); the tough guy (Hellman); the informer (Chambers); the recluse (Thoreau); the "boy on horseback" (Steffens); the émigré (Wright); the failure (Adams); the immigrant (Addams); the traveler (Gilman). These new men and women are outsiders. Their new lives are lived in fundamental ways outside the liberal consensus. Of course the critical political theorist must assume a stance outside of society if only to assess the system. But these writers assume roles in which the estrangement is both so severe and so individualized that they are extremely difficult to fully incorporate into the liberal consensus. As we indicated, the price of this alienation is very high for the construction of American political theory. Hellman and Chambers devote their lives to political judgment. The personalities they assume make judgment limited if not impossible. Thoreau leaves society in order to understand it and his place in it. Although he returns from Walden armed with the experience of his conversion and a plan for simple living, a close reading of his autobiographical travels suggests he can never live a life other than that of a recluse. Gilman too is only free when she is traveling and her political theory is an effort to institutionalize her own alienation. It is Chambers who expresses most clearly the tendency of every American autobiographer: one "is free only to the extent that he knows what he is doing and why he is doing it."

But the exile character of the American autobiographer shows that the price of genuine emancipation is extreme. Praxis, despite its use in the legitimizing tradition, is actually very rare. Perhaps the most common model is found in the transition from hustler$_1$ to hustler$_2$, but we saw how ambiguous both these roles are in relation to one another and how estranged in its essence is hustling. Most of the roles constructed permit a political theory based only on generalized alienation. Adams's dynamo, Hellman's tough guy, Steffens's honest crook, Gilman's collective living do not fit the image of individual liberation promised by conversion. There are more accommodations with a hostile or indifferent environment, efforts to avoid further crack-ups. Only with Jane Addams is the role of the immigrant as outsider transformed to genuine freedom. Only with the remembrances of childhood can many auto-

biographers conceive of life without estrangement and only through individual states of nature can the American autobiographer conceive of
a self radically different from present existence. But the pastoral self is
never reconstructed except through childhood memory.

If this is the only kind of freedom that some of the best minds of a
nation can produce, what can we say about the moral success of the
legitimizing tradition?

Introduction

1   Louis Hartz, *The Liberal Tradition in America* (New York, 1955), p. 309. Hartz's analysis, despite its boldness, is so richly presented that it is difficult to categorize. At some points (most notably in his treatment of the Whigs and Progressives) his position is quite close to that of the liberal hegemonists below. On this aspect of Hartz see Robert C. Grady, "Liberalism and the Crisis of Authority," paper presented at the Southern Political Science Association Meetings, November 1978. Other examples of consensus writings that show the wide range of interpretation are Arthur M. Schlesinger, Jr., "Epilogue: The One and the Many," in *Paths of American Thought,* ed. Schlesinger and Morton White (Boston, 1963), pp. 531–38; Seymour Martin Lipset, *The First New Nation* (New York, 1973); F. M. Coleman, *Hobbes and America* (Toronto, 1977); Robert A. Goldwin, "Of Men and Angels: A Search for Morality in the Constitution," in *The Moral Foundations of the American Republic,* ed. Robert H. Horwitz (Charlottesville, 1979), pp. 1–18.

2   Daniel Boorstin, *The Genius of American Politics* (Chicago, 1958), p. 2.

3   Robert McCloskey, "American Political Thought and the Study of Politics," in *Approaches to the Study of Politics,* ed. Roland Young (Evanston, 1971), p. 156–57.

4   See Harvey Klehr, "Marxist Theory in Search of America," *Journal of Politics* 35 (1973): 311–31.

5   Again the interpretive range is quite wide. See Werner Sombart, *Why is There No Socialism in the United States?* (1905; reprint ed., White Plains, N.Y., 1976); Earl Browder, *The Peoples' Front* (New York, 1938); Norman Thomas, *Socialism Re-examined* (New York, 1963); Selig Perlman, *A Theory of the Labor Movement* (New York, 1949). More recently, the exceptionalist thesis has been recast by Michael Harrington in his *Socialism* (New York, 1972), chap. 9.

6   Leon Samson, *Toward a United Front* (New York, 1935), p. 17.

7   Bruce Johnson, "The Democratic Mirage: Notes Toward a Theory of American Politics," *Berkeley Journal of Sociology* 13 (1968), reprinted as a Warner Modular Publication (#315), p. 9.

8   The pivotal interpretive source is Antonio Gramsci and, to a lesser extent, Raymond Williams. Examples of Gramscian-inspired American scholarship include Mike Davis, "Why the U.S. Working Class is Different," *New Left Review* 123 (October 1980): 3–45; Stanley Aronowitz, *False Promises* (New York, 1973); Todd Gitlin, *The Whole World Is Watching* (Berkeley, 1980); Harry Boyte, *The Backyard Revolution* (Philadelphia, 1982); Tom Hayden, *The American Future* (Boston, 1980); Ira Katznelson, *City Trenches* (New York, 1981). In many ways the acceptance of the liberal hegemony thesis represents the same sort of strategic decision for the Left that the exceptionalist question posed. See, for instance, the debate "Prospects for the Left," *Socialist Review* 43 (1979): 91–142. Ironically, Gramsci himself may have been an exceptionalist theorist with regard to

America. See his "Americanism and Fordism" in *Prison Notebooks* (New York, 1971), pp. 277–318.

9   Alexis de Tocqueville, *Democracy in America* (Garden City, N.Y., 1969), pp. 541, 489.

10   Irving Howe, *Politics and the Novel* (New York, 1957), pp. 161, 164.

11   Leslie Fiedler, *Love and Death in the American Novel* (New York, 1960), p. 4.

12   Daniel DeLeon, *The American as Anarchist: Reflections on American Radicalism* (Baltimore, 1978), p. 154.

13   Christopher Lasch, *The Culture of Narcissism: American Life in an Age of Diminishing Expectations* (New York, 1978), p. 50.

14   Wilson Carey McWilliams, *The Idea of Fraternity in America* (Berkeley, 1973), p. 622.

15   The propositions are from the Declaration of Independence, the Peoples' Party Platform, the Seneca Falls Platform, Martin Luther King's "Letter from the Birmingham Jail."

16   On this point, see William G. McLoughlin, "Piretism and the American Character" in *The American Experience* (Boston, 1968), Hennig Cohen, pp. 38–63.

17   James Madison, "Federalist #10" in *The Federalist Papers*, ed. Clinton Rossiter (New York, 1961), p. 79.

18   William Dean Howells called the autobiography the "most democratic province in the republic of letters," since recording "the sincere relation of what . . . has been and done and felt and thought" is open to all ("Editor's Easy Chair," *Harper's Magazine* 119 [October 1909] : 798). The sheer volume of American autobiographical effort can be seen in two bibliographies. Louis Kapan, *A Bibliography of American Autobiographies* (Madison, 1961) and Richard G. Lillard, *American Life in Autobiography* (Stanford, 1956) contain over 7,000 entries. For considerations of the general cultural significance of the autobiography in America, see Albert Stone, *Autobiographical Occasions and Original Acts* (Philadelphia, 1982); and James M. Cox, "Autobiography and America" *Virginia Quarterly Review* 47 (1971):252–77.

19   Alfred Kazin, "The Self as History: Reflections on Autobiography," in *Telling Lives*, ed. Marc Pachter (Washington, D.C., 1979), p. 75.

20   Cotton Mather, *Bonificus*, ed. David Levin (Cambridge, Mass., 1966), p. 35.

21   Kate Millet, *Flying* (New York, 1975), p. 15.

22   Benjamin Franklin, *Autobiography and Other Writings*, ed. Russel B. Nye (Boston, 1958), p. 2.

23   Henry Adams, *The Education of Henry Adams* (Boston, 1961), p. 3.

24   Tocqueville, *Democracy in America*, p. 430.

25   On this point, see G. Thomas Couser, *American Autobiography: The Prophetic Mode* (Amherst, Mass., 1979).

26   Frederick Douglass, *Narrative of the Life of Frederick Douglass* (New York, 1968), p. 83.

27   For an analysis that explores some aspects of this process, see W. C. Spenemann and L. R. Lundquist, "Autobiography and the American Myth," *American Quarterly* 17 (1965):92–110. For treatments of the autobiographical novel as an evidentiary adjunct of the sermonic tradition, see Walter B. Rideout, *The Radical Novel in the United States* (New York, 1956), chap. 7; Elizabeth Winston, "The Autobiographer and Her Readers: From Apology to Affirmation," in *Women's Autobiography*, ed. Estelle C. Jellinek, (Bloomington, Ind., 1980), pp. 93–111.

2 Hustling

1   Christopher Lasch, *The Culture of Narcissism* (New York, 1978), p. 55. The most trenchant interpretation of Franklin's autobiography is D. H. Lawrence's *Studies in Classic American Literature* (New York, 1923), pp. 13–31. For the nature of the departure of the autobiography from the religious narrative see Daniel B. Shea, *Spiritual Autobiography in Early America* (Princeton, 1968).

2   Benjamin Franklin, *The Autobiography and Other Writings*, ed. Russell B. Nye (Boston, 1958), p. 41.

3   *The Autobiography of Malcolm X* (New York, 1964), pp. 108–9.

4   Abbie Hoffman, *Soon to Be a Major Motion Picture* (New York, 1980), pp. 223, 117.

5   Franklin, *Autobiography*, pp. 7, 17.

6   *Autobiography of Malcolm X*, pp. 14, 36, 38.

7   Hoffman, *Soon To Be*, p. 24. Despite the intellectual conversion, Hoffman's emphasis on the youthful lessons of the streets led him to denigrate the college experience (pp. 17–22). Thus, although Brandeis is portrayed in part as a Bohemian alternative, Hoffman insists that he was an "outsider" among the comparatively straight students: "Sex was cut short just before going all the way. Dope was non-existent. Politics was minimal, and Brandeis, even at that, was considered 'avant garde'! Avant garde! The other campuses must have been real numb-numb joints!" (p. 28).

8   Ibid., p. 23.

9   Robert B. Sayre, *The Examined Self* (Princeton, 1964), p. 23.

10   Franklin, *Autobiography*, p. 15.   11   Ibid., p. 60.

12   Ibid., p. 26.

13   *Autobiography of Malcolm X*, pp. 79, 80–81.

14   Hoffman, *Soon To Be*, pp. 58, 77.

15   *Autobiography of Malcolm X*, pp. 99, 87.

16   Franklin, *Autobiography*, pp. 54–55.

17   *Autobiography of Malcolm X*, pp. 119, 121, 119.

18   Franklin, *Autobiography*, pp. 62–63.

19   Ibid., pp. 28–29.   20   *Autobiography of Malcolm X*, p. 68.

21   Ibid., pp. 226, 229, 232.   22   Hoffman, *Soon To Be*, pp. 280–81.

23   Franklin, *Autobiography*, p. 1.   24   Ibid., pp. 18, 21–22.

25   The plan as shopkeeper's ethics is pursued by Lawrence, *Studies in Classic American Literature*, pp. 13–31; Vernon Parrington, *Main Currents in American Thought* (New York, 1927), 1:166; Charles Sanford, *The Quest for Paradise* (Urbana, 1961), chap. 3; Sayre contends that Franklin was adopting the role of the "naif philosophical Quaker" (*The Examined Self*, p. 27).

26   Franklin, *Autobiography*, pp. 78, 83.

27   James M. Cox, "Autobiography and America," *Virginia Quarterly Review* 47 (1971):260.

28   Franklin, *Autobiography*, pp. 86, 87.

29   *Autobiography of Malcolm X*, p. 39.

30   Ibid., p. 150.   31   Ibid., p. 171.

32   Ibid., pp. 170, 198. Also see pp. 205, 212, 288.

33   Ibid., pp. 210, 191.

34   Ibid., pp. 182, 218–19. Malcolm X's depiction of black Christians as "brain-washed" reiterates the major theme of the autobiography. The Lansing black population was "brainwashed" into believing that they were part of a black bourgeoisie, blacks had been "brainwashed" into accepting a white man's religion, and Malcolm X himself had been "brainwashed" into accepting Elijah Muhammad. The lesson of the *Autobiography* is that the greatest obstacle in the search for truth is trickery on the part of others. This, of course, is the hustler's nightmare.

35.   Ibid., p. 296. Emphasis added. Malcolm X's disillusionment is all the more poig-nant in light of the fact that his brother Reginald was ejected from the Muslims for the same "acts of immorality" that were committed by Elijah Muhammad. Reginald, rejected by his family and his new church, suffered from religious delusions and was institutionalized.

36   Hoffman, *Soon To Be*, p. 98.
37   Ibid., p. 61.
38   Ibid., pp. 88, 90, 93.
39   Ibid., p. 95.
40   Ibid., p. 137.
41   Franklin, *Autobiography*, p. 93.
42   Ibid., p. 75, 107–8.
43   Hoffman, *Soon To Be*, p. 286.
44   Ibid., pp. 288–89.
45   Ibid., pp. 293–94.
46   Ibid., pp. 296, 297.
47   Ibid., pp. 297, 298.

3   Redeeming

1   Henry David Thoreau, *Walden and Civil Disobedience*, ed. Owen Thomas (New York, 1966), p. 228.

2   Ibid., p. 229.

3   *The Writings of Henry David Thoreau*, 20 vols. (Boston, 1906), vol. 6, *Correspon-dence*, p. 378.

4   Ralph Waldo Emerson, "The Transcendentalist," in *The Selected Writings of Ralph Waldo Emerson*, ed. Brooks Atkinson (New York, 1940), p. 97.

5   Attempts to develop a consistent political theory from Thoreau's writings have failed to develop a consensus. Leo Stoller, *After Walden* (Stanford, 1957), argues that Thoreau moved toward a "union of principle and expediency" after the Walden experiment, but he admits that the connection was never firmly made. Richard Drinnon, "Thoreau's Politics of the Upright Man" in *Massachusetts Review* 4 (1962):126–38, contends that Thoreau developed a consistent anarchist position, but Joseph Wood Krutch, *Henry David Thoreau* (New York, 1948) and Sherman Paul, *The Shores of America* (Urbana, 1958), place him in the tradition of liberal individualism. Truman Nelson, "Thoreau and John Brown," in *Thoreau in Our Season*, ed. John Hicks, (Amherst, 1966), pp. 134–55, sees the develop-ment of a theory of "heroic revolutionary violence." Walter Harding, *The Days of Henry David Thoreau* (New York, 1965), p. 418, denies that any such position was developed in the Brown essays. Taylor Stoehr, *Nay-Saying in Concord* (Hamden, Conn., 1979), devel-ops the intriguing argument that Thoreau attempted to develop a new ideology of "revolu-tionary abstinence." Northrop Frye finds a strong utopian strand in Thoreau ("Varieties of Literary Utopias," *Daedalus* 94 [1965]:323–47). Lawrence Bowling argues that Thoreau was resolutely antipolitical ("Thoreau's Social Criticism as Poetry," *Yale Review* 55 [1966]: 255–64). Other works emphasize the inconsistencies in Thoreau's political writings. Two of the most vituperative are Vincent Buranelli, "The Case Against Thoreau," *Ethics* 67 (1957):257–88, and Leon Edel, *Henry David Thoreau* (Minneapolis, 1970).

6   Thoreau, *Walden and Civil Disobedience*, p. 87. In this regard, Nancy Rosenblum

insists that Thoreau's militancy is so pronounced that he "offers no alternative vision of the state or community" ("Thoreau's Militant Conscience," *Political Theory* 9 [1981]:106).

7   There were other excursions as well. Thoreau made several trips to Maine (1846, 1856, 1857) to examine logging settlements and Indian tribes. Here, he claimed, "one could no longer accuse institutions and society" for our failures (*The Maine Woods,* ed. Joseph J. Moldenhauer [Princeton, 1972], p. 16). Also see *A Yankee in Canada* and the essay "Walking."

8   *The New Thoreau Handbook,* ed. Walter Harding and Michael Meyer (New York, 1980), p. 44. Krutch offers a similar assessment, in *Henry David Thoreau,* pp. 96–97.

9   Richard Lebeaux, *Young Man Thoreau* (Amherst, 1977), p. 199.

10   *The Writings of Henry David Thoreau: A Week on the Concord and Merrimack Rivers,* ed. Carl F. Hovde (Princeton, 1980), pp. 5, 13, 17, 8.

11   Ibid., p. 23.   12   Ibid., pp. 46, 74, 76.

13   Ibid., p. 123, 124.   14   Ibid., pp. 126, 130.

15   Ibid., pp. 184, 209–10, 211, 243, 259. The long commentary on friendship was added to the manuscript as late as 1848 and represents less an introduction of "sheer fudge" (Krutch, *Henry David Thoreau,* p. 96) than a final attempt on Thoreau's part to reach some accommodation with the social order in general, and perhaps with the memory of his brother as well.

16   Ibid., p. 261–62.   17   Ibid., pp. 276, 268.

18   Ibid., pp. 266, 264.   19   Ibid., pp. 123, 274, 286.

20   Ibid., pp. 317, 304, 332, 304.   21   Ibid., p. 306.

22   Ibid., pp. 50, 198.   23   Ibid., p. 322.

24   Ibid., pp. 324–25.   25   Ibid., p. 340.

26   Ibid., p. 341.   27   Ibid., pp. 383–84.

28   Here are a few examples of critical acclaim: "The structural wholeness of *Walden* makes it stand as the finest product in our literature of life-giving analogies . . ." (F. O. Matthiessen, *American Renaissance* [New York, 1948], p. 175); "By following to its uncompromising conclusion his belief that great art can grow from the center of the simplest life, he was able to be universal" (Stanley Edgar Hyman, "Henry Thoreau in Our Times," *The Promised End* [Cleveland, 1963], p. 24); "*Walden* has served as my conscience through the long stretches of my trivial days" (E. B. White, *The Points of My Compass* [New York, 1962]); see also Wendell Glick, ed., *The Recognition of Henry David Thoreau* (Ann Arbor: University of Michigan Press, 1969), and Walter Harding, ed. *Thoreau: A Century of Criticism* (Dallas, 1954) for collections of assessments of Thoreau.

29   Sherman Paul, "Resolution of Walden," *Accent* 12 (1953):103.

30   Thoreau, *Walden and Civil Disobedience,* pp. 2, 5.

31   Ibid., p. 12.

32   In "Ktaadn," which is based upon a trip he had taken while at Walden, Thoreau asked somewhat harshly why the poor immigrant, who can pay his fare to New York or Boston "could not pay five dollars more for passage to Bangor and beyond" and "be as rich as he pleases where the land virtually costs him nothing, and houses only the labor of building, and he may begin life as Adam did?" (*The Maine Woods,* p. 14).

33   Thoreau, *Walden and Civil Disobedience,* pp. 29, 33.

34   E. M. Forster, *Abinger Harvest* (New York, 1966), pp. 23, 26.

35   Thoreau, *Walden and Civil Disobedience,* pp. 44, 45.

36   John Locke, *Two Treatises of Government,* ed. Peter Laslett (New York, 1960), p. 344.

37 Thoreau, *Walden and Civil Disobedience*, p. 37.

38 Ibid., pp. 135–36. 39 Ibid., pp. 136, 137, 138.

40 Ibid., p. 139. 41 Hyman, *The Promised End*, p. 27.

42 Thoreau, *Walden and Civil Disobedience*, p. 207, 225.

43 Ibid., pp. 140, 146. 44 Ibid., pp. 97–98, 99.

45 Ibid., p. 99.

46 Henry David Thoreau, *Cape Cod* (New York, 1951), p. 282.

47 Harding, *Days of Thoreau*, pp. 277–79; Frank B. Sanborn, *Henry David Thoreau* (Boston, 1882), p. 230.

48 Thoreau, *Cape Cod*, p. 16. 49 Ibid., p. 18.

50 Ibid., pp. 20, 21. 51 Ibid., p. 22.

52 Ibid., pp. 184, 182, 116. 53 Ibid., p. 182.

54 Ibid., pp. 75, 78. 55 Ibid., p. 79.

56 Thoreau, *Walden and Civil Disobedience*, p. 50.

57 *The Writings of Henry David Thoreau* (Boston, 1906), vol. 5, *Journals*, pp. 264–65.

58 Thoreau, *Walden and Civil Disobedience*, p. 52.

59 Ibid., pp. 146, 48, 144.

60 Jean Bethke Elshtain examines the political implications of somatophobic metaphors in the context of feminist thought. "On the Liberal Captivity of Feminism," in *The Liberal Future in America*, ed. Philip Abbott and Michael Levy (Westport, Conn., 1985), pp. 63–84.

61 Perry Miller, *Consciousness in Concord* (Boston, 1958), pp. 87–101.

4 Judging

1 Cited in Whittaker Chambers, *Witness* (New York, 1952), pp. 540–42.

2 Cited in Lillian Hellman, *Scoundrel Time* (Boston, 1976), pp. 97–98.

3 The case for Hellman as an American "heroine" is taken up by Garry Wills in his introduction to *Scoundrel Time* and in Doris V. Falk's *Lillian Hellman* (New York, 1978). Also see Murray Kempton, "Witnesses," *New York Review of Books*, June 10, 1976, pp. 22–25. Kempton, who praises Hellman as "someone who knew how to act when there was nothing harder on earth than knowing how to act," also admits that he would not want Hellman "overmuch as a comrade": "She is too vain about judgmental qualities that seem to me by no means her best ones; she is a bit of a bully; and she is inclined to be a hanging judge of the motives of those whose opinions differ from her own" (p. 25). Caustically critical accounts also abound: William F. Buckley, Jr., "Who is the Ugliest of Them All?" *National Review*, January 21, 1977; Sidney Hook, "Lillian Hellman's *Scoundrel Time*," *Encounter*, February 1977; William L. O'Neill, *A Better World: The Great Schism: Stalinism and the American Intellectuals* (New York, 1982), pp. 358–66.

4 Richard Nixon, *Six Crises* (New York, 1968), p. 62; Allen Weinstein (*Perjury: The Hiss-Chambers Case*) contends that most commentators tended to see Hiss and Chambers in "iconic" terms. The most passionate, and theoretically ingenious critique of Chambers as a witness is Meyer Zelig's psychobiography, *Friendship and Fratricide: An Analysis of Whittaker Chambers and Alger Hiss* (New York, 1967). But Zelig's analysis of events in Chambers's life history, based largely on *Witness*, which leads him to a diagnosis of paranoia, are paralleled in Hiss's life as well. Also see Benjamin Jowitt, *The Strange Case of Alger Hiss* (New York, 1953) and John Cabot Smith, *Alger Hiss: The True Story* (New York,

1976) for defenses of Hiss. Hiss's own autobiography is notable only in being the most unreflective memoir in the English language (*The Court of Public Opinion* [New York, 1957]). Sympathetic statements of Chambers include: William Buckley's collection of Chambers's correspondence, *Odyssey of a Friend* (New York, 1970); Arthur Koestler, "The Complex Issue of the Ex-Communist," *New York Times Book Review,* May 25, 1952; and Lionel Trilling, "Wittaker Chambers and 'The Middle of the Journey,'" *New York Review of Books,* April 17, 1975.

5 Chambers, *Witness,* pp. 14, 449.

6 Hellman, *Scoundrel Time,* pp. 89, 94, 39.

7 Irving Howe, "God, Man and Stalin," in *Celebrations and Attacks* (New York, 1979), pp. 80, 81, 83.

8 Nathan Glazer, "An Answer to Lillian Hellman," *Commentary,* June 1976, p. 37.

9 Chambers, *Witness,* p. 798.   10 Hellman, *Scoundrel Time,* p. 94.

11 E. M. Forster, *Two Cheers for Democracy* (London, 1951), p. 68.

12 Hellman, *Three: An Unfinished Woman, Pentimento, Scoundrel Time* (Boston, 1979), p. 726. Hellman added a brief closing commentary to *Scoundrel Time* for this edition.

13 Chambers, *Witness,* p. 5.

14 Ibid., p. 611. Hiss contends that only at this point did he recognize Chambers as the Crosley he had known (*Court of Public Opinion,* p. 90).

15 Chambers, *Witness,* pp. 16, 489.   16 Ibid., pp. 194–95.

17 Elizabeth Bentley, *Out of Bondage* (New York, 1951). In fact, it was Bentley's testimony that had created such a sensation in the media. Chambers had been called before HUAC to confirm some details of what papers had called the story of the "Red Spy Queen."

18 Chambers, *Witness,* p. 6.   19 Ibid., pp. 261, 262–63.

20 Ibid., p. 507.

21 Ibid., pp. 450, 517. Hellman also treats her farm as a retreat from both politics and the dissipation of cosmopolitan life.

22 Ibid., p. 524.   23 Ibid., pp. 453, 454, 456.

24 Cited in John B. Judis, "The Two Faces of Whittaker Chambers," *New Republic,* April 16, 1984, p. 29.

25 Hellman, *Scoundrel Time,* p. 43.

26 Hellman, *Scoundrel Time* in *Three,* p. 726.

27 Hellman, *Scoundrel Time,* p. 162.

28 O'Neill, *A Better World,* p. 360; Hook, "Lillian Hellman's *Scoundrel Time,*" p. 91.

29 Hellman, *Scoundrel Time,* pp. 118, 132.

30 Ibid., p. 163.

31 Hellman, *Pentimento* in *Three,* p. 327.

32 Hellman, *An Unfinished Woman* in *Three,* p. 303.

33 Ibid., p. 284. In *Scoundrel Time,* Hellman suggests that Hammett's commitment to the Party originated from the Frank Little lynching incident. Was Hammett's radicalism an act of atonement for his activities as a Pinkerton guard for the Anaconda Company? He had been offered (and declined) $5,000 to assassinate Little (p. 50).

34. Hellman, *An Unfinished Woman* in *Three,* p. 304.

35 Garry Wills, "Introduction," *Scoundrel Time,* pp. 32–33.

36 Albert Camus, *The Rebel* (New York, 1956), p. 266.

37 Hellman, *Scoundrel Time,* p. 96.

38 Lillian Hellman, *Maybe* (Boston, 1980), p. 74.

39 Hellman, *Scoundrel Time,* pp. 96, 94.

40 Hellman, *Maybe,* p. 71.

41 Robert Edelbaum, "The Poetics of the Private Eye," in *Tough Guy Writers of the Thirties,* ed. David Madden (Carbondale, 1968), pp. 80–81.

42 Hellman, *Unfinished Woman,* in *Three,* p. 291.

43 Hellman, *Scoundrel Time,* p. 70.   44 Hellman, *Maybe,* p. 15.

45 Ibid., pp. 72–73.

46 Ibid., pp. 50–51. The inability to remember and the inability to express this quasi-amnesia is based in part on Hellman's own reticence to comprehend the motivations of others. This frustration is repeatedly noted in *Maybe* (pp. 1, 13, 64, 88).

47 Ibid., pp. 100, 101.

48 Ibid., p. 62. Hellman is quoting Sarah.

49 Hellman, *Scoundrel Time,* p. 159. Here, in the most overtly political of her memoirs, Hellman complains that in American culture remembering is considered "neurotic" (p. 159).

5 Remembering

1 Whittaker Chambers, *Witness* (New York, 1952), p. 3.

2 Lillian Hellman, *Maybe* (Boston, 1980), p. 101.

3 For an analysis of the implications of this position, see William Galston, "Defending Liberalism," *American Political Science Review* 76 (1982):621–29.

4 John Rawls regards his approach as an elevation of social contract theory (*A Theory of Justice* [Cambridge, 1971], p. 11). Both Ronald Dworkin and Bruce Ackerman employ a historical model of foundings, albeit fanciful and limited. Dworkin constructs a society of "shipwreck survivors" washed up on a desert island in need of allotting clamshells ("Liberalism" in *Public and Private Morality,* ed. Stuart Hampshire [Cambridge, 1978], p. 285). Ackerman describes a hypothetical crew of explorers aboard a spaceship (*Social Justice in the Liberal State* [New Haven, 1980], p. 38).

5 Bertrand de Jouvenal, *The Pure Theory of Politics* (Cambridge, 1963), p. 45.

6 Norman Jacobson, *Pride and Solace: The Functions and Limits of Political Theory* (Berkeley, 1978), p. 56.

7 Sigmund Freud, *A General Introduction to Psychoanalysis,* trans. Joan Rivere (New York, 1952), p. 381.

8 Herbert Lindenberger, "The Idyllic Moment: On Pastoral and Romanticism," *College English* 34 (1972):338.

9 Leo Marx's *Machine in the Garden* (New York, 1964) brilliantly describes this phenomenon but places personal fear outside the pastoral in the form of the spread of technology.

10 On the pastoral values, see Renato Poggioli "The Oaten Flute," in *Harvard University Bulletin* 9 (Spring 1957):150–54.

11 Henry Adams, *Mont-Saint-Michel and Chartres* (Dunwoody, Ga., 1978), pp. 273–75.

12 Henry Adams, *The Education of Henry Adams* (New York, 1918), p. 472.

13 Louis Auchincloss raises the question of whether Adams ever accepted the reality of the Virgin independent of human yearning in his *Henry Adams* (Minneapolis, 1971), p. 46.

14   Adams, *Education,* p. 8.

15   Ibid. See Vern Wagner's impressive textual analysis on this point (*The Suspension of Henry Adams* [Detroit, 1969], 102–19).

16   Ibid., pp. 13, 15, 12, 7. Jackson Lears emphasizes Adams's "obsession with 'feminine' values" as a sign of his problems with filial loyalty and concern with generativity, but the romance of the Quincy pastoral is unmistakably boyish. See *No Place of Grace* (New York, 1981), pp. 266–69.

17   Adams, *Education,* p. 16.   18   Ibid., p. 3.

19   Ibid., p. 4.   20   Ibid., p. 22.

21   Ibid., pp. 20, 21, 20.   22   Ibid., p. 26, 42, 43, 32, 34.

23   Ibid., pp. 44, 48.   24   Ibid., pp. 47, 48.

25   Ibid., pp. 44–45.

26   Adams, *Mont-Saint-Michels and Chartres,* p. 138.

27   *Letters of Henry Adams* (1892–1918), ed. Worthington Chauncy Ford (Boston, 1938), pp. 80, 70.

28   Adams, *Education,* p. 471.

29   Ibid., p. x.

30   Henry Adams, *Esther* (New York, 1938), p. 273.

31   Adams, *Letters,* pp. 129, 269, 296, 111, 561, 550, 463, 476, 532. See also pp. 55, 114, 145, 181, 182.

32   Adams, *Education,* p. 288.   33   Ibid., p. 351.

34   Adams, *Letters,* p. 33. See also p. 97.   35   Ibid., p. 204.

36   Adams, *Mont-Saint-Michels and Chartres,* p. 250.

37   Adams, *Education,* p. 389.

38   Van Wyck Brooks, *New England: Indian Summer, 1865–1915* (New York, 1940), p. 490.

39   Adams, *Education,* p. 39.

40   Lincoln Steffens, *The Autobiography of Lincoln Steffens* (New York, 1931), pp. 8–9.

41   Ibid., p. 3.   42   Ibid., p. 13.

43   Ibid., pp. 35, 40.   44   Ibid., p. 105.

45   Ibid., p. 108.

46   See Christopher Lasch on the significance of this incident (*The New Radicalism in America, 1889–1963: The Intellectual as a Social Type* [New York, 1965], p. 273).

47   Lincoln Steffens, *The Letters of Lincoln Steffens,* ed. Ella Winter and Granville Hicks (New York, 1938), p. 983.

48   Steffens, *Autobiography,* pp. 814, 798. Lasch insists that Steffens did see the significance of modern revolution, a point that liberals insisted upon missing (*New Radicalism in America,* p. 284). See Justin Kaplan for an assessment of Steffens as a Stalinist apologist (*Lincoln Steffens: A Biography* [New York, 1974], pp. 320–28).

49   Steffens, *Autobiography,* p. 853, 813, 815–16.

50   Richard Wright, "The Birth of *Black Boy,*" cited in Michael Fabre, "Afterword" to Wright, *American Hunger* (New York, 1977), p. 138.

51   Richard Wright, *Black Boy: A Record of Childhood and Youth* (New York, 1945), p. 228.

52   Ibid., p. 16.   53   Ibid., pp. 14–15.

54   Wright, *American Hunger,* pp. 120, 112.

55   Richard Wright, *Eight Men* (New York, 1961), p. 78.

56   Wright, *American Hunger,* pp. 1–2, 134–35.

57 Ibid., p. 2.   58 Ibid., p. 124.

59 Richard Wright, *White Man, Listen!* (Garden City, N.Y., 1957), p. 17.

60 Richard Wright, *Black Power* (New York, 1954), p. 347.

61 Richard Wright, *Pagan Spain* (New York, 1957), p. 237. See David Bakish's analysis, *Richard Wright* (New York, 1973), pp. 81–88.

6 Reforming

1 "Men do not want solely the obedience of women, they want their sentiments . . . and to have no life but in their affections" (John Stuart Mill and Harriet Taylor Mill, *Essays on Sex Equality,* ed. Alice S. Rossi [Chicago, 1970]), p. 141).

2 Estelle C. Jelinek, "Introduction: Women's Autobiography and the Male Tradition" in *Women's Autobiography: Essays in Criticism,* ed. Estelle C. Jelinek (Bloomington, 1980), p. 14.

3 Gilman, *The Living of Charlotte Perkins Gilman: An Autobiography* (New York, 1935), p. 5. Gilman, married twice, wrote under a variety of names. I have used Gilman throughout this chapter.

4 Jane Addams, *Twenty Years at Hull House* (1910; reprint ed., New York, 1961), p. 24.

5 Gilman, *Living,* pp. 8, 9.   6 Ibid., p. 10.

7 Ibid., pp. 7, 8, 10.   8 Ibid., p. 10.

9 Ibid., pp. 10, 26.   10 Ibid., pp. 42, 60.

11 *Ibid.,* p. 71. Gilman, like Franklin, kept to a rigorous daily schedule: "Oct. 5, 1881. Ice! Up at six, cold as I ever want to be. Warm up the bath and do chores as usual." Rising hours were early—6:10, 5:50, 5:55, 6, 6:55—they run. The day began with "three coal stoves to attend to, in winter; get breakfast, do chamberwork, be ready for pupils at nine. These were two girls who came to the house for tutoring; in the afternoons there were others in different parts of the city to whom I went, teaching, drawing, painting, gymnastics, and ordinary branches with cheerful enthusiasm." Often Gilman's own plan for virtue was practiced in minute detail: "I deliberately set about a course of exercises in which small and purely arbitrary decisions were sharply carried out: 'At five thirty-eight I will walk around the block.' 'I will get out of bed at thirteen minutes to seven'" (p. 56).

12 Ibid., pp. 57, 58, 59.   13 Ibid., pp. 89, 91.

14 Ibid., p. 98. The symptoms of melancholia recurred intermittently for the rest of her life. She would occasionally be forced to refuse invitations, extend writing deadlines, postpone reading heavy books. Aside from the "blank months of idleness," there is an admission of a more severe breakdown when Gilman cared for her ill mother in Oakland (p. 140).

15 Gilman was to be charged by opponents with "giving up her child," a logical consequence of feminism. Thirty years later Gilman wrote, "I have to stop writing and cry as I tell about it." (p. 163)

16 Ibid., pp. 192–93.   17 Ibid., pp. 186, 181.

18 Ibid., p. 198.

19 Charlotte Perkins Gilman, *The Home: Its Work and Influence* (1903; reprint ed., Urbana, 1972), p. 49.

20 Ibid., pp. 334–37, 340. The home is also attacked for directly contributing "food

diseases." "Home-cooking" is "poison." We die slowly from these "grease hardened particles" so lovingly made and ingested in the home (pp. 130–34).

21 Karl Marx, "Economic and Philosophic Manuscripts of 1844," in *The Marx-Engels Reader,* ed. Robert Tucker, 2d ed. (New York, 1978), pp. 82–83.

22 Gilman, *The Home,* p. 134. Gilman sees the introduction of bakers' bread and breakfast food as natural advances against the home, "this little ganglion of aborted economic processes" (pp. 318, 331–32).

23 Ibid., pp. 137, 138.

24 Addams, *Twenty Years at Hull House,* p. 25.

25 Christopher Lasch, *The New Radicalism in America (1889–1963): The Intellectual as a Social Type* (New York, 1965), p. 5. Also see Richard Hofstadter, *The Age of Reform* (New York, 1955), p. 151.

26 Addams, *Twenty Years at Hull House,* pp. 64, 94.

27 Ibid., p. 59.

28 Ibid., pp. 31, 68, 69. The episode in the West invites comparison with Thoreau's visit to the Baker Farm discussed in chapter 3.

29 Ibid., p. 73. Allen F. Davis contends that letters sent home after the bullfight show no evidence of the dramatic conversion reported in the autobiography. (*American Heroine: The Life and Legend of Jane Addams* [New York, 1973], p. 48). Perhaps Addams was reticent to share her recent experience. In any case, it is still significant that she tells the story in the mode of conversion narrative.

30 Addams, *Twenty Years at Hull House,* pp. 64, 65.

31 Ibid., p. 172.   32 Ibid., p. 95.

33 Lasch, *New Radicalism in America,* p. 33. See Staughton Lynd's rejoinder to those who would question the "validity of radical action by exploring its psychic origins" ("Jane Addams and the Radical Impulse," *Commentary 32* [July 1961]:54).

34 Addams, *Twenty Years at Hull House,* pp. 95, 172.

35 Ibid., p. 175–176.

36 Jane Addams, "Why the Ward Boss Rules," *Outlook* 58 (April 2, 1898), reprinted in *The Social Thought of Jane Addams,* ed. Christopher Lasch (Indianapolis, 1965), p. 129.

37 Ibid., p. 133.

38 Jane Addams, *The Spirit of Youth and the City Streets* (New York, 1909), pp. 5, 4.

39 Ibid., pp. 4, 7, 10, 12. Addams's analysis of prostitution in *A New Conscience and an Ancient Evil* (New York, 1912) is based in part on the perversion and exploitation of the social as well as the economic needs of displaced farm girls.

40 Addams, *Twenty Years at Hull House,* p. 119.

41 The significance of clothes for youth, even at the expense of a "lessened supply of food" is defended by Addams as a sign of desire for self-esteem in *Democracy and Social Ethics* (New York, 1902).

42 Addams, "Why the Ward Boss Rules," in Lasch, *Social Thought of Addams,* pp. 129–30.

43 Jane Addams, "A Modern Lear," in Lasch, *Social Thought of Addams,* p. 108.

44 Ibid., p. 116.

45 Ibid., pp. 119, 112.

46 Ibid., p. 122.

7 Conclusion

1 John Rawls, *A Theory of Justice* (Cambridge, 1971), p. 93.

2 Ronald Dworkin, *Taking Rights Seriously* (Cambridge, Mass., 1977), p. 272.

3 Dworkin, *Taking Rights Seriously,* p. 272.

4 Rosa Luxemburg, "The Problem of Dictatorship," in *The Essential Works of Social-ism* ed. Irving Howe (New Haven, 1976), pp. 255–56.

5 F. Scott Fitzgerald, *The Crack-Up* (New York, 1956), pp. 69, 72.

0 00 02 0377048 2
MIDDLEBURY COLLEGE